P9-CRM-549

COMPLETELY REVISED AND UPDATED

THE
NEW AGE
BABY
NAME
BOOK

BY SUE BROWDER

WARNER BOOKS

A Time Warner Company

If you purchase this book without a cover you should be aware that this book may have been stolen property and reported as "unsold and destroyed" to the publisher. In such case neither the author nor the publisher has received any payment for this "stripped book."

WARNER BOOKS EDITION

Copyright © 1974, 1987 by Sue Browder
All rights reserved.

This Warner Books Edition is published by arrangement with Workman Publishing Company, Inc., 1 W. 39th St., New York, N.Y. 10018.

Cover design by Miriam Campiz

Warner Books, Inc.
1271 Avenue of the Americas
New York, N.Y. 10020

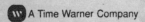 A Time Warner Company

Printed in the United States of America

First Printing, Revised Edition: October, 1987

10 9 8

CONTENTS

Preface To
The Revised Edition

This is the thoughtful parent's baby-name book. That's not to say all other name books are for nonthoughtful parents. It's just that this book was written especially for you if you not only want a special name for your baby, but also have many questions about how to choose a name that's "just right."

For example, what are the disadvantages (or advantages) of giving your baby a common name like Margaret rather than a more unusual one like Tasha? Can the name you choose have positive or negative effects on your baby's future development or success in school? What are the most common myths about naming a baby? What are the most reliable, up-to-date scientific findings? Here you'll find answers to these and many other questions, plus interesting name lore, insights into naming practices around the globe, and other intriguing facts (What are the most popular names in the United States? Where did middle names come from? Why do we have nicknames?).

This book was also written especially for you if you feel your baby will be a totally unique person* and, with that in mind, you'd like to consider a distinctive, slightly unusual name. All the old traditional favorite names are here, but so are thousands of new, contemporary names you *won't* find elsewhere—names with a bit more flair.

In the past ten years, we've seen an amazing shift to more special, distinctive names for American babies. Old stand-bys, such as John, William, Thomas, Elizabeth, Mary, and Anne, have been tumbling from the top of the popularity charts for the first time in centuries. If you'd lived in an English-speaking country between 1600 and 1800, one in every two men you met would have been called William, John, or Thomas, and about half of all women were named Elizabeth, Mary, or Anne. In name surveys conducted in New York City between 1898 and 1964, Mary consistently ranked among the top three most popular girls' names, and John was always either first or second. Yet in 1983 when twelve thousand new mothers were asked what they were naming their babies, traditional names were far less popular than ever before. While the name John still ranked fourth, William was sixteenth, and Thomas twenty-first. Anne wasn't even among the top 100 (though Anna straggled in at fiftieth). And the all-time favorite, Mary, had plunged dra-matically to thirty-seventh, far below such unusual "modern" names as Megan (sixth), Lindsay (ninth), and Tiffany (twenty-sixth). The preschool-class roster at a progressive private school in New York City's Greenwich Village sever-al years ago included girls named Chantra, Kiara, Morgan, Maya, Onawa, Shakya, Soren, and Sydney. Boys' names tend to remain more traditional, but even so in one recent

*By the way, if you feel your baby is bound to be a totally unique individual—even at birth—you're right. The odds against another baby having so much as a thumbprint identical to your baby's are said to be astronomical—an estimated 63 billion to one. The latest child-development research shows that each baby even has breathing and sleeping rhythms as unique as a snowflake.

survey Jared, Travis, and Dustin were more popular than Edward or Charles.

What to make of all this? Could this dramatic shift, especially in girls' names, be a direct reflection of women's liberation and this country's rapid social change in the seventies? Quite possibly so. Wilbur Zelinsky, Ph.D., a human geographer at Penn State, believes that variations of first-name choices over time are a sensitive indicator of American cultural patterns. In times of strict social conservatism, Zelinsky notes, parents tend to give their babies the traditional names; in times of rapid social change, we see a surge of individualism and diversity—and a preference for fresh, new names.

This modern shift in naming is probably also due in large part to the fact that Americans suddenly have a much larger pool of names to choose from. Not only do we see and hear new names every day in the news (names like Mikhail and Yuri now flow easily off many Americans' tongues), but baby-name books are also changing as never before. When I wrote the first edition of this book in the early 1970s, unusual, pretty names from other cultures, such as Tamika, Lian, or Shani, were seldom listed in American name books. For the most part, baby-name books then were comprised of such common names as Susan, Carol, and Jane plus many uncommon names we've all heard of but few of us like, such as Adolph, Attila, and Aloysius.

The dire shortage of new, short, distinctive, and pleasant-sounding names in the early 1970s prompted me to write this book. I wanted to give new parents like you (and at the time me), a real choice.

When I began searching for unique names from around the world, I had to glean them from newspaper birth records and dusty scholarly journals. Today practically every baby-name book contains at least a few of the names I unearthed during my long hours in the library.

Names I found—such as Abebi (from Nigeria and meaning "we asked for her and she came to us"), Tani (from Japan, meaning "valley"), and Kala (one of the 1,008 names for the Hindu god Siva and meaning "black" or "time")—are now almost as routinely listed in today's name books as Linda, Mary, and John.

For this new edition, I've added thousands of brand-new, contemporary names that have never appeared in an American name book before, including the most recently coined names in this country, as well as many names from other countries.

A friend once asked, "Doesn't it annoy you that so many other baby-name books are now partial clones of yours?" Frankly, I think it's terrific. I'm pleased that expectant parents at last have a choice of names. If you do wind up calling your baby John, William, or Mary, it's because you love that name better than all the others—not because you have no other option. Now, thanks to the many additions and revisions in this new edition, I'm also confident that *this* book—as the original of its kind—is once again the most complete, detailed, accurate, and authoritative source of distinctive, contemporary names you'll find anywhere.

—SEB, October 1986,
Roxbury, Connecticut

INTRODUCTION

Choosing A Name for the Twenty-first Century

The Yoruba-speaking people of Nigeria have a proverb: "Consider the state of your life before you name a child." And that is essentially what many American parents are doing today as they seek more distinctive, contemporary names for their children.

Here you will find meanings and pronunciations (when useful) for thousands of names from cultures around the world—African, Oriental, East Indian, Russian, European, Latin American, South American, Scandinavian, Eskimo, Hawaiian, and North American Indian. In addition, Americans are constantly creating new names, which may reflect not only our independence and creativity but also changing cultural consciousness, and these newly created names have been collected from newspaper birth columns. You may want to use the names exactly as they are listed. Or you may decide to use them as a base for creating a totally personalized name, in which case the section on "How to Create a Name" and "Choosing a Name to Reflect Your Roots" will give you pointers.

Being Up to Date

When choosing a contemporary name, you'll want to consider a few modern fashions. As Americans, many of us are seeking out distinctive, slightly unusual names for our babies.

1

Some Americans are creating unique names on their own, but many are dipping into traditional name pools from other cultures. Today's babies are being given names that weren't even listed in traditional U.S. name books twenty years ago—such as Kirsten (a Scandinavian form of Christina), Natasha (traditionally Russian), and Hans (the German form of John).

Interestingly enough, this trend toward more distinctive, special names seems to have suddenly become worldwide (possibly because of the incredible impact of television, which introduces us to new names every day). In West Germany, where babies' names must be "approved" by local village registrars, parents who've grown weary of ordinary German names like Hans, Anna, and Klaus have actually gone to court to win the right to give their babies names with more flair. So far German judges have turned down such names as McDonald (too closely associated with McDonald's hamburgers for the judge's taste), Agla (the name of a German soap powder), and Oma (a brand of camera), as well as names with built-in titles, such as Princess Anne and Lady Diana. But West German courts *have* allowed parents to use the names Merlin and Pepsi-Carola. In Barcelona, a Spanish couple went all the way to Spain's constitutional court to win the right to name their baby girl Lola. (The stuffy registrar had argued that Lola wasn't a "real" name but only a nickname for Dolores). And in Italy (where authorities don't fuss with names), such American TV shows as *Dallas* and *Dynasty* have had their impact: Little baby girls named Sue Ellen, Pamela, Crystal, and Alexis are now being pushed about in prams on the sidewalks of Rome.

In France, where town halls keep lists of "permissible" names, registrars are also under attack by parents who want names more unusual than the traditional Jacques and Pierre. Though French judges have rejected such "ice-cream flavor" names as Cerise (cherry) and Vanille (vanilla), one judge did allow a mother and father to call their baby boy Sinbad.

Even in China, there's a strong movement away from traditional monikers and toward more special, distinctive names. Noting there are so many Zhangs in China that if they declared independence, they'd be the seventh most populous country in the world, *The New York Times* recently reported that the Chinese government has even issued a manual to help its citizens choose more unusual names.

Popular Short Forms

To find distinctive names, American parents are often doing as the Spanish couple above did: They're using what were once considered only nicknames as formal given names. Newspaper records show Carrie becoming more popular than Caroline, and Stacy more often used than Anastasia. Many of these "shortened" names are listed as independent names. This trend toward using nicknames may also be the product of Americans' characteristic informality and a loss of the superstitions that created nicknames in some cultures in the first place. Nicknames were originally used (and still are in a few remote parts of the world) to hide one's real name from evil spirits, the idea being that—as in the fairy tale "Rumpelstiltskin"—one has only to know another's name to control him. Believing this, people in some relatively primitive tribes still consider it quite rude to ask someone his or her name, and when asked their own name will often simply reply, "I forgot it" or "I have none."

Another modern development is the practice of using what were formerly exclusively boys' names for girls. Many traditionally masculine names, like Lindsay, Harper, and Darcy, are more popular today for girls than for boys, no doubt the result of the reduced emphasis on stereotyped masculine and feminine roles. The same practice can be found in many other cultures (most American Indian names, for example, can be used by both boys and girls). For this reason, traditional boys' names that have been widely adopted by girls are listed in the girls' section.

Unique Choices

We are also seeking names with deep personal meaning for us and, of course, for our children. Years ago, parents rarely knew that Barbara meant "stranger," and even if they did, the meaning was just an interesting bit of trivia having nothing to do with them or their child personally. But since the early 1970s—and especially since the stunning success of Alex Haley's *Roots*—parents of all heritages, from African to Scotch-Irish, have increasingly sought names with more personal meaning. This trend, though relatively recent to the United States, is traditional in many other cultures where a child's name is considered part of his soul and so has profound personal significance.

A Hopi Indian called Quoiavma, or "Sunrise," once told me his name was a picture. "It means," he said, "the golden sun coming up over the misty mountains and glimmering on hazy smoky-blue waters, while the morning birds chirp in the rustling green trees." Once, Sunrise recalled, he rose before dawn to take photos from the floor of the Grand Canyon, and when he showed the pictures to his clansmen, they said, "That is your name." The modern return to heritage names is one attempt to regain lost meaning, and in this book I've tried wherever possible to get beyond a name's literal meaning to show you the "picture"—connotations and traditions—that brought the name into being.

Names are listed here by nationalities, so that you may choose a name to reflect your family roots. If your last name were Leibowitz, for example, you might want to give your little girl the pretty Polish name Melcia instead of the English equivalent Amelia, or Henka rather than Harriet.

Or perhaps you would like to name your baby after a favorite relative, but somehow his name (John, for instance) seems too ordinary. You might consider one of the many variations of John—the Russian Ivan, the Irish Shane or Sean, or the Swedish Jens. Many names are listed to help you if you have mixed feelings about naming your baby son "junior." Fewer babies are named junior today than fifty years ago, perhaps because many parents feel that each child deserves a unique, individual name of his own. (More about the pros and cons of naming a son "junior" in Chapter One) If the father's name were Daniel, you might compromise between Daniel and a totally different name by calling the baby Dani, the modern Israeli form of Daniel, used for both boys and girls. If the baby were a girl, you could name her Daniela, or one of the modern or international forms of Daniela: Dana, Danice, Danit, Danett, Dania, or Danya.

More Pointers

About twenty common-sense rules have been established, telling you how to pick a name, but basically they all boil down to this: The name should sound pleasant and not leave open strong possibilities for embarrassing or derogatory nicknames like Piggy or Fatso. The old rules that a name should clearly designate sex and not be too unusual, as I have pointed out, have disappeared. Generally, for the sake of euphony, it is suggested that children with two- or three-syllable family names should receive two given names, one with one syllable and the other with two syllables. One-syllable family names (Smith and Jones, for example) often go best with two- or three-syllable names. Avoid rhyming your child's first name with his or her last. And watch out for embarrassing initials. Superstition has it that if your child's initials spell a word, she'll be lucky. But a little girl whose initials spell MUD or RAT may not feel blessed. The composer Arthur Seymour Sullivan (of the Gilbert and Sullivan musical team) always found his initials mortifying— with good reason.

How many names should your baby have? Though there has been a trend toward choosing single names (especially among entertainers, who are increasingly choosing single names like Madonna and Cher), most name experts advise that because of society's increasing complexity, a middle name is practically essential. If you have a common surname, you may even want to select three given names for your child to avoid identity mix-ups. It's not uncommon in other parts of the world (among the Chinese, for example) for a child to have as many as ten names, each bestowed to commemorate an important event, such as entering school, graduating, getting married, and so forth. Some Americans, of course, have been given long strings of names for other reasons. Years ago, Mr. Jackson Ezekiel David James Nathaniel Sylvester Willis Edward Demosthenes Hender-

son of Charlotte, North Carolina, was so named because
his mother hoped one of her son's rich-uncle namesakes
would remember the boy in his will. Unfortunately for
J.E.D.J.N.S.W.E.D.H., the wealthy old men all died without giving him a cent. Which brings us to a last rule: In case
of family disputes, pick the name you and your mate like
best.

Individual Tastes

One final word. These entries have been carefully selected to screen out names that sound awkward or unusual to
Americans. For those seeking a more unusual heritage or
ethnic name, there are boxes throughout the book that
include names I felt only a few parents would be interested
in. The Yoruba name Apara, for instance, is included as a
main entry because it's short, easy to pronounce, and quite
distinctive. In the box on page 55, however, you'll find
other, longer Yoruba names, such as Malomo, Kosoko,
Banjoko, Durosimi, and Akisatan. A few names (especially
those in the boxes) may seem weird or even comical to
American tastes. But for this reaction the Yoruba have still
another proverb: "He who does not understand the cry of
the palm bird complains of the noise it makes."

CHAPTER 1

The Psychology of Naming Your Baby

After working hard to build her career as a lawyer, Joanne is about to have her first baby at age thirty-five. Not content with just one book, she's brought home armloads of books from the library and has even dug out half a dozen magazine articles on how to choose the best name for her baby.

Unfortunately, the more Joanne reads, the more uncertain she feels. "Several articles say the name I choose can affect the grades my child will get in school," Joanne says. "I don't honestly see how a child's name alone could affect how her teachers treat her... but, still, I do worry. Also, if my baby's a girl, I was thinking of calling her Kayla or Shanna, but then I saw a psychologist quoted who insists unusually named kids are unpopular and have emotional problems. I don't know. Maybe I should just listen to my mother. She wants me to call the baby Kathy or Michael."

Joanne is hardly alone. Many thoughtful, loving parents are concerned about the psychological impact a particular name may have on their baby's future. Clearly, our names are important to us. Scientists have observed that when you hear your own name spoken—even when you're asleep—your brain waves become twice as active as when you hear someone else's name. The late psychologist Gordon Allport contended that a child's name is the focal point around which he organizes his self-identity throughout life. But what does modern psychological research tell us about

7

choosing the very best name for a baby? What are the pros and cons, for example, of giving your baby an unusual name like Shanna rather than a common one like Kathy? Can the name you choose affect your baby's future school grades or emotional development (as some so-called experts ominously warn)? Should you play it safe and opt for an ordinary name like Dick or Jane?

When trying to answer such complex questions, it's not nearly enough to simply glance at findings from one or two poorly designed name studies done twenty or thirty years ago and then try to draw up guidelines for naming your baby (which is what far too many "experts" intent on drawing up hard-and-fast naming rules have done). Findings from a scientific study done in a lab, while frequently interesting, don't always translate directly and easily to hard-and-fast naming "how-tos" in the real world. So let's analyze the latest scientific findings about the psychology of names to see what this research tells you (if anything) about how to choose the very best name for your special baby.

Stereotypes: How Much Will Your Child's Name Determine How Others See Her?

Articles about names often note that, whether you like it or not, others will judge and stereotype your child by her name. Depending on the study cited, you'll see that people generally consider Bertha a "fat" name, Brian "macho and dynamic," Justin "vigorous," Rebecca "sweet," April "spritely," Kevin "popular and virile," and Harvey something of a klutz. Percy is reportedly a "weak" name, whereas Eric is perceived as "very strong."

In a 1963 study reported in the *British Journal of Psychiatry*, a British psychologist found that John is nearly always thought to be trustworthy, Robin young, and Tony sociable. Agnes and Matilda were considered unattractive, Ann passive. The most unusual name in this study—Grizelda—received the largest number of mixed ratings, a phenomenon the researcher chalked up to the fact that people probably had no views either way. When asked whether Grizelda was trustworthy, sociable, or kind, respondents jotted down "yes" or "no" more or less at random. This finding suggests that unusual and rare names are less quickly stereotyped. In other words, a child with a distinctive name may be able to "write her own meanings" on her name more easily than a child given a common name people already have many preconceived notions about.

Other common girls' names and their stereotypes (drawn from several different studies) include:

- Amanda—cultured
- Amy—active
- Angela—attractive and a bit willful
- Ann—ladylike and honest but rather plain
- Emily—a wallflower
- Jennifer—young but old-fashioned
- Jessica—beautiful and ambitious
- Katharine—determined, strong-willed, and pretty
- Lisa—popular but frail
- Margaret—trustworthy and kind but a bit dowdy
- Mary—womanly, active, and wholesome
- Patricia—plain-looking
- Vicky—very sexy and popular

Stereotypes for boys' names include:

- Anthony—tall, thin, and elegant
- Benjamin—not to be trusted
- Charles—popular and masculine but not very athletic
- Christopher—intelligent and hardworking
- Cyril—old and unattractive
- David—good, strong, wise, serious, sociable, masculine
- Harold—weak, foolish, passive, and humorless
- Ian—young and honest but unaggressive
- James—an all-around winner
- Kevin—virile and quite popular
- Robert—shy and lacking in confidence
- William—honest but unattractive and unassertive

What can you make of these "results" and other stereotypes? Some "experts" imply that giving your baby an unpopular name like Bertha or Harold may handicap your child for life. They argue that we tend to see ourselves as others see us, and so a name with negative connotations can hamper a child's emotional development. Such warnings can be particularly angst-provoking for parents who take them seriously. Shouldn't you be quite concerned about saddling your child with a negatively stereotyped name?

No. When naming your baby, there are several reasons *not* to take "findings" like those mentioned above too seriously.

For one thing, overly simplified stereotypes like these reveal only how a bunch of people viewed these names *on average*. When you look at the research more closely, you find that nearly every name had both advocates and detractors. In the *British Journal of Psychiatry* study, for example, only 35 percent of the people polled thought a boy named William would be good-looking, but those 35 percent *did* think he'd be handsome. (And let's face it, anytime any of us has a trait, talent, or ability one in three people applaud, we're doing pretty well.) Also, such stereotypes apply only to names in the *abstract*; once anyone actually *meets* bright-eyed, perky, adorable baby William, any preconceived negative ideas about his looks will no doubt instantly vanish. Also, name "images" change over time. Now that England has a cute Prince William, a lot more people will probably stereotype the name as "cute."

Another reason not to take such findings too seriously is that stereotypes can vary—considerably on some scores—depending on how the name is spelled (suggesting these generalities about names are hardly set in stone). Intriguingly, 90 percent of those in the British study thought a girl named Ann would be young. But when an *e* was added, making the name Anne, the number who considered her young plunged to 78 percent. Would Lynda be rated as "feminine and energetic" as Linda has been? Would Caren, Karin, Karen, and Caryn each be stereotyped in exactly the same ways? If the findings of this study are any indication, probably not.

How people stereotype a name also depends on whether they perceive the bearer as upper-, middle-, or lower-class. Dr. Richard L. Zweigenhaft, a psychologist at Guilford College in Greensboro, North Carolina, asked his psychology students to judge a number of names, including McKinley and Talmadge. McKinley was generally rated as "upper-class," "overconfident," "intolerant," and "cold"—the picture of aristocratic insensitivity and aloofness. In contrast, Talmadge was considered "lower-class," "bad," "weak," "stupid," "uncertain," "weak-willed," "cowardly"—in short, everything unpleasant. But the ratings changed dramatically, depending on whether the students thought the baby's father was an unemployed laborer or a physician. If the father was a physician, the name McKinley was rated as more "good," whereas Talmadge was considered more "strong" and "strong-willed" than if the students believed the father was an unemployed laborer.

Also, name stereotyping studies rarely—if ever—take into account the effect of nicknames. How, for example, would the stereotypes of McKinley's name change if all his friends called him Mack? Or what if Talmadge was often called just Tal?

As you can see, there are countless subtle variables to consider before you can say with any certainty that Harold is a "bad" name and James is a "good" one. In fact, so many variables contribute to stereotyping that it's really not worth worrying too much about it. Certainly, if you read that a certain name—Cyril, for example—was rated very negatively by nearly everyone (as, unfortunately, Cyril was in one study), you might want to avoid that name or consider using a shorter version or alternative spelling, such as Cyrill or Cy. Generally, though, most names get such mixed reviews that the findings are of more use to scientists who are trying to devise more name studies than they are to you as a parent. No scientist yet has ever found that calling a baby Cyril or any other name will doom him to an unhappy future or that calling a boy David will guarantee his future success.

Will the Popularity of Your Child's Name Affect Her Grades in School?

When reading about names, you'll invariably read of a study done by psychologists John W. McDavid and Herbert Harari (now both at California State University in San

Diego), which supposedly "proves" you'd better give your child a popular name if you want her to do well in school. The more you think about it, the more worrisome this pronouncement may become. After all, what exactly *is* a popular name? No one really knows. The fact is, name fads shift—often quite dramatically—from year to year.

Let's look at this study closer to see what was actually found. McDavid and Harari asked eighty elementary school teachers to grade short paragraphs written by fifth- and sixth-graders. The essays were all on the topic "What I Did All Day Last Sunday." Supposedly, the only difference in these "comparable" essays was that four names on the tests (David, Michael, Lisa, and Karen) were "popular" among the teachers, whereas the other four names (Elmer, Hubert, Adelle, and Bertha) were "unpopular." Papers by Michael or David received a full grade higher than those by Elmer or Hubert. And Karen and Lisa were given a grade and a half higher than the supposedly outcast, unpopular Bertha.

But there are major problems with this study if you take it as serious "proof" (as do many authors of popular articles and books about names) that you'd better give your child a familiar, "popular," or socially "desirable" name if you want her to do well in school.

First, one of the so-called undesirable names—Adelle— actually received the *highest* grade of all. This finding, if reported at all, is generally skipped over with the lame excuse that the teachers probably considered the name Adelle "scholarly" and "academic." But the fact that Adelle *did* get a better grade than the popularly named kids leaves the often-drawn conclusion that kids with uncommon or out-of-vogue names do poorly in school open to question.

Second, what if this study—which has been cited *ad nauseam* as "proof" against unpopular names—was, in fact, flawed? Suppose Lisa's essay really *was* subtly better in some way than Bertha's, and Lisa's higher grade had little, if anything, to do with her first name. Writers who report this study seldom bother to tell you that the essays were not the same. David wrote about "The Store," Michael about "Tarzan," Elmer about "The Anniversary," and Hubert about "Kites." Adelle wrote about "Shopping" and

Lisa about "Walking the Dog." Bertha's topic was "Planting Seeds" (hardly the liveliest subject). As researchers Louisa Seraydarian and Thomas V. Busse point out in *The Journal of Psychology*, not only is it possible that the essays *weren't* comparable, but the teachers in the McDavid-Harari study also weren't given any specific criteria for grading the essays. The vaguer and more unspecified a task, Drs. Seraydarian and Busse note, "the more likely it is that irrelevancies (e.g., first names) might affect the task."

Third, to be accepted as scientific "fact," a study has to be reproduced—and the same results found—by other teams of scientists. Yet in 1981 when Drs. Seraydarian and Busse, then at Temple University, tried to duplicate the McDavid-Harari findings, they couldn't. In the Temple University study—which involved 60 children's names, 10 essays, and 180 teachers—popular or unpopular names had *no* good or bad effects on the grades fifth-graders received. Though the children's names were prominently displayed on the papers, many teachers later admitted they hadn't even *noticed* them.

In short, no psychologist can say with great certainty that you should call your little boy David or Michael (as opposed to Hubert) if you want him to do well in school. Until scientists prove that a child's first name can seriously affect what grades he receives, it seems wisest—and certainly less anxiety-provoking—just to choose the name you like best.

Should It Be Shanna or Kathy?
Unusual versus Ordinary Names

Thirty to forty years ago, scientists thought an unusual, distinctive name would make a child unpopular in school and harm her emotional development. It was thought that children with uncommon names like Riza or Blair would have fewer friends than children with ordinary names like Susan or David. Some experts even insisted an unusual name alone would launch a child on a path of crime!

Happily, these silly notions have gone by the wayside. The most recent research reveals that, far from being a handicap, an unusual name can be quite an advantage.

Clinical psychologist C.R. Snyder, co-author of *Uniqueness:*

The Human Pursuit of Difference, argues that a child's name is one of his or her "uniqueness" traits. "To have self-esteem," Dr. Snyder says, "all human beings have to feel special. If you make people too similar to others, you threaten their uniqueness and their self-esteem will take a nose-dive." Dr. Snyder points out that *any* name helps a child establish a unique identity. But a distinctive name that makes a child stand out a little more from the crowd may actually help the child in his or her struggle to feel individual and special.

Sports heroes, singers, and film stars have long recognized the publicity value of having a distinctive name. Would Yogi Berra have been as memorable on and off the baseball diamond if he'd gone by his real name—Lawrence Peter Berra? Would Cary Grant have been a sex symbol as Archie Leach? Or would Bo Derek have rated a "10" had she stayed Mary Cathleen Collins? Probably not.

An unusual name may be especially advantageous to a child born in the upper-middle or upper class. As Guilford College psychologist Richard Zweigenhaft notes in a *Journal of Social Psychology* article, a child already privileged by birth may see his distinctive name as just another positive way he stands out. Research on upper-class children who go on to fulfill their promise of birth strongly supports this theory. To see whether an unusual name had any effect on later success, Dr. Zweigenhaft chose 436 male names at random from *The Social Register*, which has been called the "best guide to the membership of the national upper class." Half the men had unusual first names like Urie and Cornell, whereas the other half had common ones like William and John. Of those thirty men who actually went on to become listed in *Who's Who*, twenty-three—or a whopping 77 percent —came from the group with unusual names.

Past studies showed that children with unusual names did worse on IQ tests and had lower self-esteem. Again, more recent studies have not borne this out. Indeed, one study reported in *The Journal of Social Psychology* found unusually named college women actually scored *higher* on many variables, including capacity for status, sociability, social presence, and self-acceptance, than did women with ordinary names.

Nor should you worry that giving your child an unusual name will make her unpopular. One often-reported 1966 study *did* suggest that kids with uncommon names might be less popular with their peers. But that study included only fifty-nine children (all Jewish) who knew one another. In a much more extensive study done in 1979, Dr. Busse looked at 1,548 children from many racial, ethnic, and religious backgrounds. Comparing kids with ordinary names to those with unusual ones, he found no relation between a child's first name and her popularity. There is simply *no* proof that a special, unique, or distinctive name will doom your child to a life of unpopularity.

Lest we replace the myth that an unusual name *always* harms a child with a new myth that an unusual name *never* hurts, however, we should point out that there's a clear difference between giving a child a downright comical name like Ima Pigg or Hong Fong Dong (which is bound to provoke vicious teasing from schoolmates) and a pretty or distinctive name like Kala or Jared, which will likely just help a child feel more special.

What About Unisex Names or Calling Your Son "Jr."?

Another old naming rule that's now gone, thanks to recent research, is the notion that your child's name should clearly denote his or her sex. The old idea was that if you gave your child a sexually ambiguous name (like Robin, Lee, Dana, or Harper), he or she would have trouble establishing a sexual identity and would likely suffer serious psychological problems (a phenomenon known as "the boy-named-Sue syndrome").

This notion has now been discarded. In his carefully controlled studies of Wesleyan University students reported in 1980, Dr. Zweigenhaft compared students with sexually ambiguous or misleading names (such as Dana, Leslie, and Ronnie) with students whose names were decidedly masculine or feminine. All the students had taken the California Psychological Inventory (CPI), which tests psychological health on eighteen scales. Students with unisex names were *just* as psychologically healthy as students whose names clearly denoted their sex. As a matter of fact, girls with sexually ambiguous names scored higher than other girls on "capacity for status," whereas boys with unisex names scored higher than other boys on the "well-being" and "good impression" scales. Dr. Zweigenhaft's conclusions are very clear. He writes, "there is no evidence in these data to support the dire predictions for the 'boy-named-Sue syndrome.'" Case closed.

What about naming your son after his father with "Jr." attached? Research has generally shown this isn't such a good idea. Most studies have found boys intensely dislike being given their father's name (although Dr. Busse did find in one study that boys named for their fathers *liked* their names and also got along well with other boys). Dr. Zweigenhaft found in his 1980 studies that juniors scored significantly lower than other boys on a number of psychological measures, including capacity for status, well-being, responsibility, tolerance, and intellectual efficiency.

It's important to remember, of course, that such findings are for all juniors *on average*. Any one specific junior (yours, for example) may actually score way above other boys in these areas. If you do name a son junior, the most important thing is to make sure your son has a sense of individuality. Thus, if a boy is named Thomas Jones, Jr., it's advisable to give him a distinctive nickname (like T.J., for example) to emphasize the fact that he's still unique and special.

Intriguingly, when Dr. Zweigenhaft looked at the psychological scores of boys named after their fathers, but whose junior status was designated with Roman numerals rather than Jr., (as in John Smith II or John Rockefeller III), he found these boys were as well adjusted as boys not named for their fathers. Dr. Zweigenhaft speculates that a boy with a II, III, or IV after his name may see himself as one link in a long chain of respected, admirable high achievers, and may therefore see himself as quite special. "In contrast," he writes, "the person with Jr. attached to his name may or may not be part of a long line of many. His title reminds us, and him, that he is younger, most likely smaller (at least for the first 15 years of his life) and lesser in status than the real thing, the person he was named after."

When you examine all the latest psychological findings about names, one fact becomes obvious: You needn't worry about making some dreadful blunder when naming your baby. The latest scientific research has shown that choosing a name for your child is a lot less perilous—and hence a lot more fun—than psychologists of the past believed.

CHAPTER 2

How to Create a Name

Creating a totally original name for a child is traditional in many cultures. The Chinese have few "common" first names because each child is believed too special to be given a name many others have used before. The same is true of some American Indians, who believe a person's name is his soul and so must be totally personal. In fact, it was said of many an Indian paradise that you had only to tell the gods your name to be admitted. Among these Indians, then, if two people accidentally ended up with the same name, one of them would choose a new one. The Purim Kukis, a tiny Tibeto-Burmese tribe in China, actually have clan monopolies on names, and if anyone takes a name from another clan, he is fined a pig and a pot of rice brew, but allowed to keep the name.

In many cultures original names are created from an event in the father's life. The Miwok Indian name Lipetu, for example, means "bear going over a man hiding between rocks," referring to a close call the father had with the animal. Or the child might be named for an event at birth; for instance, the Miwok girl called Huyana ("rain falling") was probably born during a rainstorm. Another favorite custom, that of naming children for the first object one of the parents sees after birth, accounts for unusual names like the Zuni Indian Taci ("washtub") and Tiwa ("onions").

The ways to create your own name are limited only by

your imagination. But the most common methods include the following.

Anagrams

Creating a name anagram involves taking a word that has special meaning to you and switching the letters until you have a pleasant-sounding name. "Peace" might become Capee or Ceepa, "earth" can be switched to Retha, and so forth.

Telescoping from Contemporary Newsmakers or Famous Namesakes

Telescoping simply involves dropping letters from a word until you arrive at a suitable name. If you want to telescope from the name of a person you admire—Martin Luther King, Jr., for example—you might shorten the name to Marin or Marnin. Or Kahlil Gibran can be changed to Kabran. You might also telescope and then juggle the letters to create a name. Hence, Golda Meir might be shortened to (Go)lda Me(ir), which can then become Melda.

Telescoping from Trends

This process simply involves using the first letters of words to create a name. You might create a "world peace" telescope from the words *peace, interdependence, enlightenment,* and *trust,* producing the name Piet. Or you might create the "unspoiled nature" telescope Tesa from the words *trees, earth, streams,* and *air.* Another possibility is to use first letters from a favorite saying, or book, movie, or song title.

Inversions

To create a name by inversion, you switch the syllables in a familiar name. Examples are Mary to Ryma, the flower name Dahlia to Liadah, Marco to Comar, the Spanish Blanco to Coblan, and Donald to Alddon.

Names from the Father's Name

A boy, of course, can be named after his father by adding "junior" or a Roman numeral, or by shortening the father's name. Donald might name his son Donal or Doni. Similarly, a girl can be named after her father by adding one of dozens of feminine suffixes. The combinations are virtually endless. For example, from the name John a girl might be called Joni, Jonie, Joney, Jony, Jonine, Jonisa, Jonitta, Jonitte, Jonit, Jonica, Jonitka, Jonitsa, Joniki, Jonanne, Jonille, Jonsay, Jonette, Jonetta, Jonia, Jonya, or Jonalee to name only a few. These, in turn, could be spelled with an initial *John* in place of *Jon*, two *n*s instead of one, and so forth.

Names from the Mother's Name

The most popular way to name a boy after his mother (especially in the upper classes) is to use her maiden name. Thus, a boy may be named Ward, Grey, Parker, Potter, Richardson, Davis, Ross, Cole, Sanders, Taylor, or Johnson. Again, as with the father's name, the mother's name can be shortened and used with male suffixes. Hence, the name Mary, transformed into a boy's name, could become Marston, Marton, Marten, Marnett, Marsin, Marson, Marald, Mardy, Marle, Marley, Marrand, Marick, Marwin, Marris, Marty, Marren, Marnand, and so forth. In the same way, Maria could become a feminine Mari, Marine, Marissa, Marica, or Maritsa, to name but a few. See examples from the preceding section for other common feminine suffixes.

Inventing Names by Combining Those of the Parents

This method of making up names is practically self-explanatory. The parents' first or first and middle names are written down, and letters are dropped, added, or juggled until a pleasant name is formed. Joseph and Ellen might name their little girl Joselle, or Daniel and Susan might call their boy Dansan. The first letters of the parents' names could also be used to form a new name. For instance, Gerald and Ida Adams might call their daughter Gia.

Apheresis

Apheresis involves dropping unaccented syllables from the beginning of a name. Since this has already been done with many familiar names (Tilda from Matilda, Beth from Elizabeth), if you want to create a new name using this method you'll probably have to use an unusual name to start with. Examples of apheresis using unusual names are the Hebrew Arella to Rella, the Russian Amaliya to Maliya or Liya, and the American Indian name Aponi to Poni.

Apocopation

Apocopation is apheresis reversed. You drop unaccented last syllables to create a new name. Again, we have common examples, such as Elisa from Elisabeth or Nicol from Nicholas. You might shorten the Swahili Azizi to Azi, the Irish Delano to Delan, or the Russian Lidiya to Lidi.

Diminutives

After using apocopation, you might choose to create a diminutive by adding a pet ending. For example, you might drop the final syllable of Arna and add the suffix -ette to produce Arnette (just as mothers of the past changed Susan into Susette). The more common Sharon becomes Shari, Sharie, Shary, Sharita, Sharette, Shareen, and so forth. The examples under "Names from the Mother's Name" give you typical masculine endings to get you started, whereas common feminine endings are listed under "Names from the Father's Name."

Combinations

Combinations are made almost exactly like names invented by combining those of the parents, except that you go a step further and create a new name with a specific, personal meaning. For instance, Avra could be created by combining the two Hebrew names Avirice, meaning "air" or "atmosphere," and Burura, meaning "clean" or "pure." The name Avra, then, might express your hope for the future—a clean atmosphere with pure, fresh air.

Sex Switches and Respellings

Sex switches and respellings are becoming increasingly common today. Examples of boys' names already being used for girls include Harper and Sydney, Gari from Gary, and Darsey from Darcy. Respelling usually involves changing *i* to *ie* or *y* or vice versa, *k* to *c* or the reverse, or *e* to *i* or *y*, producing examples like Karin, Carin, Caren, Caryn, Karyn, Ellyn, Robyn, Kari, Karie, Kary, and so forth. Another possibility is to capitalize a letter in the middle of a name, creating names like MariAnne and ArLene or to hyphenate a name like Sue-Ellen.

CHAPTER 3

Choosing a Name That Reflects Your Roots

This chapter will give you a general overview of names that have been collected from other cultures, including their traditions, customs, and naming practices.

African

Naming customs vary greatly in Africa, but the types of names most commonly found denote the time of birth ("born on Sunday"), the order of birth ("first-born daughter"), a physical characteristic, or a recent family incident. Sadly, because of Africa's generally high infant mortality rates, mothers in Ghana and many other countries do not name a child until it has survived seven days, and many names express the parents' concern that the baby will die. Some children are, in fact, believed to be reincarnated spirits who quickly enter and leave this world, and such infants are given what are called "born-to-die" names in an attempt to prevent them from returning to the spirit world. Kaya, a common Ghanaian name, means "stay and don't go back (don't die)," while the Yoruba name Kosoko translates as "there is no hoe (to dig a grave with)."

Some of the most fascinating African names come from Yoruba and Umbundu proverbs. Examples are Cilehe, from "just let it stink, let it be," meaning if you bother it, you will make it worse; Kanene, from "a little thing in the eye is big"; and Ayondela, "a little tree bends and bends, as we all bend toward death." Among the Ibo-speaking people of Nigeria, short-sentence names are popular and include names such as Dumaka ("help me with your hands") and Nnamdi ("my father is alive").

Other African names commemorate the spirits. The Ibo god Chi, for instance, gives rise to such names as Cinese ("Chi is protecting"), Cis (which simply means "Chi"), and Chinelo ("thought of Chi"). Chi, a personal god thought to stay with a person from conception until death, is believed to be the cause of myriad misfortunes as well as successes.

Included here are Hausa, Ibo, Umbundu, Bari, Yoruba, Swahili, and other African names, as well as several early Afro-American names. Some names reflecting African roots can also be found among Arabic entries.

American Indian

Today American Indians may very well be named John, William, or Robert. But traditional American Indian names are far more colorful and often contain hidden stories. The Miwoks, one of the largest groups of Indians in California, for example, have in their heritage many extremely colorful names, which reveal much about traditional Indian life and the Miwok's once close partnership with the natural world. These names often imply far more than their literal meanings. To a person who understands Moquelumnan (the Miwok language), the name Memtba simply means "to taste." But if you'd ask a Miwok named Memtba what his name really means, he might say, "Tasting farewell-to-spring seed after it has been mashed with the pestle, but while it's still in the mortar." Probing still deeper, you might find the name describes what Memtba's mother was doing when she felt her first labor pain. To a stranger, the name Luyunu simply means "to shake the head sideways." But to Luyunu's friends, his name is really "bear taking off a leg or arm of a person while eating him," implying the child has the strength of a vicious bear.

The complexity of the meanings behind Indian names has

led American Indian names to often be misunderstood. An American Indian name that translates into English as "sweaty blanket" does not indicate that its bearer had a dirty bed, but that he was a tireless rider.

Many imaginative, ecological names taken from plants, animals, the stars and moon, and other natural phenomena come to us from the American Indians. It's because of the American Indians' detailed observations and close associations with nature that we have such names as Taipa meaning "valley quail spreading its wings as it alights," and Tiponya, "great horned owl sticking her head under her body and poking an egg that is hatching." Such names may refer to an actual event or to a dream one of the baby's parents had.

Because of a strong belief in each person's individuality and unique soul, an American Indian following traditional practices would seldom take one of his parents' names. Instead, his name might mirror a proud event in his father's or grandfather's life. Wakiza ("desperate fighter"), for example, may refer to a battle won without weapons, and Kijika ("walks quietly") to a time the older man noiselessly sneaked up on a deer in the forest. Similarly, a child born during a storm might be given a name as imposing as Shappa ("red thunder") or as whimsical as Lokni ("rain coming through a small hole in the roof").

In contrast (though the practice has diminished over time), some Eskimos still believe that they *must* give a newborn a recently deceased relative's name, since the dead return to this world only through their names. In the same Eskimo families, however, it is taboo to name a child after a living relative, because the name would then be saddled with two bodies, one of which it is believed would have to die.

Because of the tendency to create new names, there are no "most common" American Indian names. The most typical names, however, are nature names, magical names taken from the gods, war and peace names, and names that simply have pretty meanings, such as Halona ("happy fortune") and Onida ("the looked-for one").

Arabic and Moslem

The fact that Arabic and Moslem names have remained virtually unchanged for over two thousand years may account for their strongly felt influence on names in many other cultures. Nearly every country has a version of the Arabic Leila ("born at night"), and a high percentage of Swahili names are simply slight variants of the Arabic.

Many popular Arabic names come from the ninety-nine qualities of God listed in the Koran: Karim ("generous"), Kamil ("perfect"), Hakeem ("wise"), Kadar ("powerful"), and Nasser ("victorious"). In addition, these are often prefixed with *Abdul*, *Abdel*, or *Abd*, each meaning "servant of." Abdel Nasser, as an example, means "servant of the victorious One." Moslem names, on the other hand, are usually derived from those of the Prophet Muhammad's descendants or immediate family: Ali, Hashim, and Hussein for boys, and Fatma, Aisha (also spelled Ayasha), and Hinda for girls. The Prophet's name, with its estimated five hundred variations, is often considered the most popular name in the world, and a pious Moslem saying goes, "If you have a hundred sons, name them all Muhammad."

Following religious names in popularity are those describing an abstract quality or virtue. Girls are named Amineh ("faithful"), Marid ("rebellious"), and Zarifa ("graceful"), whereas boys are called Sharif ("honest"), Nabil ("noble"), and Zaki ("intelligent"). Similar are Rafi ("exalting"), and Yasar ("wealth"), names which, according to Orthodox Moslems, Muhammad disdained because they were too proud.

Although less common than a century ago, animal names are also used today. Typical are Hamal ("lamb") and Numair ("panther"). Nature names like Rabi ("fragrant breeze") and occupation names such as Harith ("ploughman") are also common.

To avoid using a person's name too casually, considered the peak of rudeness, Arabs often attach prefixes to names. In this way, Sharif's father might be called Abu Sharif ("father of Sharif"), and his mother Um Sharif ("mother of Sharif") instead of by their own given names. Similarly,

Bin, Binte, or Ibn ("daughter of" or "son of") followed by the father's name is often used in place of a child's true given name.

Chinese

Chinese parents create an original name for each child, usually making certain all the names in the family "go together." Thus, Precious Jade's sisters might be named Precious Jewel and Precious Peace. Also, unlike in most other cultures, Chinese first and middle names are selected to have a good combined meaning, the idea being that a good name enhances social status.

In the past some parents selected the most repulsive names they could think of, examples being names that translate into English as "swine urine" and "cat vomit," hoping that evil spirits would be fooled into thinking the child was unloved and would leave him alone. Occasionally even today, parents give boys girls' names to deceive the demons, who supposedly prefer to harm males.

Because Chinese names are so individual, few common names exist, and to have a true Chinese name, you should create one of your own. A few Chinese names are included to give you possible ideas and words to work with, such as Mu Lan ("magnolia blossom") and Mu Tan ("tree peony blossom"). However, you will probably want to use a good Chinese-English dictionary, too. One reminder: When studying Chinese names, don't forget that Chinese surnames are written first and the given names last.

Hawaiian

Many contemporary Hawaiian names are adaptations of English or Biblical names. Some are similar to the English names, such as Dorisa for Doris, whereas others have been changed more significantly (Akoni for Anthony, for example). Although Hawaiians have many short names, they also have some of the longest in the world, and the custom of giving a child an English first name with a Hawaiian middle name sometimes produces fascinating combinations. One example is David Kekoalauliionapalihauliuliokekoolau Kaapuawaokamehameha, nicknamed Kekoa Kaapu. While such names often seem odd to outsiders, they usually have melodic, picturesque meanings, the above being "the fine-leafed koa tree on the beautiful green ridges of the Koolau (mountains)." The same boy's sister was named Kapuale-huaonapalilahilahiokaala, or "the lehua flower blooming on the steep ridges of Mount Kaala."

In this book you will find shorter names with similarly pretty meanings. Alaula ("light of early dawn" or "sunset glow") and Aolani ("heavenly cloud") are typical and can be given to both boys and girls.

Many pretty Hawaiian names are created by the parents from an incident at birth. For instance, if a father looked up and saw a seagull shortly after his daughter was born, he might name her Iwalani ("heavenly seabird") or perhaps Iulani ("the highest point of heaven"). The names listed in this book, therefore, are only samples of the many names you can create. Some of the most commonly used elements in Hawaiian names include: Lani ("sky" or "heavenly"), Pua ("flower"), Olu ("gentle"), Mele ("a song" or "poem"), Lei ("wreath" or "child"), Ipo ("darling"), Iao (name of a star), Kapu ("sacred"), Malu ("peace"), Nani ("beautiful"), and Ola ("life" or "health"). Two common names, in fact, are combinations from this list: Pualani, which means "heavenly flower," and Puanani, "beautiful flower." Another example: Melei, from Mele plus Lei, meaning "song child."

Hindustani

Most Hindu names come from the many Hindu gods, who are actually manifestations of the One God. Common boys' names include Kistna, Hanuman, Siva, Rama, Narain, and Valli, while Devaki, Devi, Sakti, and Ratri are popular for girls.

Although high castes were once legally forbidden to marry anyone with a "plebeian" nature name, girls today are often named after rivers, flowers, trees, animals, and stars. Like some Chinese and African people, some Hindus believe an ugly name will trick demons into thinking the child is not worth notice. Such parents may name a child Klesa ("pain") or Kirwa ("worm").

The many suffixes added to Hindu names make the combinations and variations of one name almost endless. For example, in the Punjab, where children are named after common words, Nath ("lord"), may become Natha, Nathi, Natho, Nathan, Nathu Rai, Nathu, and Nathi Mall, to name only a few variations. Most of the entries in this book are simple forms of Hindu names, and to create your own name you might add any of about sixty suffixes used today, some of which can be considered names themselves. The more common ones are: Rai ("prince"), Lal ("cherished"), Ram ("god"), Mall or Sena ("warrior"), Singh or Simha ("lion"), Autar ("incarnation"), Das or Dasa ("slave"), Gupta ("protector"), Guha ("secret"), Varma ("shield"), Putra ("son"), Datta ("gift"), Vala ("mine" or "from"), Tirtha ("ford"), Sagara ("ocean"), Pandita ("scholar"), Ananda ("bliss"), and Ji ("soul" or "life"). For example, to create your own contemporary name, you might take Kali, which is another name for the goddess Sakti, and add the suffix *das* to create Kalidas, meaning "slave of Kali" or "devoted to Kali." Or since the Hindus often split one long name in two, you might pick one of the above elements as a middle name.

Japanese

The most typical Japanese girls' names denote virtue, with examples being Setsu ("fidelity"), Shizu ("quiet" or "clear"), and Sumi ("the refined"). Similarly, many other names have an implied virtue meaning. For instance, Umeko, meaning "plum-blossom child," also connotes wifely devotion, whereas a name from the lotus blossom implies all the Buddhist concepts of a heaven where immortal souls sleep enveloped in lotus buds until they are admitted to paradise.

The Japanese also use order-of-birth and number names for children. Hence, we find Ichi, meaning "one," all the way up to Man, or "ten thousand." The smaller numbers often indicate order of birth, the higher ones, such as eighty, a hope for longevity; very large round numbers, such as ten thousand, were once considered good omens. Numeral names, of course, leave opportunities for whimsy, as in the family of children named "ten dollars," "one hundred dollars," and "one thousand dollars," or the boy called "1-2-3-4-5-6-7-8-9-10."

The most common girls' names include Chika or Chikako ("near"), Kiku ("chrysanthemum"), Suzu ("little bell"), and Taka or Takako ("lofty"). Common for boys are Taro ("first male"), Jiro ("second male"), Saburo ("third male"), and Akio ("bright boy").

You can create your own boys' name by using any of a number of prefixes, the most common of which are *Toku* ("virtue"), *Masa* ("good"), *Zen* ("just"), *Michi* ("righteous way"), *Yu* ("courage"), and *Shin* ("faithful"). Masataro, for example, means "good first-born male," and so forth. You will find other major elements to use with these prefixes in the regular name lists. Similarly, you can create your own girls' name by adding the suffixes, *-ko*, *-yo*, or *-e* to regular name elements. Thus, Kiku and Suzu might become Kikuko and Suzuyo.

Jewish

Jewish people traditionally give their children two first names, one purely Hebrew (the *shem hakodesh*, or holy name) and the other secular. In America, the holy name is often only used in the synagogue.

If you're Jewish, how names are commonly bestowed in your family often depends on your family's roots. Among orthodox Ashkenazic Jews (who hail from Germany, Austria, Poland, and Russia), it's considered bad form to name a child after a living relative. This taboo springs from an ancient superstition that naming a baby after a living person will rob the original namesake of a full life and may upset the spirit of the dead. It's considered especially poor judgment to name a baby after an older relative; it's believed the angel of death might confuse the two names and when it's time for the older relative to die might take the baby by mistake. When orthodox Ashkenazic Jewish parents name a child after a favorite relative it is one who is deceased. Often they'll borrow only the first letter of the relative's name. Thus, it's understood that baby Michael is named in Uncle Murray's honor.

Conversely, among Sephardic Jews (from France, Italy, Spain, and Portugal), it's customary and quite common to name a baby after a living relative.

In Israel, where the most common name today is Moshe, it has become popular to choose a name which sounds unmistakably Israeli, yet is easy for Gentiles to pronounce and remember. Names of this type often end in *n* and have no more than four consonants: Doron, Rimon, Givon, and the like. In Israel, as in the United States, the trend is toward shortened names. Zlatopolsky becomes Paz, and Taranto, Tal. Other formerly long names include Dan, Gal, Kol, Nir, Niv, and Ziv. At one time, animal names like Lieb, or "lion," were widely used, but the modern trend is toward plant and flower names, such as the feminine Nurit, meaning "little yellow flower."

Hebraizing names by rearranging the letters is popular in Israel and was recommended by the late Moshe Sharett as well as other leaders. Thus, Kleinman becomes Kenan, Neurath becomes Nur, and so forth. You will find many of these shortened forms in the name list, as well as longer names you may want to abbreviate yourself. (Of course, names from the Torah and Bible also have Hebraic roots.)

Russian

Several years ago Russians were urged to give their children Russian-sounding names like Ivan, Vladlen, Vladislav, Anna, Vera, and Sofia. In fact, more foreign-sounding names were even ridiculed, the Russian *Gazette* commenting that names like Azalia, Ella, Alfred, and Henry are not only unpatriotic but ludicrous. According to a recent article in the daily *Pravda*, the four most popular names for girls in Russia are currently Yelena, Natalya, Olga, and Irina, while the big favorites for boys are Sergei, Aleksei, Aleksandr, and Oleg. But as in the United States, popular names in Russia shift from year to year. Several years ago Alexander and the feminine equivalent Alexandra (both of which are commonly shortened to Sasha) were so popular that one Russian remarked, "If you yell 'Sasha' on a Moscow street, twenty men and a couple of women will look around."

Unlike people in many other nations, the Russians seldom name their children after political figures for fear the child's namesake may fall out of favor. Many women named Stalina hastened to change their names after Stalin was posthumously denounced in 1956 and again in 1961. One man named Melsor (a telescope name from *M*arx, *E*ngels, *L*enin, *S*talin, and *O*ctober *R*evolution) actually went so far as to drop the *s* from his name and become simply Melor.

No other people in the world use pet forms, variations, and nicknames more extensively than do the Russians. A man named Ivan Ivanovich Ivanov (the Russian equivalent of John Doe), for example, might be called by any of forty or fifty different names, including Vanya, Vanechka, Ivanyshka, Vanyashka, Vanka, Vanyatka, Vanykha, Vanushka, Vanushechka, Vanek, Vanka, Vanko, and Yanka. Likewise, a girl named Agneshka, the Russian development or equivalent of the English Agnes, can be called Nessa, Nessia, Agnita, Agnya, Gusya, Nyusha, Ahniya, Nyushka, and Agnesa, all of which are in a sense her names. In addition, each pet name has an implied meaning. Names ending in -*ka*, for instance, are used in anger, while those ending in -*usha* or -*ya* are special terms of endearment.

Scandinavian

Many Scandinavian names refer to leadership in battle, to bravery, or to Norse mythology. The Swedish Lars means "crowned with laurel," a victory symbol, Akin is "descent of the eternal king," and Bodil means "commanding." You'll rarely find peace names from Scandinavia, the exceptions being names that start with *Fred* (such as Fredrik, meaning "peaceful ruler," often shortened to Frits).

The Scandinavians have given the world a number of individualistic names, such as Hamar ("a symbol of man's ingenuity") and Einer ("individualist" or "nonconformist").

These northern countries are also great sources of short, masculine names—Alf, Alrik, Arens, Garth, Arni, Sven, Lars, and Jens, for example. You can find many lovely Norwegian, Swedish, and Danish girls' names, too, including Arla, Disa, Gressa, Meri, Beda, Blenda, Birgitta, and Gretchen.

While many Scandinavians, particularly Norwegians, have common Biblical names, such as John, Peter, Ester, and Evelyn, it is fashionable today to give children names with a more Nordic flavor. Common names include Björn, Jens, Josef, Knut, Lars, Sven, Erik, Gunnar, Hans, Nils, Rolf, Olaf, and Karl. Popular for girls are Katrina, Ingrid, Helga, Dorotea, Jonina, Else, Astrid, Signe, Britta, Karin, Margareta, and Rakel.

Slavic

Slavic names include Polish, Slovak, and Czech or Bohemian names. At first glance, some names used in these countries may appear awkward. But the Slavic practice of pronouncing words with the stress on the first syllable and with the soft *sh* instead of *s* and *zh* in place of *z* makes these names almost melodic. Anezka becomes AH-nehzh-kah, and Anicka is pronounced AH-neesh-kah.

Many typical boys' names end in *-slav* or the Polish *-slaw*, which means "glory." In addition to Jaroslav ("glory of spring"), other glory names include Budislav ("future glory"), Ladislav ("glorious government"), Miroslav ("glorious peace"), Vaslav ("glorious wealth") and Vladislav ("glorious ruler"). Some of the more popular Czech names are Radomil ("love of peace"), Bohdan ("God-given"), Bohumir ("peace of God"), as well as Filip, Jan, Jakub, Josef, Karel, Jiri, Pavel, Tomas, and Vilem. Common names for girls are Bela, Ludmila, Maria, Rusalka, Anezka, Svetla, and Zofie. Many Slavic girls' names are created by simply adding *-a* to a boy's name, making Pavela from Pavel, for instance.

Although Polish names typically end in *-slaw* (masculine) or *-slawa* (feminine), these are usually replaced by shorter nicknames. The Polish name Hortensja, for example, is often shortened to a prettier Tesia (TE-shuh) and Giertruda frequently becomes just Truda.

Spanish

Spanish names are usually taken from the calendar of saints, and a "typical" name in Mexico, Spain, and other Latin countries will have religious connotations. For girls, Maria is so popular that additional names relating to some quality of Mary, the mother of Jesus, have been added to differentiate among the thousands of Maria Garcias and Maria Chavezes. For this reason, you will find Maria de los Dolores ("Mary of Sorrows"), which is often shortened to Lolita, Lola, or simply Dolores; Maria de la Cruz ("Mary of the Cross"); and many similar names. Widely popular forms of such Virgin Mary names include: Luz and Lucita, from Maria de la Luz ("Mary of the Light"), Carmen ("Mary of Scarlet"), Jesusa ("Mary of Jesus"), and Suela from Maria del Consuela ("Mary of Consolation"). The popular name Pilar, meaning "pillar," used for both boys and girls, also refers to Mary, who stands as the base or pillar of the Christian religion.

Occasionally you will see combinations of other names with Maria, a technique you may want to use to create your own Spanish name. Thus, Maria plus Flora gives you Mariflor. Other examples are Maria and Ramona, which blend to create Marona, and Maria plus Linda, Marinda.

The most popular Spanish boys' names have as many pet forms (or nicknames) as English names do. Francisco, for example, has at least sixteen Spanish variations, some of the most common being Chico, Paco, Pancho, Curro, and Paquito. The favorite names for boys throughout the Spanish-speaking world include Juan, José, Pablo, Pauel, Pedro, Rafael, Mario, Manuel, Jaime, Luis, Jesus, and Miguel.

Turkish

Because of intense national pride, the Turks have been encouraged to exchange names with foreign derivations for names derived exclusively from Turkish. Cemal ("beauty"), Halim ("gentle" or "patient"), and Kabil (a form of Cain, meaning "possessed" or "possession"), have been discarded in favor of the Turkish Cahil ("young"), Deniz ("sea" or "storm"), and Halil ("intimate friend"). As a result, the old source of Turkish names—the Koran—is less popular today than it was in the past. Still quite common, however, are the Koran names Hasan, Mehmet, Ali, Ibrahim, Osman, and Suleyman.

Turkish given names are traditionally more important than in some other cultures because surnames were not used in Turkey before the 1930s. Hence, like the Chinese and many American Indians, Turkish people often change or add to a boy's name at each important event in his life. A boy, therefore, could receive names upon birth (the umbilical names), circumcision, his first day of school, graduation, and marriage, as well as several nicknames. Girls' names, in contrast, tend to be fewer and less changing.

CHAPTER 4

Choosing an Astrological, Magical, or Numerological Name

People from cultures around the globe have believed names have magical powers and that just by bestowing a certain name, you can instill positive traits in your baby. It's such "magical" (perhaps even subconscious) thinking that may have given rise to such American names, first used by the Puritans, as Faith, Hope and Charity.

Astrological names, for example, are bestowed according to time of birth in the hopes that such names will be lucky and work in harmony with the stars. A child born under Leo might be given a name meaning "lion," the symbol of that sign of the zodiac, or one meaning "sun," the star that governs Leo.

Oriental astrologers believe a lucky horoscope balances the basic elements—earth, fire, air, water, metal, and wood— to allow the universal order to work smoothly throughout a person's life. In China, if the astrologer who casts the baby's horoscope on the third day of life finds too many wood influences, he may correct this "evil" by giving the baby a metal name (because metal conquers wood) or a name meaning "earth" (since earth produces—and controls—metal ores). Astrological earth names, for example, include Clay ("of the earth"), Blair ("child of the fields"), and Ertha or Eartha (both meaning "child of the earth"). A child with too many wood influences may also be given a fire name, such as Edan (meaning "fire") because fire burns up wood.

THE TWELVE SIGNS OF THE ZODIAC

SIGN	SYMBOL	ELEMENT	BIRTH-STONE	FLOWER	COLOR	RULING PLANET
Aries *(March 21-April 20)*	Ram	Fire	Diamond	Daisy	Deep red	Mars
Taurus *(April 21-May 20)*	Bull	Earth	Emerald	Lily-of-the-Valley	Deep yellow	Venus
Gemini *(May 21-June 20)*	Twins	Air	Pearl	Rose	Violet	Mercury
Cancer *(June 21-July 22)*	Crab	Water	Ruby	Water Lily	Light green	Moon
Leo *(July 23-August 22)*	Lion	Fire	Sardonyx	Gladiolus	Light orange	Sun
Virgo *(August 23-Sept. 23)*	Virgin	Earth	Sapphire	Aster	Dark violet	Mercury
Libra *(Sept. 24-Oct. 23)*	The Balances	Air	Opal	Cosmos	Yellow	Venus
Scorpio *(Oct. 24-Nov. 22)*	Scorpion	Water	Topaz	Mum	Red	Mars
Sagittarius *(Nov. 23-Dec. 22)*	Archer	Fire	Turquoise	Narcissus	Light purple	Jupiter
Capricorn *(Dec. 23-Jan. 20)*	Goat	Earth	Garnet	Carnation	Deep blue	Saturn
Aquarius *(Jan. 21-Feb.19)*	Water Bearer or Sage	Air	Amethyst	Violet	Light blue	Uranus
Pisces *(Feb. 20-March 20)*	Fish	Water	Bloodstone	Daffodil	Dark purple	Neptune

Likewise, if a baby's horoscope contains too many metal influences, the baby may be given an "aquatic" name (such as Rea, meaning "a stream") because water rusts and erodes metal. Some astrologers also believe metal names, with meanings like "iron" or "hammer" improve a baby's health and fate.

Other names stemming from ancient Oriental magic beliefs include Japanese color names like Akako ("red") and material names like Tetsu ("iron"). The color red, believed to cure diseases and ensure good health, was once considered a potent protector, while the material names probably date back to an ancient idea that demons and evil spirits were born in the Stone Age and hence feared metals, especially iron. It was thus believed that if a tiny baby girl were named Tetsu, the evil spirits would shun her for a child with a less frightful name.

Many magical or astrological names are included in this book. Not only are there magical names of all the above types, but also some delightful magic names used in incantations to summon or exorcise spirits, plus a few deity names from the Egyptian *Book of the Dead*, often considered the original record of magic. A fascinating group of magic names are those of the English Gypsies, who've long had a close kinship with fortune-telling and the supernatural.

In many cultures down through history, numbers have also been believed to have magical powers or some ability to influence fate. In Japan, where round numbers were once thought to be good omens, children are still occasionally named Sen ("thousand"), Michi ("three thousand"), or Yachiyo ("eight thousand generations"). Lest these examples seem merely an unusual Oriental custom, you should know that a man in Stanford, California, was named 4E Chittenden, and another American's birth certificate name read Willie ⅝ Smith.

Many other beliefs are embodied in numerology, begun by the Greek philosopher Pythagoras, whose fascination with ciphers led him to number the letters of the alphabet. The result was numerology. One success story involves commentator and columnist Hedda Hopper, who supposedly was a loser as Elda Furry, a bit more successful as the married Elda Hopper, but never really began to achieve fame until a numerologist selected the name Hedda.

There are no "numerologically good" first names as such because the complete name must be counted. To do this, add the numbers of the letters in a name, including the middle and last names, according to this chart.

1	2	3	4	5	6	7	8	9
A	B	C	D	E	F	G	H	I
J	K	L	M	N	O	P	Q	R
S	T	U	V	W	X	Y	Z	

You will probably come up with two digits—81, for example. Add the digits together to get the name's destiny number, in this case 9 (8 plus 1). If you have two digits, which add up to another two digits—98, for example, which gives you 17—simply keep adding until you get a number under 10, in the latter case 8 (1 plus 7). Eleven is seldom reduced to 2 because 7 and 11 are considered master numbers, bestowing great intelligence and leadership abilities.

Generally the qualities associated with each number are as follows: 1, creative; 2, friendly, a follower; 3, artistic; 4, home-loving, peaceful; 5, a traveler, seeker of truth; 6, scholar, with a social conscience; 7, intelligent, a leader; 8, ambitious, organized; and 9, just, righteous, a conscientious objector.

Magic names can be fun to play around with. And who knows? By fiddling around with a name's numerology or astrological influence, you may give your child even more than an interesting name.

PRONUNCIATION GUIDE

Of course, you can pronounce your baby's name however you please. Some parents, for example, pronounce the name Elisa as e-LEES-ah, whereas others prefer ee-LIGH-zah. Nevertheless, for those who would like to choose a name from another culture and also retain its traditional pronunciation, many pronunciations are included. The symbols used represent the following sounds.

A	*a* as in *at*
AH	*a* as in *father*
AW	*aw* as in *hawk*
AY	*ay* as in *say*
E	*e* as in *met*
EH	almost *a* as in *mate*, only shorter
I	*i* as in *bit*
IGH	*i* as in *rise*
O or OH	*o* as in *note*
OW	*ow* as in *how*
OO	*oo* as in *moon*
OO:	*oo* as in *foot*
UH	*u* as in *under*
ZH	*z* as in *azure*

Occasionally a name will contain a single consonant as a separate syllable. Such syllabic consonants are designated by a period after the letter (example: K.). Accented syllables are indicated by capital letters, except in some Hindu and Oriental names, which have no accented syllables.

CHAPTER 5

Girls' Names

A

Aba (ah-BAH) Ghanaian: "born on Thursday."

Abebi (ah-bay-BEE) Yoruba, Nigeria: "we asked for her and she came to us."
Abeni

Abina (ah-bee-NAH) Akan, Southern Ghana: "born on *Benada* (Thursday)."
Abana, Abena

Abiona (ah-BEE-o-nah) Yoruba, Nigeria: "born during a journey." Also a boys' name.

Abira (ah-BEE-ah) Hebrew: "strong."
Adira

Abital (ah-BEE-tahl) Hebrew: "my father is dew." Popular in Israel for girls and boys.
Avital

Ada Old English: "happy"; or from Latin: "of noble birth"; or from Hebrew: "an ornament."
Adda, Addi, Addie, Adi, Aida

Adamina Hebrew: "daughter of the red earth." Astrological name for a girl born under one of the earth signs: Capricorn, Taurus, or Virgo.

Adamma (ah-DAHM-mah) Ibo, Nigeria: "child of beauty."

Adara Greek: "beauty"; or Arabic: "virgin," the symbol of the astrological sign Virgo.

Adelle Old German: "noble."
Adaline, Addi, Addie, Addy, Adela, Adele, Adelina, Adeline, Adella, Aline, Edeline (English); *Ada, Adela, Adele, Adelka, Dela* (Czech); *Adele, Adelina* (French); *Akela* (Hawaiian); *Adel* (Hungarian); *Adelina* (Italian); *Ada, Adelaida, Ela* (Polish); *Adel, Adela, Adelina, Adeliya* (Russian); *Adelita, Alita, Dela, Lela* (Spanish)

Aderes (ah-de-RAYS) Hebrew: "an outer garment" or "a cape."
Aderet

Adesina (ah-DAY-see-nah) Yoruba, Nigeria: "the coming of this baby has opened the way (for more children)." Often used in Nigeria when the parents have waited a long time for a child.

Adia (ah-DEE-ah) Swahili: "gift" or "present," implying the child is a gift from God.

Adie (ah-dee-AY) Hebrew: "an ornament."
Ada, Adiella

Aditi (ah-dee-tee)—Hindi: "free and unbounded." In Hindu lore Aditi is the mother of the gods and is often asked to bestow blessings on children and cattle or to grant protection and forgiveness.

Adoette (ah-do-AY-tuh) North American Indian: "big tree." Among the Indians, this name was probably given to a child born beneath a tree or believed to be akin to a tree spirit.

Adrienne Latin: "dark one." Commonly used in the United States and France.
Adri, Adria, Adriana, Adrie, Adriena (English); *Adriane* (German); *Adriana* (Italian)

Adya East Indian from *Teluga Adivaram:* "Sunday." Given to a girl born on Sunday.

Agata Greek: "good" or "kind." A truly New Age name, Agata is already used around the globe in Bulgaria, Ireland, Czechoslovakia, Italy, Latvia, Poland, Portugal, Russia, Rumania, Sweden, Spanish-speaking countries, and the United States.
Ag, Agatha, Aggi, Aggie, Aggy, Agna, Agneta, Agnetta, Agnessa (English); *Agathe* (French, German); *Agathi* (Greek); *Agi, Agota, Agotha* (Hungarian); *Agnesina* (Italian); *Aga, Agatka, Atka* (Polish); *Agueda* (Portuguese); *Agafia, Agasha, Ganya, Gasha, Gashka* (Russian)

Agate "the agate stone." The magical agate stone was once believed to cure the bites of scorpions and snakes, soothe the mind, drive away polluted air, and stop thunder and lightning. The stone was also believed to make one independent, an eloquent writer and speaker, and a favorite of princes. Wearing an agate around one's neck allegedly gives one victory over enemies.

Agnella An Italian form of Agnes.

Agnes Greek: "pure." First made popular by Saint Agnes, a third-century virgin martyr. From the twelfth to sixteenth centuries, Agnes was one of the commonest names in England and in the sixteenth century it was among the top three (the others being Elizabeth and Joan). Lately this name has gone out of favor: in one study of stereotypes, only 12 percent of those asked thought an Agnes would be good-looking, although the name was characterized by 63 percent as "kind" and by 80 percent as "trustworthy."
Aggi, Aggie, Agna, Agneti, Anesse, Annice, Annis, Nesa, Nesi, Nessa, Nessi, Nessie, Nessy, Nesta, Neysa (English); *Agnessa* (Bulgarian); *Agnesa, Agneska, Anezka, Anka* (Czech); *Agnies* (French); *Agni* (Greek); *Agne, Agnella, Agnesca, Agnese, Agnola, Anete, Hagne* (Italian); *Agne, Agniya* (Lithuanian); *Aga, Agnieszka, Jaga* (Polish); *Ines, Inez* (Portuguese); *Agnessa, Nessa, Nessia, Nyusha* (Russian); *Ines, Inez, Necha, Necho, Nesho, Ynes, Ynez* (Spanish); *Agneta* (Swedish, Norwegian)

Ahava (ah-HAH-vah) Hebrew: "beloved."
Ahuda, Ahuva

Ah Kum (ah-koom) Chinese: "good as gold."

Ah Lam (ah-lahm) Chinese: "like an orchid."

Aida Old English: "happy." Popularized in Italy by the Verdi opera of the same name. See Ada.

Ailene Anglo-Irish: "light bearer."
Aileen, Ailey, Aili, Aleen, Alena, Alene, Eileen, Eleen, Elene, Ileana, Ileane, Ilena, Ilene, Leana, Lena (English); *Aila, Aili* (Finnish); *Ailinn* (Portuguese)

Aimee French form of Amy, "loved one."

Aisha (ah-EE-shah) Arabic: "life." See Ayasha.

Aiyana (eye-YAHN-nah) North American Indian: "eternal bloom."

Ajuji (ah-JOO-jee) Hausa of Africa: "refuse-heap child." The Hausa of Africa usually give this name to the surviving child of a woman whose other children have died. According to the tradition, when the baby is born, the grandparents take the child out to the refuse heap, the *juji*, and pretend to throw it away. After this gesture to the demons, the mother rushes out and reclaims her child.

Akako (ah-KAH-ko) Japanese: "red." This was once a magical name, red being considered a charm to cure diseases, particularly blood ailments. In one ancient Japanese tale, a powerful tree spirit is conquered because men attacking it painted their faces red, wore red shirts, and tied a red cord about the tree's trunk. Although the superstition is no longer believed, the name remains.

Akanke (ah-kahn-KEH) Yoruba, Nigeria: "to know her is to pet her."

Akela (ah-KAY-lah) Hawaiian form of Adelle, "noble."

Aki Japanese: "born in autumn."

Akilah (AH-kee-lah) Arabic: "intelligent" or "logical."

Alake (ah-lah-KAY) Yoruba, Nigeria: "one to be petted if she survives." Often bestowed on an unhealthy child.

Alala Greek: "Mars's sister" or "war goddess." Astrological name for a girl born under Aries or Scorpio, the signs ruled by the fiery planet Mars.

Alamea (ah-luh-MAY-uh) Hawaiian: "ripe" or "precious."

Alameda (ah-la-MAY-dah) North American Indian: "cottonwood grove"; or Spanish: "promenade."

Alana (uh-LAH-nuh) Hawaiian: "an offering" or "light and buoyant."

Alani (ah-LAH-nee) Hawaiian: "orange" or "orange tree." Refers in particular to the oahu tree, with its oblong fragrant leaves, which are used for scenting cloth. Also a boys' name.

Alaqua (ah-LAH-quah) North American Indian: "sweet gum tree."

Alauda Gallic: "lark."

Alaula Hawaiian: "light of early dawn" or "sunset glow." Like most Hawaiian names, this one is given to either sex.

Alberta Old English: "noble and brilliant." A feminine form of Albert.
Albertina, Albertine, Alli, Allie, Berta, Berti, Bertie, Berty, Elberta, Elbertina, Elbertine, Elbi, Elbie, Elby (English); *Alba, Berta* (Czech); *Albertina* (German); *Alverta* (Greek); *Albertina* (Italian); *Albertine* (Latvian); *Albertyna, Alka, Berta* (Polish); *Berta, Bertunga* (Spanish)

Albina Latin *albinus*: "blond" or "white." Used today in many countries, including Italy, Russia, Portugal, Czechoslovakia, and the United States.

Alba, Albinia, Alvina, Alvinia (English); *Alva, Bela, Bina* (Czech); *Alwine* (German); *Ala, Albinka* (Polish); *Alvina* (Russian)

Aleeza Hebrew: "joy" or "joyful."
Aliza, Alizah, Alitza, Alitzah

Aleka (ah-LAY-kah) Modern Greek form of Alexandra, "helper and defender of mankind."

Alena (ah-LAY-nah) Modern Russian form of Helen.

Aleta (ah-LAY-tah) Contemporary Spanish name meaning "little winged one." Derived from Latin.
Alida (English)

Aletea (ah-leh-TEH-uh) Modern Spanish name meaning "the truth."

Alexandra Greek: "helper and defender of mankind." Once used primarily in Russia, now common worldwide.
Alex, Alexa, Alexine, Alexis, Alli, Lexi, Lexie, Lexine, Lexy, Sandi, Sandie, Sandy, Sandra, Zandra (English); *Alekko, Aleksi, Aleksey, Sander* (Bulgarian); *Ales, Leska, Lexa* (Czech); *Alexandrie, Alexius* (French); *Alexis, Alexius* (German); *Aleka, Alexiou, Ritsa* (Greek); *Alexa, Elek, Eli, Lekszi* (Hungarian); *Alessandra, Alessio* (Italian); *Aleska, Ala, Alka, Ola, Olesia* (Polish); *Alya, Aleksey, Aleks, Aleksasha, Alesha, Lelya, Lesya, Oleksa, Olesya, Sasha, Sasa, Shura, Shurka* (Russian); *Alejandra, Alejandrina, Jandina* (Spanish); *Dina, Drina*

Alexis Popular form of Alexandra in the United States and Germany. See Alexandra.

Algona (ahl-GO-nah) North American Indian: "valley of flowers."

Alhena (ahl-HEE-nuh) Arabic: "a ring." This name refers to a third-magnitude star in Pollux, part of the constellation of Gemini, the twins.

Ali Modern U.S. form of Alice or Alison.

Alice Greek *alethia*: "truthful."
Aleta, Aletha, Ali, Alicea, Alicia, Allie, Alis, Alisa, Alissa, Alisha, Alithia, Ally, Allyce, Allys, Alyce, Alycia, Ellie, Elsie, Elsa (English); *Alisa* (Bulgarian); *Alica* (Czech); *Alix* (French); *Adelicia, Alexia, Alexie, Elschen, Else, Ilse* (German); *Alike, Aliz, Alizka, Lici* (Greek); *Alika* (Hawaiian); *Alisz, Aliz, Alizka, Lici* (Hungarian); *Ailis* (Irish); *Alise* (Latvian); *Ala, Alisia* (Polish); *Elica, Eliza* (Rumanian); *Alisa, Alya* (Russian); *Elza* (Slavic); *Alicia, Elsa, Licha* (Spanish); *Alicia, Elsa* (Swedish)

Alicia Modern U. S. form of Alice, also popular in Italy, Sweden, and Spanish-speaking countries. For other forms, see Alice.
Aleesha, Alisha, Alysha

Alida Latin: "small, winged one"; or Spanish: "noble."
Aleda, Aleta, Alita, Dela, Elida, Elita, Leda, Leeta, Lela, Lita, Oleda, Oleta (English); *Alette* (French); *Aletta* (Italian); *Adelina, Adelita, Aleta, Aletta* (Spanish)

Alike (ah-LEE-keh) Ibo, Nigeria: from the longer name Alikecopeleabola, "girl who drives out beautiful women." Bestowed because the child is lovely.
Aleeka, Alika

Alile (ah-LEE-leh) African: "she weeps." Given by the Yao-speaking people of Malawi to a child born into unfortunate circumstances.
Aleela, Alila

Alima (ah-LEE-muh) Arabic: "skilled in music and dancing." Another meaning is "sea maiden," making this an appropriate name for a girl born under a water sign: Cancer, Scorpio, or Pisces.

Alina "bright" or "beautiful." Popular in Poland and Russia. An alternate source is Celtic: "fair."
Aleen, Aleena, Aleene, Alena, Alene (English); *Alya, Lina* (Russian)

Alisa Modern Israeli name meaning "a joy." See also
Aleeza.
Alissa, Alyssa

Alita (ah-LEE-tah) A Spanish form of Adelle, "noble."

Alka (AL-kah) Polish form of Alexandra.

Alkas (AHL-kahs) North American Indian: "she is afraid."

Alleen Dutch name meaning "alone."

Allison, Alison Irish Gaelic: "small and truthful."
*Ali, Alie, Alli, Allie, Allyson, Alyson, Lissi, Lissie,
Lissy* (English); *Allsun* (Irish)

Alma (AHL-mah) Spanish and Italian name that literally
means "soul" or "spirit," with a connotation of nour-
ishment. In other words, the child feeds one's soul or
lifts the spirit.

Almira (ahl-MEE-ruh) Hindi: "clothes basket." The Hindus
believe that God is manifested in everything, and thus
children in India are often named after common household objects. Each time the name is pronounced, God's
name is spoken, an act considered a step toward salvation. In Arabic this name means "fulfillment of the
Word" or "truth without question."

Alnaba (ahl-NAH-bah) Navaho Indian: "wars passed each
other." In the Navaho tradition of naming girls after
events of war, this name indicates two battles raged in
opposite directions.

Aloha (ah-LO-hah) This familiar Hawaiian name has connotations of love, affection, mercy, kindness, charity,
greetings, and farewell.

Alohi (ah-LO-hee) Hawaiian: "shining" or "brilliant." Also
a boys' name.

Alona (ah-LO-nah) Hebrew: "oak tree." The masculine
form is Alon.

Altsoba (ahlt-SO-bah) Navaho Indian: "all are at war."

Aludra (uh-LOO-druh) Greek and Arabic: "virgin." Astrological name for a girl born under Virgo, the virgin.

Alumit (ah-loo-MEET) Hebrew: "girl" or "secret." Modern Israeli name.
Alma, Aluma, Alumice

Alverta Modern Greek form of Alberta, "noble and brilliant."

Alzubra (ahl-ZOO-bruh) Arabic: Refers to a tiny star of the fifth magnitude in the constellation Leo, the lion. Hence, given to a child born under that sign.

Am (uhm) Vietnamese: "lunar" or "female principle." The latter refers to the Oriental concept of the universe, which states that in the beginning two sources of energy existed—male and female—and from these the world was born.

Ama (AH-mah) Akan, South Ghana: "born on Saturday," from the word *Memenda* ("Saturday").

Amadika (ah-mah-DEE-kah) Southern Rhodesian: "to be beloved." Popular among the Wataware people, this is a name a mother gives to herself if her life has been filled with tragedy; the connotation is "once my husband loved me, but he doesn't anymore."

Amalia (ah-mah-lee-ah, with the stress falling on one of the first three syllables, depending on the language) Currently used in Hungary, Poland, Rumania, Germany, Holland, Spain, and the United States, this international name is derived from the Gothic word *amala*, meaning "industrious." See Amelia and Emily.

Amaliya (ah-mah-LEE-yah) Russian form of Amy.

Amanda Latin: "lovable" or "worthy of love."
Manda, Mandi, Mandie, Mandy, Mandaline (English); *Amandine* (French); *Amata* (Spanish)

Amara (ah-MAH-rah) Esperanto form of Mary, "bitter." Esperanto is an artificial international language devised

DAY-OF-THE-WEEK NAMES

Americans have been known to name their children after the day on which they were born—especially if that day happens to be Tuesday. Actress Tuesday Weld is probably responsible for bringing this day-of-the-week name into vogue, though her real name was Susan Kerr Weld.

In other countries (especially in Africa), naming a girl after her birth day is even more fashionable. In addition to Ama, for example, other Ghanaian day-of-the-week names for girls are:

AKOSUA—
"born on Sunday"
AJUA—
"born on Monday"
ABMABA—
"born on Tuesday"
EKUA—
"born on Wednesday"

ABA—
"born on Thursday"
EFUA—
"born on Friday"
AMA—
"born on Saturday"

by Polish oculist and philologist Ludwig Zamenhof (1859–1917). Esperanto, which is fairly easy for people who speak many different languages to master and read, means literally "one who is hoping." Zamenhof's hope was that the entire world would one day be united by a common language.

Amaris "child of the moon"; or Hebrew: "God has promised." In astrology the moon is the ruler of the sign Cancer, the crab. Early astrologers believed Cancer was the constellation through which souls passed from heaven into human bodies.

Amata (ah-MAH-tah) Spanish form of Amy, "beloved."

Amaui (uh-MOW-ee) Hawaiian: "thrush," referring to a gentle Hawaiian thrush which is a dusky olive brown.

Amayeta (ah-mah-YEH-tah) Miwok Indian: "big manzanita berries."

Amber Arabic: "jewel"; or Old French: "fierce one." The amber, a semi-precious jewel made of fossil resin and containing bits of plants, insects, and feathers, was used in ancient magical healing rites.

Ambika (ahm-BEE-kah) Hindi: "the mother." One of the more than one thousand Hindu names for Sakti, goddess of power and destruction.

Amelia Gothic *amala:* "industrious"; or Latin: "flatterer." *Amali, Amalia, Amalie, Amelina, Amelita, Ami, Amie, Amilia, Amy, Emelie, Emelina, Emeline, Emelita, Emilia, Emilie, Emily* (English); *Amalia* (Czech); *Amalie, Emilie* (French); *Amalia, Emilia, Ilma, Mali, Malika, Malcsi* (Hungarian); *Ama, Amelcia, Melcia* (Polish)

Ami Modern U.S. spelling of Amy, "beloved."

Amina (ah-MEE-nah) Arabic: "peace" or "security." The name of the prophet Muhammad's mother.

Amineh (a-MEE-na) Arabic: "faithful."

Amira (ah-MEE-ruh) Hebrew: "speech" or "utterance."

Amissa (ah-MEE-suh) Hebrew: "friend" or "truth."
Amisa

Amma (ah-mah) Hindi: "mother goddess."

Amoke (ah-mo-KEH) Yoruba, Nigeria: "to know her is to pet her." Popular nickname in Nigeria.

Amy Latin: "beloved." Also a short form of Amelia.
Aimy, Ame, Ami, Amie (English); *Aimee, Amelie* (French); *Amalia, Amadea* (Italian); *Ema* (Rumanian); *Amaliya* (Russian); *Amata, Amada* (Spanish); *Amata* (Swedish)

An (an or ang) Vietnamese: "peace," "safety," or "security."

Anaba (ah-NAH-bah) Navaho Indian: "she returns from war." See Alnaba.

Anabela (ah-nuh-BEL-ah) Hawaiian form of Annabelle, "graceful" or "beautiful."

Anala (ah-NAH-luh) Hindi: "fire." Another name for the Hindu god Agni, god of fire. Also a boys' name.

Ananda (ah-nuhn-dah) Hindi: "bliss." Often used in India as a name component to create new names.

Anastasia Greek: "of the Resurrection." Very popular in Russia (where it's pronounced ah-nah-stah-SEE-ah), this name was introduced into Russia through the Greek Orthodox Church. Made famous by the Grand Duchess Anastasia, a member of Czar Nicholas's family who, some say, escaped death when the family was assassinated during the Russian Revolution of 1918.
Anastace, Anastice, Anastyce, Anstice, Stacey, Staci, Stacia, Stacie, Stacy (English); *Anastazia, Stasa, Staska,* (Czech); *Anastasie* (French, German); *Anya, Asya, Nastasya, Nastka, Nastusya, Nastusha, Stasya, Tasenka, Taska, Tasya* (Russian, Latvian, Lithuanian); *Tasia* (Spanish)

Anda Spanish: "going." Used in most Spanish-speaking countries. The variation *Andeana* means "a walker" or "a goer."

Andrea Latin: "womanly"; or Greek: "A man's woman." Feminine form of Andrew or Andreas; one of the most popular girls' names in the United States.
Andreea, Andreana, Andree, Andri, Andria, Andriana (English); *Andree* (French); *Aindrea* (Irish)

Andulka (AHN-dool-kah) Czechoslovakian form of Ann, "graceful." See Ann for other forms.

Ane (AH-neh) Hawaiian form of Ann.

Anela (ah-NEL-ah) Hawaiian: "angel." Used by early Hawaiian Christians to designate the few pagan gods they still believed in.

Anevay (ah-neh-VIGH) North American Indian: "superior."

Anezka (AH-nehzh-kah) A very popular form of Ann in Czechoslovakia. See Ann for other variations.

Angela Greek: "angel" or "one who brings good news." Popular in the United States, Greece, Germany, and many other countries.
Angel, Angele, Angelina, Angelle, Angi, Angie, Angy (English); *Andela* (Czech); *Angele* (French); *Angelika* (German, Lithuanian); *Angelica, Angeliki* (Greek); *Aingeal* (Irish); *Angelina, Anhelina, Gelya, Lina* (Russian)

Angeni (ahn-GAY-nee) North American Indian: "spirit angel."

Angie Popular U.S. form of Angela, often used as an independent name.

Anila (uh-nee-lah) Hindi: "the wind god," referring to the Hindu god with whom the forty-nine godlings of the wind are associated. Also a boys' name.

Aniweta (ah-nee-WAY-tah) Ibo, Nigeria: "Ani (a spirit) brought it." This is typical of many Ibo short-sentence names, which often refer to the child's birth, future, or a hope of the parents. Also a boys' name.

Ann, Anna, Anne Hebrew: "graceful." A truly international name, this is used in Russia, Bulgaria, France, Italy, Germany, Czechoslovakia, Poland, and Spanish-speaking countries, as well as in the United States.
Ana, Anette, Anita, Anni, Annie, Annina, Anny, Hanna, Hannah, Nan, Nanci, Nancy, Nanna, Nina (English); *Andulka, Anicka, Anuska, Andula* (Czech); *Annikki* (Finnish); *Annette* (French); *Anitte, Annchen, Anneli, Anneliese, Anni, Hanne, Nettchen* (German); *Nani, Noula* (Greek); *Ana, Ane* (Hawaiian); *Anci, Aniko, Annus, Annuska, Nina, Nusi* (Hungarian); *Annetta,*

Annina (Italian); *Anya, Anyuta, Asenka, Aska, Asya, Hanna* (Latvian); *Anikke, Annze, Ona, Onele* (Lithuanian); *Ania, Anka, Hania, Hanka* (Polish); *Anicuta* (Rumanian); *Anninka, Annuska, Anya, Asenka, Asya, Nyura* (Russian); *Anica, Anita, Nana, Nita* (Spanish); *Chana, Channa, Hana, Hannah* (Yiddish)

Anona Latin: "yearly crops." Earth name appropriate for a girl born under one of the earth signs: Capricorn, Taurus, or Virgo.

Anthea (ahn-THAY-ah) Greek: "lady of flowers."

Antonetta (ahn-to-NET-tah) Swedish and Slavic form of Antonia, "priceless."

Antonia Latin: "priceless."
Netta, Netti, Nettie, Nety, Toney, Toni, Tonia, Tony, Toinetta, Toinette (English); *Antoinette, Antonie, Toinette, Toinon* (French); *Antonina, Anta, Nina, Tola, Tolsia* (Polish); *Antonette, Antonina, Tonya, Tosky, Tosya* (Russian); *Antonieta, Antonina, Antuca, Tona* (Spanish); *Antonetta* (Swedish)

Anya Popular in Latvia, Estonia, Russia, and the Ukraine. See Ann.

Anzu (AHN-zoo) Japanese: "apricot," the emblem of the fair sex. In Western lore the apricot symbolizes timid love.

Aolani (ow-LAH-nee) Hawaiian: "heavenly cloud."

Apangela (ah-pahn-GAY-lah) Umbundu, Angola: from the proverb "*(W)a pangela ka mali ungende,*" or "one who intends not to finish her journey." The people of Angola take many names from proverbs; this one has a possible connotation that the child may not live.

Apara (ah-PAH-rah) Yoruba, Nigeria: "one who comes and goes." One of many African born-to-die names (see box).

Aponi (ah-PO-nee) North American Indian: "butterfly." The

AFRICAN BORN-TO-DIE NAMES

So many African infants die at birth that parents have created elaborate superstitions in the hopes they can help their babies escape early death. *Abiku*, or born-to-die names, are common in many African languages. According to an old superstition, certain children are the incarnations of evil spirits, which enter and leave the world. *Abiku* names are bestowed on such children to keep them from dying. Other Nigerian born-to-die names are:

AKISATAN—"rags are not finished (with which to bury you)"

BANJOKO—"sit down (or stay) with me," meaning "don't desert me"

DUROSIMI—"wait and bury me," meaning "don't die before me"

DUROSOMO—"stay and play the child"

KOSOKO—"there is no hoe (to dig a grave with)"

MOLOMO—"don't go back (to the spirit world)"

MATANMI—"do not deceive me"

Some of these names are now used in the United States by parents who read the meaning of the name outside its original death connotation. The name Rotimi, for example, which means "stay by me," could be given to any healthy child.

Pima Indians believed that the Creator took the form of a butterfly and fluttered all over the world until he found the best place for man.

April Latin: "open" or "born in April." Astrological name for a baby born either under Aries (the ram) or Taurus (the bull).
Aprilette, Aprille, Averil, Averill, Averille, Averyl, Avril (English); *Aprili* (Swahili)

Aquene (ah-KAY-neh) North American Indian: "peace."

Arabela Latin: "beautiful altar." Spanish form of Arabella.

Arella (ah-RAY-luh) Hebrew: "angel" or "messenger."
Arela

Arete (ah-RAY-teh) Modern Greek form of Grace, meaning "graceful" or "lovely."

Aretha Greek: "best."
Areta, Aretta (English); *Arette* (French); *Arethi* (Greek)

Ariel (ah-ree-AYL) Hebrew: "lioness of God."
Ariela, Ariella

Arista (ah-REE-stuh) Latin: "harvest." Astrological name for a girl born under the sign of Virgo, the virgin, maiden of the harvest.

Ariza (ah-REE-zuh) Hebrew: "cedar panels." Used today especially in Israel.
Arza, Arzice, Arzit

Arna (AHR-nah) Hebrew: "cedar tree."
Arnice, Arnit

Arnina (ahr-NEE-nuh) Many meanings have been given for this name: "mountain," "singer," "to shine," and "messenger." Currently used in Israel as well as the U.S.
Arni, Arnice, Arnit

Artha (ahr-tah) Hindi: "wealth" or "worldly prosperity," a goal which practical as well as spiritual Hindus regard as one of the four ends of man.

Asa (AH-sah) Japanese: "born in the morning."

Asabi (ah-sah-BEE) Yoruba, Nigeria: "one of select birth."

Asela (ah-SEH-lah) Modern Spanish name meaning "slim ash tree."

Ashley Old English: "one from the ash-tree meadow." Popular in the United States.

Asisa (ah-SEE-sah) Hebrew: "juicy" or "ripe."

MAGIC NAMES

Throughout time, man attributed magical powers to names. One of the most famous magical names—*Agla*—is said to be taken from the first letters of the Hebrew phrase *Ataw Gebor Leolam Adonai*, which means "Thou art mighty forever, Lord." The words were used as a charm by rabbis and some Christians to exorcise demons until the sixteenth century. The same magic name was also used in Germany, where it was thought to be derived from *Allmächtiger Gott, lösch'aus*, meaning, "Redeem, Almighty God." Another powerful magical name, used by occultists in hexagram rituals to banish and invoke spirits, is *Ararita*, taken from the first letters of the words in an incantation meaning, "One is His Beginning; One is His Individuality; His Permutation is One." Another magic name used to invoke spirits is *Belatha*, meaning "Thou Essence, Air Swift-streaming, Elasticity!"

Asiza (ah-SEE-zah) African: "forest spirit." The African Dahomey believe the asiza are spirits who dwell in the forests and grant magical powers to men.

Asoka (ah-sho-kah) Hindi: "non-sorrow flower." The non-sorrow flower allegedly blooms orange or scarlet when touched by the foot of a gentle maiden.

Asta Old Norse: "divine strength"; or Greek *aster*: "like a star," referring to the aster flower. Very popular today in Norway. See Astrid.

Astera "the aster flower." Popular Israeli flower name, from the aster which because of its star-shaped leaves has been called the starflower.
Asteria, Astra

Astrid Old Norse: "divine strength." One of the most popular names in Denmark.
Asta, Astrud, Astyr

Atara (ah-TAH-ruh) Hebrew: "a crown."
Ataret

Atida (ah-TEE-duh) Hebrew: "the future." Jewish name used in Israel as well as the U.S.

Atira (ah-TEE-rah) Hebrew: "a prayer."

Aud (owd) Norwegian: "deserted" or "empty." Because of the current Norwegian preference for names with a distinctly Scandinavian sound, this is one of the most popular names in Norway.

Audey Modern U.S. form of Audrey.

Audrey Old English: "noble strength."
Audey, Audi, Audie, Audree, Audri, Audrie, Audry

Aulii (OW-lee) Hawaiian: "dainty."

Averill Old English: "born in April." Astrological name for an Aries child.
Averyl, Avril, Avrill

Avi (AH-vee) Hebrew: "my father" or "my God." Modern Israeli name.

Aviva (ah-VEE-vah) Hebrew: "springtime," with the connotation of youthfulness and freshness.
Avivah

Avivi (ah-VEE-vee) Hebrew: "springlike." Modern Israeli name related to Aviva.
Avivice, Avrit

Awanata (ah-wah-NAH-tah) Miwok Indian: "turtle." The turtle is prominent in some Indian myths. The Korusa, for example, believe that in the beginning there was only the Old Turtle swimming in a limitless ocean. He dove down, brought up a mouthful of dirt, and created the world.

Awendela (ah-wayn-DAY-lah) North American Indian: "early day." Given to a child born just before dawn.

Awenita (ah-way-NEE-tah) North American Indian: "a fawn."

Ayame (ah-YA-me) Japanese: "iris." The iris is the Oriental emblem of the warrior and the Japanese flower of May. In astrology the iris is the "herb" of the moon, which governs the sign Cancer.

Ayasha (EYE-ish-ah) Arabic: "life." Common Moslem name that varies slightly throughout the Moslem countries of India, Turkey, Jordan, Persia, Egypt, and Arabia. Ayasha was one of the prophet Muhammad's favorite wives. *Aisha, Asha, Ashia*

Ayelet (ah-yeh-LAYT) Hebrew: "deer" or "gazelle."

Ayita (ah-YEE-tah) North American Indian: "the worker."

Ayoka (ah-YO-kah) Yoruba, Nigeria: "one who causes joy all around." Often bestowed as a nickname.

Ayondela (ah-yohn-DAY-lah) Umbundu, Africa: "a little tree bends and bends, as we all bend toward death." Many African names derive from proverbs revealing some philosophy of life.

Azami (ah-zah-mee) Japanese: "thistle flower." In the Orient the thistle symbolizes defiance and surliness.

Aziza (ah-ZEE-zah) Swahili: "precious."

Azize (uh-ZEEZ) Turkish: "dear," "precious," or "rare."

---- B ----

Babara (BAH-buh-ruh) Hawaiian form of Barbara, "stranger."

Baka (bah-kah) Hindi: "crane." The crane is a symbol of longevity.

Bakula (bah-koo-lah) Hindi: "the bakula flower." Accord-

ing to Hindu myth, the bakula bursts into bloom when
sprinkled with wine from the mouth of a beautiful girl.

Balala (BAH-lah-lah) Mashona, Southern Rhodesia: "You
must eat much to grow." Often bestowed on a frail
child.

Balaniki (bah-lah-NEE-kee) Hawaiian form of Blanche.

Barbara Latin: "a stranger" or "foreigner." When the
barbarians attacked Rome, Romans thought the barbar-
ians' speech sounded like "barbarbarbarbar." Thus,
Barbara came to be the name for anyone not like the
Romans.
*Bab, Babb, Babette, Babica, Babita, Barba, Barbette,
Barbi, Barbie, Barbra, Barby* (English); *Bara, Barbora,
Barborka, Baruska* (Czech); *Barbe* (French); *Babette*
(German); *Voska* (Greek); *Babara* (Hawaiian); *Varvara,
Varenka, Varka, Varya, Vava, Vavka* (Russian); *Varina*
(Slavic); *Barbro* (Swedish)

Barika (ba-REE-ka) Arabic: "bloom" or "be successful."
Popular Swahili name.

Batini (bah-TEE-nee) Swahili: "innermost thoughts."

Batya (bah-TEE-uh) Hebrew: "daughter of God." Modern
Israeli name.
Basia, Basya, Batia

Beatrisa (beh-ah-TREE-sah) Latin: "she makes others hap-
py." Spanish form of Beatrice.
Bea, Beatrice, Bee, Trixi, Trixie, Trixy (English); *Blaza,
Blazena* (Czech); *Beatrix* (French, German, Italian);
Beatrise (Latvian); *Beatriz* (Portuguese); *Beatriks, Beatrisa*
(Russian); *Beatriz, Bebe, Ticha, Trisa* (Spanish)

Behira (beh-HEE-rah) Hebrew: "light," "clear," or
"brilliant."

Bel Hindi: "the sacred wood apple tree." It is said the
branches of the sacred wood apple cannot be broken or
used for firewood except by Brahmins.

Bela (BYEL-ah) Old French: "white, fair-skinned one." Widely used in Czechoslovakia.
Blanche (English)

Belicia Spanish form of Isabel, "dedicated to God." See Isabel for other forms.

Belinda Old Spanish *bella-linda*: "pretty."
Bel, Belle, Linda

Bella Old English: "nobly bright" or "beautiful." Popular in Hungary as a Hungarian form of Alberta.
Bela, Belle

Belloma Latin: "warlike" or "war goddess." Astrological name for a girl born under Aries or Scorpio, which are ruled by the war planet Mars.

Bena North American Indian: "pheasant." The exact tribe from which this name comes has been lost.

Bene (BEH-neh) African: "born on Fenibene," referring to one of the eight days in the African Kalabari-Ijaw market week.

Benita (beh-NEE-tah) Latin: "blessed." Spanish form of Benedicta, which is in turn a feminine form of Benedict.
Bena, Benni, Bennie, Binnie, Dixie (English); *Benoite* (French); *Benicia* (Spanish)

Bernadette French: "as brave as a bear." A female form of Bernard, originally from France but now equally popular in the United States.
Berna, Bernadine, Berneta, Bernetta, Bernette, Bernita, Berni, Bernie, Berny (English); *Bernarda, Bena, Dina, Ina* (Polish); *Bernardina* (Italian, Portuguese, Spanish)

Beta Czechoslovakian form of Elizabeth, "dedicated to God."

Beth Once used as a nickname for Elizabeth, Beth is now one of the one hundred most popular girls' names in the United States.

WHAT IF YOUR BABY GROWS UP HATING HER NAME?

When naming your baby, one fear may be that your child will grow up hating the name you choose. Relax. Psychological studies consistently show that happy, well-adjusted people who like themselves also tend to like their names, no matter what they are and even if it takes a while.

Gertrude, for example, is commonly disliked by many children. One writer named Ann Bayer confessed in *Seventeen* magazine several years ago that as a little girl she absolutely abhorred her middle name Gertrude: "When I confided it to anyone, the reaction was always the same: a screech of horror followed by giggles followed by a sympathetic glance and then a final snort of amusement." But as this woman grew up and came to fully appreciate her own uniqueness, she also grew to like her middle name. She writes, "I can't say that I'm crazy about its original German meaning—"spear maiden"—but the name has a certain headstrongness, a kind of I'm-Gertrude-wanna-make-something-of-it quality that appeals to me. Whenever I write a story I always name the heroine Gertrude. It has become my hallmark, a code word for the part of me that's most unique."

It's generally best not to inflict a humorous name on a child. Calling twins Pete and Repeat might be amusing at first, but the joke soon grows stale. Likewise, rhyming names such as Mary Perry or Ronson Johnson may make a child the butt of jokes at school. Still, even an odd name won't *necessarily* cause a child to want to change it. Until his death in the 1950s, a Wisconsin man named Oofty Goofty Bowman (after a circus clown) insisted he always liked his name and never tried to conceal it by using initials.

Many children (especially teen-age girls) go through a stage when they dislike their name, no matter what it is.

Girls named Tia and Krishna want more ordinary names, while those called Sara and Emily wish their names were more exotic. Though parents sometimes worry when their daughter suddenly wants to change her name, psychologists say this may actually be a sign of healthy growth: The adolescent is developing a strong, unique personal identity and part of this evolving independence may involve considering a whole new name.

Most kids, once they get through their rebellious teenage years, settle down and come to love the names they once detested. But for those who don't, it's fairly easy in most states to change one's name by simply going to court. About 50,000 Americans change their names each year. Why some people choose the new names they do, however, often remains a mystery. A clerk in the New York State Supreme Court tells of a Mr. Murphy who had grown weary of his last name, which he found "too Irish and too common." So he petitioned the court to change his name—to Kelly.

Bethany Aramaic: "house of poverty." This popular modern U.S. name actually comes from the name of a village near Jerusalem.

Beti (BAY-tee) English Gypsy: "little" or "small."

Betula (beh-TOO-luh) Hebrew: "girl" or "maiden."

Bian (BEE-uhn) Vietnamese: "to be hidden" or "secretive."

Bianca Popular Italian, Spanish, and Hungarian form of Blanche, "white, fair-skinned one." Popularized in the United States by Bianca Jagger, actress. See Blanche.

Bibi (bee-bee) Arabic: "lady." A Swahili term of politeness.

Bina (BEE-nuh) Hebrew: "understanding" or "intelligence"; or Arapaho Indian: "fruits." This is an example of

how the same name can develop and be used by widely
different cultures.
Buna (Israeli)

Binti (BEEN-tee) Swahili: "daughter."

Birgit A popular Norwegian form of Bridgett. A variation,
Bergitte, is one of the most popular names in Denmark,
as is Birgitta in Sweden. See Bridget.

Bitki (BIT-kee) Turkish: "plant."

Blanche Old French: "white, fair-skinned one."
Blanch, Blanshe (English); *Bela, Blanka* (Czech); *Bianca*
(Italian, Spanish, Hungarian); *Branca* (Portuguese); *Blanca*
(Spanish); *Blanka, Blenda* (Swedish)

Blom Afrikaans, South Africa: "flower."

Blum (bloom) Yiddish: "flower."
Bluma

Bly North American Indian: "high"; or Afrikaans: "happy." Among some Indians, this name was often bestowed
in the hopes the child would grow tall. Also a boys'
name.

Bo Chinese: "precious." Popularized in the United States
by actress Bo Derek. Also a nickname for Bonita.

Bobina (bo-BEE-nah) Czechoslovakian form of Roberta,
"brilliantly famous."
Berta, Roba

Bohdana (bo-DAH-nah) "Given by God." Popular in the
Ukraine as the feminine form of Bohdan. Bohdan
Chmelnyckyj was a famed seventeenth-century Cos-
sack leader.
Danya

Bona Hebrew: "a builder."

Bonita Spanish: "pretty."
Bo, Boni, Bonie, Nita

Bonnie Middle English: "good."
Bonni, Bonny, Bunni, Bunnie, Bunny

Brandy Old English: literally "to burn wine." Quite popular in the United States from the strong, sweet liqueur.
Brandi, Brandie

Bridget Irish Gaelic: "strength" or "protecting."
Berget, Bergit, Bridgid, Brietta, Brighid, Brigid, Brigit, Brita, Brydie (English); *Bergette, Brigide, Brigitta, Brigitte* (French); *Brigette, Brigitta* (German); *Berek* (Greek); *Brigada, Brigida* (Italian); *Brigita* (Latvian); *Birgitta, Birget* (Norwegian); *Bryga, Brygida, Brygitka* (Polish); *Brigida, Gidita* (Spanish); *Birgitta, Biddy* (Swedish)

Brita Form of Brittany especially popular in Norway.

Brittany Latin: "from Britain."
Bret, Brett, Brit, Britt, Britta, Brittni

Brona Greek *Berenike:* "coming before victory." Modern Czech name.
Berenice (English)

Brooke Old English: "dweller by the brook." Masculine name now often used for girls in the United States. Popularized by actress Brooke Shields.

Bua (BOO-uh) Vietnamese: "hammer," "written charm," or "amulet." In Vietnam such metal names are often thought to bring luck or good health.

C

Cai (kay) Vietnamese: "female."

Caitlin Popular modern U.S. name, this is actually an Irish form of Katherine. See Katherine for more information.

Calida (kah-LEE-dah) Spanish: "warm" or "loving."

Caltha Latin: "marigold" or "yellow flower."
Cal, Calli, Callie, Kal, Kalli, Kallie, Kaltha

Cam (kam) Vietnamese: "orange fruit," or "to be sweet."

Camila Latin: "a young attendant at a ceremony," refer-
ring to the beautiful ceremonial girl who helped in
ancient pagan rites. Popular in Spanish-speaking countries.
*Cam, Cami, Cammi, Cammie, Cammy, Milli, Millie,
Milly* (English); *Kamila* (Czech); *Camille* (French);
Kamila, Kamilla (Hungarian, Latvian); *Camilla* (Italian);
Kamilka, Kamilla, Milla (Polish)

Camilla Modern U.S. name meaning "born free." Also
Italian form of Camila or Camille.

Candi Latin: "brightly white." Popular Spanish form of
Candida or modern U.S. form of Candice.

Candice Greek: "glowing white"; or Latin: "brightly white."
Popular modern U.S. name.
Candace, Candee, Candi, Candie, Candy

Candra "moon." Astrological name for a child born under
the sign of Cancer, ruled by the moon. In the tarot
pack, Pisces corresponds to the card of the moon.

Caprice Italian: "fanciful one."

Cara Vietnamese: "diamond" or "precious jewel"; or
Italian: "beloved"; or Irish Gaelic: "friend."
Carina, Carine, Kara, Karina, Karine

Cari Turkish: "flowing like water." Also a contemporary
U.S. name, which began as a variant spelling of Carrie,
a nickname for Caroline, "womanly."

Carita Latin *caritas:* "charity." Especially popular in Italy.

Carlota Spanish and Portuguese form of Charlotte. One of
the most popular names in Portugal.

Carly Popular modern U.S. form of Caroline, "little, womanly one."
Carli, Carlie, Karli, Karlie, Karly

OVIMBUNDU PROVERB NAMES

Among the Umbundu-speaking people of Africa, babies are often given names that are shortened forms of popular proverbs. Some examples of these fascinating names are:

CAIMILE (chigh-MEE-lee) from the sorrowful saying "*Ca imile li loluka; epota li citiwe li kunduka*," "A tree bears fruit, the fruit falls to the ground; a family has children, and they all die."

CAKUSOLA (chah-koo-SOH-luh) "If you loved, you followed the messenger," given to a child born shortly after the parents have been honored in some way.

CATAVA (chah-TAH-vah) from the saying "*Ca tava otulo; ca patala olongembia*," "It consented sleep; it protested pain." Loosely translated, this means she wanted to sleep, but was in too much pain to do so.

CILEHE (chee-LAY-heh) from "*Ci lehe no; oi kaile*," "Just let it stink, let it be." Loosely translated, this saying means if something is bad, just leave it alone or you will make it worse. Another version of the same saying is "Let it stink, it is his own," meaning we all must handle our own problems.

CINOFILA (chee-noh-FEE-lah) from the proverb "*Ocina o fila te nda o ci lia*," "A thing you die for only if you eat it." The saying is used to describe the hunter who overcomes all obstacles to find meat.

CIYEVA (chee-YAY-vah) "You hear it, but you don't do it."

COHILA (cho-HEE-luh) From "*Ca uhila onene, kutima ku vala*," "It is silent on the part of the young, at heart it hurts." In other words, the young are quiet about the things that hurt them.

Carmen Spanish: "crimson"; or Latin: "a song." A shortened form of Maria del Carmen, referring to Mary, mother of Jesus.
  Carma, Carmia, Carmina, Carmine, Carmita, Char-

maine, Karma, Karmia, Karmina, Karmine, Karmita
(English); *Carmine* (Italian); *Carmencita* (Spanish)

Carna Hebrew *Karnis*: "horn." Often used today in Israel.
Carniela, Carniella, Carnis, Carnit, Karniela, Karniella,
Karnis, Karnit

Caroline, Carolyn Latin/French: "little, womanly one."
Cari, Carla, Carleen, Carlene, Carli, Carlie, Carline,
Carly, Carol, Carole, Carri, Carrie, Carroll, Cary,
Caryl, Charla, Charleen, Charlena, Charlene, Charline,
Kari, Karie, Karla, Karleen, Karli, Karlie, Karly,
Karoline, Lina, Line, Sharleen, Sharlene, Sharline
(English); *Karolina, Karola, Karla, Karlinka* (Czech);
Lina (Finnish); *Charlotte* (French); *Charlotte, Karla,*
Karoline, Lina, Linchen, Line, Lottchen (German);
Karolina, Lina, Linka (Hungarian); *Carla, Carlotta*
(Italian); *Karlene* (Latvian); *Karolina, Karolinka, Ina,*
Inka (Polish); *Carlota, Lola, Tota* (Spanish); *Lotta*
(Swedish)

Caron French form of Karen, "pure."

Carrie Popular modern U.S. form of Caroline.
Cari, Carri, Cary, Kari, Karie, Kary

Catherine Greek: "pure." One of the most popular names
in the world. See Katherine for more than seventy
variations.

Cecilia Latin: "dim-sighted." Used not only in the United
States but also Czechoslovakia, Italy, Portugal, Rumania,
and Spanish-speaking countries. Feminine form of Cecil.
Cecely, Cecyl, Cecyle, Cele, Celia, Celie, Cicely, Cicily,
Cissi, Cissie, Cissy, Sissi, Sissie (English); *Ceciliia,*
Sesiliia (Bulgarian); *Cecilie,Cilka, Cile* (Czech); *Cecile,*
Cecily (French); *Cacilia, Cecilie, Cilli, Cilly* (German);
Kikilia (Hawaiian); *Cecilija* (Latvian); *Cecylia, Cesia*
(Polish); *Cecilla, Chela, Chila* (Spanish); *Celia* (Swedish)

Celeste Latin: "heavenly."
Celesta, Celestina, Celestine, Celia (English); *Celestin,*
Celestyna, Tyna, Tynka (Czech); *Celestine, Celeste,*

Celie (French); *Celestina* (Italian, Portuguese, Spanish); *Cela, Celek, Celestyna, Celina, Celinka, Celka, Cesia, Inka, Inok* (Polish); *Cela, Celestyn, Celestyna, Celina, Celinka, Cesia, Inka, Selinka* (Russian)

Cella Italian form of Francesca, "free one" or "from France."

Cerella (se-RAY-luh) "of the spring." Astrological name for a girl born under one of the spring signs: Aries, Taurus, or Gemini.
Cerelia

Cerise French: "cherry."
Cherise

Chandi (chahn-dee) Hindi: "angry" or "fierce." One of the more than one thousand names for the Hindu goddess Sakti. Another variation used in India is *Chanda*, sometimes loosely translated as "the great goddess." For more information, see Sakti.

Chandra (CHAHN-druh) Hindi: "moon," or "moon god." For astrological implications, see Candra.

Channa (chah-nuh) Hindi: "chickpea." According to traditional Hindu mythology, all herbs, plants and trees (including the chickpea) were "fathered by heaven, mothered by earth, and rooted in the primeval ocean."
Chana, Shana, Shanna

Charlotte French: "little womanly one." Like Caroline, this name is a feminine form of Charles. Popularized in England around 1761, when George III married Charlotte Sophia of Mecklenburg-Strelitz, and further in 1774, when Goethe used the name for his heroine in *The Sorrows of Young Werther.*
Carla, Carli, Carlie, Carly, Carlene, Charleen, Charlene, Charline, Charyl, Cheryl, Karla, Karli, Karlie, Karline, Karly, Lola, Loleta, Loletta, Lolita, Sharleen, Sharlene, Sharline, Sheree, Sheri, Sherri, Sherrie, Sherrill, Sherry (English); *Karla, Karlicka* (Czech); *Lolotte* (French); *Karla, Lottchen, Lotte, Lotti* (German); *Karlotta* (Greek);

Sarolta (Hungarian); *Sarlote* (Latvian); *Lottie* (Polish); *Carlota* (Spanish, Portuguese)

Chavi (CHAH-vee) English Gypsy: "child" or "daughter."
Chavali

Chaya (ki-YAH) Hebrew: "life" or "living."
Kaija

Chelsea Old English: "ship's port." Popular modern U.S. name.
Chelsey, Chelsi

Chenoa (chay-NO-ah) North American Indian: "white dove," with the connotation of peace in nature.

Cher French: "dear," or "beloved." Popular modern U.S. name from the French name Cherie.

Chika (chee-KA) Japanese: "near," possibly in the sense of near and dear.
Chikako

Chilali (chee-LAH-lee) North American Indian: "snowbird."

Chimalis (chee-MAH-lees) North American Indian: "bluebird."

Chiriga (chee-REE-gah) Wahungwe, Africa: "she is the girl of poor parents." Derived from the words *ka riga*, "to rob of everything."

Chitsa (CHEET-sah) North American Indian: " fair one."

Chizu (CHEE-zoo) Japanese: "a thousand storks." In Japan the stork was once a symbol of longevity, and the name is a holdover from this belief. The round number— one thousand—gives added luck.
Chizuko

Cho Japanese: "butterfly."

Cholena (cho-LAY-nah) North American Indian: "bird."

Choomia (CHOO:-mee-ah) English Gypsy: "a kiss."

Christel German form of Christina.

Christina Greek *christianos*: "Christian." With all its variations, this is one of the most popular names in the world.
Chris, Chrissie, Chrissy, Christi, Christie, Christy, Chrystal, Crystal, Cristina, Kris, Krissi, Krissie, Krissy, Tina, Tinah (English); *Crystina, Krista, Kristina, Kristinka, Tyna* (Czech); *Kristia* (Finnish); *Christine, Crestienne* (French); *Christa, Christiane, Christel, Chrystel, Stina, Stine, Tine* (German); *Christina, Tina* (Greek); *Kriska* (Hungarian); *Cristin, Cristiona* (Irish); *Cristina* (Italian); *Krista, Kristine* (Latvian); *Krysia, Krysta, Krystyna, Krystka, Krystynka* (Polish); *Cristina* (Portuguese); *Khristina, Khristya, Tina* (Russian); *Kirsten, Kirstin, Kristin* (Scandinavian); *Christiana, Cristy* (Spanish)

Chu Hua (chuh hwah) Chinese: "chrysanthemum." In China the chrysanthemum is the flower of autumn and October. In Far Eastern astrology, it is the flower of Scorpio.

Chuma (CHOO-mah) Mashona, Southern Rhodesia: "bead."

Chun Chinese: "spring."

Cilka (CHEL-kuh) Czech form of Cecilia, from Latin meaning "dim-sighted."

Cipriana (see-pree-AH-nah) Greek *kupris*: "from the island of Cyprus." The Zuni Indians borrowed this name from Spanish, changing it to Sipiana.

Claire Latin: "brilliant" or "illustrious." Modern form of the older name Clara, Claire is often used in the United States and France.
Clair, Clairine, Clarita, Clare, Clari, Clarie, Clarina, Clarine, Clarice, Clarissa, Clarisse (English); *Klara* (popular in many languages, including Bulgarian, Czech, Polish, Russian, and Swedish); *Clairette, Clarette* (French); *Clarissa, Klarissa* (German); *Klarika* (Hungarian); *Chiara, Clarissa* (Italian); *Clareta, Clarisa, Clarita* (Spanish)

Cocheta (sho-CHAY-tah) North American Indian: "the unknown."

Connie Originally a nickname for Constance, but has become popular in the United States as a given name in its own right.
Conni, Conny

Constance Latin *Constantia*: "firm, constant."
Con, Conni, Connie, Conny, Constancia, Constanta, Constantia (English); *Constanz, Konstanze* (German); *Dina, Kosta, Kostatina, Tina* (Greek); *Concettina, Constantia, Constanza* (Italian); *Konstantin, Kostenka, Kostya, Kostyusha, Kotik* (Russian); *Constancia, Constanza* (Spanish)

Cora Greek: "maiden."
Cori, Corie, Corri, Corrie, Corry, Kora, Kori, Korrie, Korry, Corella, Corene, Coretta, Corette, Corrina, Correne, Correen

Cornelia Latin: "yellowish" or "cornel tree." Used around the globe—in the United States, Portugal, Rumania, and Spanish-speaking countries.
Cornela, Cornella, Cornelle, Cornie, Neely, Nell, Nelli, Nellie, Nelly (English); *Kornelia* (Czech); *Cornelie* (French); *Kornelia, Nele* (German); *Melia, Nelia* (Spanish); *Kornelis* (Swedish)

Courtney Old French: "one who lives at the court or on the farm." In a study at Guilford College in Greensboro, North Carolina, people stereotyped the name Courtney as extremely "strong," "smart," "upper-class," "attractive," "overconfident," "strong-willed," "creative," and "a leader." Currently one of the most popular names in the United States, given to newborns more often than Lisa or Mary.

Crystal Latin: "as clear as crystal." Popularized in the United States and many other countries in the '80s by

Krystal Carrington, a character on the TV series *Dynasty*.
Chrys, Chrystal, Cristel, Cristol, Krys, Krystal, Kristol

Cynthia Greek: "moon." Astrological name for a girl born
under the sign of Cancer, which is ruled by the moon.
Cindi, Cindie, Cindy, Cyndi, Cyndie, Cynth, Cynthie
(English); *Kynthia* (Greek); *Cintia* (Portuguese); *Cinta*
(Spanish)

D

Dacey Irish Gaelic: "a Southerner." Modern U.S. name
once used only for boys, now popular for girls.
Daci, Dacie, Dacy, Dasey, Dasi, Dasie, Dasy

Dagania Hebrew: "corn" or "ceremonial grain."
Dag, Dagi, Dagana, Daganya

Daggi Form of Dagmar popular in Estonia.

Dagmar Old German: "glorious day," "famous thinker,"
or "glory of the Danes." Used in Czechoslovakia,
Germany, Denmark, Sweden, the United States, and
many other countries.
Dagmara, Dasa (Czech); *Dagi, Daggi, Dagmara*
(Estonian); *Daga* (Polish)

Dagny Old Norse: "day." Feminine form of Dag, very
popular in Norway.

Dalila (dah-LEE-lah) Swahili: "gentle."

Dalit (dah-LEET) Hebrew: "to draw water" or "a tree
branch." Used in Israel.
Dalice

Damita Spanish: "little noble lady."

Dana Celtic: "from Denmark." In Celtic mythology Dana
was the mother of the gods. Originally a boys' name,
but popular today as a girls' name in the United States

and Scandinavia. In Hebrew this name is a form of
Daniel.
Daina, Dayna

Danett Modern U.S. name created from Daniela, "God is
my judge." A feminine form of Daniel.
Danetta, Danette, Dani, Danie

Danielle Hebrew: "God is my judge." A popular variation—
Daniela—is used in the United States, Czechoslovakia,
Poland, and Spain.
*Danela, Danella, Danelle, Danila, Danilla, Danille,
Danyelle* (English); *Daniell* (French); *Dania, Danit,
Danya* (Hebrew); *Danielka, Danka* (Polish); *Danila,
Danikla, Danya* (Russian)

Danya (DAHN-yah) Modern U.S. name also popular in the
Ukraine and Israel. See Danielle.

Darda Hebrew: "pearl of wisdom." Another meaning for
this modern Hungarian name is "dart."

Darsey Irish Gaelic: "black man"; or Old French: "from
the fortress." Modern U.S. development of the boys'
name Darcy, now popular for girls.
Darcey, Darci, Darcie, Darsi, Darsie

Daru (DAH-roo) Hindi *devadaru*: "divine daru," referring
to a species of pine or cedar. An ancient Hindu sacrifi-
cial post was said to be carved from daru wood.

Dasha (DAH-shah) Popular Russian pet form of Dorothy,
from the Greek for "gift of God." See Dorothy.

Dawn Middle English: "daybreak." Popular modern U.S.
name.

Deborah Hebrew: "a bee." First became a favorite Christian name in the seventeenth century, when it was
adopted by the Puritans.
Deb, Debi, Debbi, Debbie, Debby, Debora, Debra

TIME-OF-BIRTH-NAMES

Many parents like to give their babies names with extra-special meanings. One way they're doing this is by giving their babies names that reveal when they were born. Baby girls born early in the morning are now often called Dawn, Dawna, or Dawnette, whereas girls born in spring are sometimes called April or Aprille.

Time-of-birth names have had a long, respected tradition in other countries. In Japan, for example, girl babies are called Asa ("born in the morning"), Cho ("born at dawn"), Yoi ("born in the evening"), and Sayo ("born at night"). The Arabic name Laila (also spelled Leila and Layla) is also used not only by Americans, but also by Arabs and Swahili-speaking people for a girl "born at night."

(English); *Devora* (Bulgarian, Greek, Russian); *Deboran* (German); *Dwora* (Yiddish)

Dede (DEH-de) Ochi and Ga, Ghana: "first-born daughter."

Deedee Hebrew: "beloved." The abbreviated form *Didi* is often used in Israel as a pet form of Jedidiah. Also a boys' name.

Degula (deh-GOO-lah) Hebrew: "excellent" or "famous."

Dela Spanish form of Adelle, "noble."

Delle (dehl or DEH-luh) Hebrew: "a jar." Another name for the constellation Aquarius, the water bearer, and given to a child born under that sign.

Delora "from the sea coast." Used for a girl born under one of the water signs: Cancer, Scorpio, or Pisces. Also a form of Dolores.

Delu (day-LOO) Hausa, Africa: "first girl born after three boys." Another name given in this situation is *Iggi*.

Dena (DAY-nah) North American Indian: "a dale" or "a valley." Because American Indian names were often recorded sloppily, the exact tribe from which this and many other Indian names come has been lost.

Derora (deh-RO-rah) Hebrew: "flowing brook," "freedom," or "bird," referring in particular to the swallow. Modern Israeli nature name.
Derorice, Derorit

Deva Hindi: "divine." Hindu name for the moon goddess.

AFRICAN ORDER-OF-BIRTH NAMES

Order-of-birth names are common in many countries. In Africa such names can become quite specific, as some of the following indicate:

ALABA Yoruba, Nigeria: "second child born after twins."
BOJO Bari, Southern Sudan: "despiser of her twin," for a first-born female twin.
DO Ewe, Ghana: "first child after twins."
DOFI Ewe, Ghana: "second child after twins."
DOTO Zaramo, Tanzania: "second of twins."
KAKO Bari, Southern Sudan: "girl born after one daughter has died."
KEHINDE Yoruba, Nigeria: "second born of twins."
PONI Bari, Southern Sudan: "second-born daughter."
JWAN Bari, Southern Sudan: "third-born daughter."
PITA Bari, Southern Sudan: "fourth-born daughter."
SUKOJI Bari, Southern Sudan: "first-born daughter following a son."
TWIA Fante, Ghana: "born after twins."

Devaki (dah-vah-KEE) Hindi: "black." Hindu name for the goddess who was the mother of the powerful god Krishna. Krishna was such an energetic baby that when only twenty-seven days old, he kicked a demon to death. His energy continued into later life; he is said to have had 16,108 wives and 180,008 children.

Devi (DAY-vee) Hindi: "goddess." One of the many names for the Hindu goddess of power and destruction, Sakti.

Devora (day-VO-rah) Russian form of Deborah, "a bee." See Deborah.

Dezba (DEHZ-bah) Navaho Indian: "going to war."

Diana Latin *Diana:* "goddess," referring to Diana, the Roman goddess of the hunt. Popularized around the world, most recently by Princess Diana.
Deana, Deanna, Di, Diahann, Dian, Dianna, Dyan, Dyana, Dyane (English); *Diani* (Portuguese)

Dickla (dee-KLAH) Hebrew: "a palm tree" or "date tree." Used especially in Israel.
Dikla, Diklice, Diklit

Dina Popular around the world as a nickname for many longer names, including the Greek Kostantina and the Russian Dinah. In some parts of Africa this is given as a nickname to a boy who is always seeking a comfortable place to sit, the meaning being "he sat down wherever he went."

Dinka Dinka *jieng*: "people." The Dinka are a tribe of about a million people who have lived since remote times on the plains around the Southern Nile. Concerned about equality among men, the Dinka believe if a man hoards more possessions than he needs, he upsets the balance of nature.

Disa Old Norse: "active sprite"; or Greek: "double." Modern U.S., Danish, and Swedish name.

Dita (DEE-tah) Czech form of Edith, meaning "rich gift."
   See Edith.

Diza Hebrew: "joy."
   Ditza, Ditzah

Doba (DO-bah) Navaho Indian: "there was no war." With
   few exceptions, Navaho girls' names commemorate
   war or, in this case, peace.

Dodie Hebrew: "beloved." Comes from the same source as
   the masculine name David.
   Doda, Dodi

Dolores Spanish: "sorrows." A shortened form of the Vir-
   gin Mary name Maria de los Dolores, "Mary of the
   Sorrows," referring to the seven tragic events in Mary's
   life.
   Delora, Delores, Deloris, Delorita, Lola, Lolita (English);
   Dolore (Hawaiian); *Doloritas, Dolorcitas, Lola, Lolita*
   (Spanish)

Domini Once a pet form of Dominique, "belonging to
   God," or a variation of Domina, "lady," but now used
   today as an independent name in the United States.

Dominique Latin: "belonging to God." Once a French
   form of Dominica, this name has surpassed its original
   in popularity.
   Dom, Domini, Dominic, Dominica (English); *Doma,
   Domek, Dominik, Dumin* (Czech); *Dominik* (German);
   Dominik, Niki (Polish); *Dominika, Domka, Mika*
   (Russian); *Dominga* (Spanish); *Chumina*

Doni U.S. creation from Donna, "lady," or Donalda, "ruler of the world."
   Donie, Donni, Donnie

Dooriya (DOO-ree-yuh) Irish *Deire*: "the deep." Romantic
   English Gypsy name referring to the sea.
   Dooya

Doris Greek: "bountiful" or "one from the ocean."
Dori, Doria, Dorice, Dorise, Dorri, Dorrie, Dorris, Dory (English); *Dorisa* (Hawaiian)

Dorit (do-REET) Hebrew: "a generation." Currently used in Israel as well as the U.S.
Dorice

Dorothy Greek *Dorothea*: "God's gift." Popular in many forms around the world.
Dode, Dodi, Dodie, Dody, Doll, Dolley, Dolli, Dollie, Dolly, Dora, Dori, Dorolice, Dorothea, Dorothia, Dorthy, Dory, Dosi, Dot, Dotti, Dottie, Dotty (English); *Dora, Dorka, Dorota* (Czech); *Dorothee, Dorette, Doralice, Dorolice,* (French); *Dore, Dorchen, Dorle, Dorlisa, Thea* (German); *Theadora* (Greek); *Dorte* (Norwegian); *Dorka, Dorosia, Dorota* (Polish); *Dol, Dorotthea* (Rumanian); *Dasha, Doroteya, Dorka, Dosya* (Russian); *Dorotea, Teodora* (Spanish); *Lolotea* (Zuni Indian)

Dory French: "golden-haired one." Originally a boys' name, now being used in the United States for both sexes.
Dori, Dorri, Dorrie, Dorry

Dosya (DOHS-yah) Popular Russian pet form of Dorothy.

Drina (DREE-nah) Popular Spanish form of Alexandra, "helper and defender of mankind."

Drisana (dree-SAH-nah) Sanskrit: "daughter of the sun." Might be given to a girl born under Leo, the lion, which is ruled by the sun. The name is often shortened to *Drisa*.

Duci (DOO-tsee) Modern Hungarian name meaning "rich girl." Form of Edith.

Dudee (DOO-dee) English Gypsy: "a light" or "a star."

Durva (DOO.R-vah) Hindi: "durva grass," a Hindu name referring to a holy grass used in ceremonial worship.

Duscha (DOO-shah) Russian: "soul." Used as an endearing term, as we in the United States use the terms "honey" and "sweetheart."

Dyan Popular contemporary U.S. form of Diana, "goddess."

Dyani (d.YAH-nee) North American Indian: "a deer." The deer was generally not considered as admirable as more ferocious animals like the bear, but a Tsimshiau Indian proverb states, "A deer, although toothless, may accomplish something," meaning don't judge by outward appearances.

————————————— E —————————————

Eartha Old English: "child of the earth." Nature name for a girl born under one of the earth signs: Capricorn, Taurus, or Virgo.
Erta, Ertha, Herta, Hertha

Ebony Popular contemporary U.S. name meaning "blackness."

Edda "poetry" or "composer (or singer) of songs." Popular in Iceland.

Edena (e-DEN-ah) Hawaiian development of Edna.

Edith Old English: "valuable gift."
Dita, Eda, Ede, Edie, Editha, Edithe, Ediva, Edyth, Edythe, Eyde (English); *Dita, Ditka, Edita* (Czech); *Editha* (German); *Edi* (Hawaiian); *Duci, Edit* (Hungarian); *Edetta, Edita* (Italian); *Edite* (Latvian); *Eda, Edka, Edda, Edyta, Ita* (Polish)

Edna Hebrew *'ednah*: "rejuvenation."
Edena (Hawaiian)

Ega (AY-guh) Yoruba, Nigeria: "palm bird," from the proverb, "He who does not understand the cry of the palm bird complains of the noise it makes."

Eirene (ee-REH-nee) Old Norse: "peace." Scandinavian name.

Ela Polish form of Elvira, "white," or "blond." Also a short form of the Polish Melania, "dark in appearance" or simply "black" or "dark."

Eleni (eh-LEH-nee) Popular modern Greek version of Helen, "light" or "torch." See Helen.

Elese (e-LES-e) Old German *Elsa:* "noble." A Hawaiian form of Elsie.

Eli (AY-le) A form of Ellen, "light," used in Norway.

Elidi (eh-LEE-dee) "gift of the sun." Astrological name for a child born under Leo, which is ruled by the sun. Also appropriate for girls born under the other two fire signs, Aries and Sagittarius.

Eliora (eh-lee-O-ruh) Hebrew: "the Lord is my light." Modern Israeli and Jewish name.
Eleora

Eliska (EL-izh-kah) Czech development of either Alice, from the Greek for "truthful," or Elsie from the Old German for "noble." In Czechoslovakia the *s* in this name is pronounced like the *z* in *azure*.

Elizabeth Hebrew *Elisheba*: "dedicated to God." Because this name is associated with Elizabeth, the mother of John the Baptist, it's one of the most popular names in the world.
Bess, Bessi, Bessie, Bessy, Beth, Betsey, Betsi, Betsy, Bett, Betta, Bette, Betty, Buffa, Elsa, Else, Elsi, Elsie, Elisa, Elissa, Eliza, Elyse, Elyssa, Libbi, Libbie, Libby, Lisa, Lisbet, Lisbeth, Liz, Lizabeth, Lizbeth, Lizzi, Lizzie, Lizzy (English); *Elisveta* (Bulgarian); *Alzbeta, Beta, Betka, Betuska, Eliska* (Czech); *Betti, Elisabet,*

Elsbet, Elts, Etti, Etty, Liisa, Liisi (Estonian); *Babette, Elisa, Elisabeth, Elise* (French); *Betti, Bettina, Elisabet, Elsbeth, Elschen, Else, Elis, Ilse, Lisa, Lise, Liese, Lisette, Lieschen, Liesel* (German); *Elisavet* (Greek); *Boski, Bozsi, Liszka, Liza, Zizi* (Hungarian); *Eilis* (Irish); *Betta, Bettina, Elisa, Elisabetta, Lisettina* (Italian); *Elizabete, Lisbete* (Latvian); *Elzbieta* (Lithuanian); *Ela, Elka, Elzbieta, Elsbietka, Elzunia, Eliza, Liza* (Polish); *Isabel, Izabel* (Portuguese); *Elisabeta* (Rumanian); *Betti, Elisavetta, Lisenka, Lizanka, Lizka, Yelizaveta, Yelisabeta* (Russian); *Elspeth* (Scottish); *Belicia, Belita, Elisa, Isabel, Isabelita, Liseta, Ysabel* (Spanish)

Ellama (EL-lah-mah) Hindi: "mother goddess," referring to the Hindu goddess worshiped as the guardian of South India.
Elamma

Ellen Popular today in the United States. See Helen.

Elli Estonian form of Helen "light" or "torch."

Elma (el-MUH) Turkish: "apple."

Elsa Popular Swedish and Spanish form of Alice, "truthful." See Alice.

Else (AYL-se) Old German *Elsa*: "noble." Very popular today in Denmark.

Elvira Spanish: "elf like"; or Latin: "white" or "blond." Used around the world—in Sweden, Spain, Russia, Hungary, Latvia, the United States and other countries.
Elvire (German); *Ela, Wira, Wirke* (Polish)

Elza Hebrew: "God is my joy." Popular in Israel. In Russia, the same name is occasionally used as a form of the Old German Elsa, "noble."

Ema Hawaiian form of Amy, "beloved" or Emma, "universal."

Emily Gothic *amala*: "industrious"; or Latin: "flatterer."
See also Amelia.
Amalea, Amalie, Ameldy, Amelia, Amella, Em, Ema,
Emera, Emi, Emie, Emilie, Emily, Emilyn, Emlyn,
Emlynne, Emma, Emmi, Emmie, Emmy (English); *Emiliia*
(Bulgarian); *Ema, Emilie, Emilka, Milka* (Czech); *Emilie*
(French); *Amalie, Amma, Amilia, Amilie, Emmi* (German);
Emalia, Emele (Hawaiian); *Emmali* (Iranian); *Eimile*
(Irish); *Emilia* (Italian); *Aimil* (Scottish); *Ema, Mema,*
Neneca, Nuela (Spanish)

Emuna (eh-MOO-NUH) Hebrew: "faithful."
Emunah

Enola (ay-NO-LAH) The interpretation by some experts
that this North American Indian name is simply "alone"
spelled backward seems unsatisfactory because of the
Indian tradition of bestowing names deeply and personally meaningful. No other explanation, however, could
be found.

Erica, Erika Old Norse: "eternal ruler" or "always powerful." The spelling Erika is extremely popular around
the world—in the United States, Czechoslovakia, France,
Germany, Hungary, Latvia, and Sweden.

Erin Irish Gaelic: "from Ireland"; or Old Norse *eir*: "peace."
Popular Irish name now used extensively in the United
States.
Eri, Erina, Erinn, Erinna, Eryn

Estrella Astrological name meaning "child of the stars."

Etenia (ay-TAY-nee-ah) North American Indian: "the
wealthy."

Etty Estonian form of Elizabeth, "dedicated to God." See
Elizabeth.

Eva (AY-vah) Hebrew: "life-giving." Used in Portugal,
Germany, Italy, Spanish-speaking countries, Denmark,

Greece, Bulgaria, Hungary, Rumania, Russia, Austria, Serbia, Sweden, Norway, and the United States.
Eba, Ebba, Eve, Evelina, Eveline, Evelyn, Evlyn (English); *Evicka, Evka, Evuska* (Czech); *Evaine* (French); *Evchen, Evy* (German); *Evathia* (Greek); *Evi, Evike, Vica* (Hungarian); *Ewa, Ina, Lina* (Polish); *Yeva, Yevka* (Russian); *Evita* (Spanish); *Chava* (Yiddish)

Evangelia (eh-vahn-GEE-lee-ah) Modern Greek form of Angela,"angel" or "one who brings good news."
Angela, Lia, Litsa

Eyota (eh-YO-TAH) North American Indian: "the greatest." Often a boys' name.

Ezrela (ehz-RAY-luh) Hebrew: "God is my help" or "God is my strength." Modern Israeli name.
Ezraela, Ezraella

---------------------------- **F** ----------------------------

Falda Icelandic: "folded wings."

Fanya (FAHN-yah) Popular Russian form of Frances, "free one." See Frances.

Fatima Arabic: The meaning of this name is unclear; although it may mean "weaned," the name is so associated with Fatima, the favorite daughter of Muhammad, that it has come to mean simply "daughter of the Prophet." Popular throughout the Moslem world, including Arabia, Jordan, Egypt, Iran, Turkey, and India. Fatima is believed to have lived from 606 to 632 A.D. and was married to Ali.
Fatimah, Fatma

Fayina (figh-EE-nah) Russian and Ukrainian form of Frances or Francesca, "free one." See Frances.

Fayola (fah-YO-lah) Yoruba, Nigeria: "good luck" or "walks with honor."

Felcia (FEL-shuh) Polish form of Felicia or Felice, "happy."
Fela, Felicia, Felka (Polish)

Felda Old German: "from the field." Appropriate for a girl
born under one of the earth signs: Capricorn, Taurus,
or Virgo.

Femi (FEH-mee) Yoruba, Nigeria: "love me."

Flo North American Indian: "like an arrow." Used for both
boys and girls.

Flora Latin: "flower." A truly international name, Flora is
used in the United States, Russia, Bulgaria, Sweden,
Norway, Germany, and many other countries.
Flo, Flore, Flori, Florie, Flory, Florri, Florrie, Florry
(English); *Kveta, Kvetka* (Czech); *Flore* (French); *Flo-
ra, Lora, Lorka* (Russian)

Frances Latin: "free one" or "from France."
*Fan, Fani, Fanni, Fannie, Fanny, Fran, Franci, Francie,
Frankie, Franni, Frannie, Franny* (English); *Franca,
Francka* (Czech); *Francoise* (French); *Franz, Franze,
Franziska* (German); *Fotina* (Greek); *Ferike, Franci*
(Hungarian); *Cella, Francesca* (Italian); *Fraka,
Franciszka, Frania* (Polish); *Francise* (Rumanian); *Fe-
dora* (Russian); *Chica, Francisca, Paca, Pancha,
Panchita, Paquita* (Spanish)

Franci Modern U.S. and Hungarian form of Frances, "free
one" or "from France."

Fredericka Old German: "peaceful ruler."
Freda, Fredi, Fredie, Frederica, Frederika (English);
Bedriska (Czech); *Frederique* (French); *Frida, Fritze,
Fritzinn* (German); *Frida, Frici* (Hungarian); *Fredrika*
(Norwegian); *Fryda, Fryderyka* (Polish)

Frida (FREE-duh) Modern U.S., Hungarian, and German
form of Fredericka, "peaceful ruler."

———————————— G ————————————

Gada (GAH-dah) Hebrew: "happy" or "lucky"; or Aramaic: "luck." Currently used in Israel. Also a plant name in Hebrew.

Gafna (GAHF-nah) Hebrew: "vine."

Gala (GAH-lah) Old Norse: "singer." Scandinavian name.

Gali (gah-LEE) Hebrew: "a hill," "a mound," "a spring," or "a fountain." Currently used in Israel.
Gal, Galice, Galit

Galina (gah-LEE-nah) Russian development of Helen, "light," or "a torch." This name, originally from Greek, came into Russia through the Greek Orthodox Church. See Helen.

Galya (GAHL-yah) Hebrew: "God has redeemed." Also used in Israel as a boys' name. In Russia, this is a popular pet form of Galina.

Ganesa (guh-NAY-shuh) Hindi: "god of good luck and wisdom." In the Hindu religion Ganesa is depicted as a rotund, pink god, with an elephant's head and a snake tied about his potbelly. He has four hands, one holding either a shell or a water lily, the others holding a discus, an ax, and a modaka (a sweet riceball, which is his favorite food). Once while riding on his rat, Ganesa was said to be frightened by a snake. He fell and his tummy burst. Dozens of modakas flew out, but he stuffed them all back inside him and retied the snake about his middle. The moon, who saw the whole episode, laughed and incurred Ganesa's wrath.

Ganit (gah-NEET) Hebrew: "garden."
Gana, Ganice

Gari Teutonic: "spear" or "spear maiden." Like many contemporary girls' names, this one is a feminine form of a masculine name—in this case Gary.

Gauri (GO-ree) Hindi: "yellow" or "fair." One of the many names for the Hindu goddess Sakti. This name refers to either the yellow harvest or the yellowish gauri buffalo, both associated with the goddess. See Sakti for further information.

Gavrilla (gahv-REE-luh) Hebrew: "a heroine" or "strong."

Gazit (ga-ZEET) Hebrew: "hewn stone." Modern Israeli name also used in other parts of the world.

Geela (GEE-lah) Hebrew: "joy."

Gelya (GAYL-yah) Russian form of Angela, "angel," or "one who brings good news."

Gemini Greek: "twin." Astrological name for a girl born under Gemini, which is symbolized by the twins and ruled by Mercury.
Gemina, Geminine, Mini

Georgia Latin: "farmer." A feminine form of George.
Georgena, Georgene, Georgetta, Georgette, Georgiana, Georgina, Georgine (English); *Jirca, Jirina, Jirka* (Czech); *Georgienne, Georgette* (French); *Georgina, Georgine* (German); *Gruzia, Gyorci* (Hungarian); *Gerda* (Latvian); *Georgina, Gina* (Russian); *Georgina, Gina, Jorgina, Yoya* (Spanish)

Gerda (GAIR-dah) Originally Scandinavian, from the Old Norse for "protection" or "enclosure," Gerda is used today as a Latvian form of Georgia and an Estonian form of Gertrude.

Germaine Latin: "the German," which in turn comes from the Celtic for "the shouter." Originally a French name, now used in many parts of the world.
Germana, Germain, Jermaine

Geva (GAY-vah) Hebrew: "hill." This modern Israeli name is also a place name in the Bible.

Gianina (jah-NEE-nah) Popular Italian form of Jane, "God is gracious." See Jane.

Gilada (gee-LAH-duh) Hebrew: "my joy is eternal" or "my hill is a witness."

Gilda Old English: "covered with gold." Popularized in the United States by actress Gilda Radner.

Gina Japanese: "silvery." According to an ancient Oriental superstition, the evil spirits and demons were born during the Age of Stone and hence feared the influence of metals. Though this belief is no longer common in Japan, metal names like Gina remain. In other parts of the world, Gina is a shortened form of many longer names, including Regina ("queen"), Eugenia ("well-born" or "noble"), and Virginia ("maidenly").

Ginger Latin *gingiber*: "the ginger spice" or "the ginger flower." See Virginia.

Girisa (gee-REE-shah) Hindi: "mountain lord." One of the many Hindu names for the god Siva. Also used in India as a boys' name.

Gisa (GEE-suh) Hebrew: "hewn stone"; or Teutonic: "gift." *Gissa, Giza, Gizza*

Giselle Old German: "a pledge" or "a hostage." *Gisela, Gisele, Gisella* (English); *Giza, Gizela* (Czech); *Gizi, Gizike, Gizus* (Hungarian); *Gisela* (Italian, Spanish); *Gizela* (Latvian)

Gita (GEE-tah) Yiddish: "good." Also a Slavic form of Margaret, "a pearl." See Margaret.

Gitana Spanish: "gypsy girl."

Gizi (GEE-zee) Hungarian form of Giselle, "a pledge" or "a hostage." See Giselle.

Gladi (GLAH-dee) Hawaiian form of the flower name Gladys, meaning "gladiolus."

Gleda (GLAY-dah) Icelandic name meaning "make happy" or "make glad."

Golda Old English: "golden-haired." Popularized throughout the world by former Israeli Prime Minister Golda Meir.
Goldi, Goldie, Goldina, Goldy

Grace Latin: "graceful" or "lovely."
Grazielle (French); *Gratia* (German); *Arete* (Greek); *Gracia* (Hungarian); *Grazia, Graziosa* (Italian); *Graca* (Portuguese); *Engracia, Gracia, Graciana* (Spanish)

Greer Latin: "watchful." Once a nickname for Gregoria, this is now used in the United States as an independent name.

Gressa (GRAY-sah) Norwegian nature name meaning "grass."

Greta German and Austrian form of Margaret, "a pearl." See Margaret.
Gretal, Gretchen, Grete, Gretel, Grethal

TRAIT NAMES

Some parents believe (perhaps subconsciously) that they can instill certain positive traits in a child by giving their baby such a name as Grace, Hope, Prudence, or Ernest. The Puritans, of course, carried this practice to extremes by calling their babies such names as Fear-Not, Search-the-Scriptures, and Flie-Fornication. This practice of giving a baby a name with "magical" powers was carried to an all-time high (or low, depending on your viewpoint) by a Rhode Island couple in the 1700s. The name they bestowed on their tiny son? Through-Much-Tribulation-We-Enter-Into-The-Kingdom-Of-Heaven Clapp. Reportedly, whenever the boy told anyone his full name, the person invariably replied, "Amen."

Gunda (GOON-dah) "warrior" or "battle maiden." Very popular today in Norway.

Gurit (goo-REET) Hebrew: "young animal," referring in particular to the lion cub. In astrology the lion is the symbol of the sign Leo.
Gurice

———————————— H ————————————

Habibah (hah-BEE-bah) Arabic: "beloved." The masculine form of this name is Habib, and the Hebrew equivalent is Haviva.

Hadiya (hah-DEE-yah) Swahili: "gift."

Hagia (hah-GEE-uh) Hebrew: "joyful" or "festive." In the Bible Hagia is masculine, but the name is used today for girls.
Hagit, Hagice

Haley Irish Gaelic: "scientific" or "ingenious." Originally used for boys, this is now a common girls' name in the United States.
Hali, Halie, Halli, Hallie, Hally

Halona (hah-LO-nah) North American Indian: "happy fortune."

Hama Japanese: "shore." Popular Japanese name.
Hamako

Hana Japanese: "flower" or "blossom"; Arapaho Indian: "sky" or "black cloud." Also a Czech and Polish form of Hannah, "graceful."

Hania (hah-NEE-uh) Hebrew: "resting place." Similar to the Israeli names Hanice and Hanit, which mean "spear."
Haniya

Hannah Hebrew: "graceful." A Hebrew form of Ann, this traditional Biblical name has dozens of variations throughout the world. See also Ann.
Hana, Hanna (English); *Hana, Hanicka, Hanka* (Czech); *Hanni* (Finnish); *Hanna, Hanne, Hannele, Hanni* (German); *Anci, Aniko, Annuska, Nina, Ninacska, Nusi* (Hungarian); *Hana, Hania, Hanka* (Polish)

Hara Hindi: "seizer." Feminine form of the Hindu name Hari, one of the 1,008 names for the god Siva, the destroyer in the Hindu triad of gods.

Harper Old English: "harp player." A boys' name now used in the United States for girls. Famous namesake: *To Kill a Mockingbird* author Harper Lee.

Harriet Old German *Haimirich*: "ruler of the house or home."
Harriette, Harriott, Henrietta, Henriette, Hetti, Hettie, Hetty (English); *Jindraska* (Czech); *Henriette* (French); *Henriete* (Latvian); *Henia, Henka, Henrieta* (Polish); *Enrieta* (Rumanian); *Enriqueta, Kika, Queta* (Spanish); *Arriet* (Swedish)

Hasana (hah-SAH-nah) Hausa, Africa: "first-born female twin." Among the Hausa people of Nigeria, this name is always given to a first-born female twin. The second-born, if a girl, is called Huseina, and if a boy, Husseini.

Hasina (hah-SEE-nah) Swahili: "good"; or Hebrew: "strong."

Hateya (hah-TEH-yah) Miwok Indian *hate*: literally "to press with the foot." The connotation is "bear making tracks in the dust."

Heather Middle English: "flowering heath," referring to the heather flower or shrub. The purple heather is considered symbolic of admiration and beauty in solitude, and the white blossom supposedly protects one against danger. Popular contemporary U.S. flower name.

Hedda Old German: "strife in battle."
   Heda, Heddi, Heddie, Heddy, Hedi, Hedy (English);
   Hedvick, Hedvika (Czech); *Hede* (German); *Eda* (Pol-
   ish, Spanish)

Hedia (hay-DEE-ah) Hebrew: "the voice (or echo) of God."
   Hedya

Hedy Greek: "sweet" or "pleasant." Also a variation of
   Hedda.

Heidi Old German: "noble and cheerful." Once a nickname for the German Adelheid, Heidi has become an
   independent name and is now one of the one hundred
   most popular names in the United States.

Helen Greek *helene*: "light" or "torch." This name became popular worldwide due to the fame of Helena,
   the mother of the Emperor Constantine, the subject of
   legends. It was said that Helena discovered the true
   cross of Jesus and was the daughter of the British king
   known in the nursery rhyme as Old King Cole.
   *Elaine, Elana, Elane, Elayne, Eleanore, Elena, Eleni,
   Elenora, Elenore, Elle, Ellen, Elli, Ellie, Elly, Ellyn,
   Ellynn, Elnora, Helena, Helene, Ileana, Iliana, Lana,
   Lena, Lenore, Leonora, Leonore, Leora, Liana, Liora,
   Nell, Nelli, Nellie, Nelly, Nora, Norah* (English); *Elena*
   (Bulgarian); *Alena, Elena, Elenka, Hela, Helena,
   Helenka, Heluska, Jelena, Lenka* (Czech); *Hele, Leena,
   Lenni* (Estonian); *Helli* (Finnish); *Elaine* (French); *Elli,
   Lena, Lene, Leni* (German); *Eleni, Elenitsa, Nitsa*
   (Greek); *Ila, Ileana, Ilka, Ilona, Ilonka, Iluska, Lenci*
   (Hungarian); *Eleanora, Leonora* (Italian); *Ale, Aliute*
   (Lithuanian); *Alena, Alenka, Elena, Galina, Galinka,
   Galka, Galya, Halina, Jelena, Leka, Lelya, Lena,
   Lenka, Lili, Nelya, Olena, Olenko* (Russian) *Elenor,
   Eleonor, Leni, Leonor* (Spanish); *Chaim* (Yiddish)

Helga Old German: "pious" or "religious." Very popular
   today in Norway and Iceland.

Helki Miwok Indian *hele*: "to touch." The more colorful connotation is "jacksnipe digging into the ground with its bill." The jacksnipe supposedly comes out of hiding only in winter. Also a boys' name.

Helli Finnish form of Helen, "light," or "torch." One of the most popular names in Finland.

Helmine Old German: "unwavering protector." Popular today in Germany. A form of Wilhelmina, the masculine form of which is William.
Billi, Billie, Min, Minni, Minnie, Minny, Valma, Velma, Wilhelmina, Wilhelmine, Willamina, Wiletta, Wilette, Willi, Willie, Wilma, Wilmette, Wylma (English); *Vilma* (Czech); *Mini* (Finnish); *Guilette, Mimi, Minette, Wilhelmine* (French); *Mina, Minchen, Minna, Wilhelmina* (German); *Mina, Minka* (Polish); *Guillerma, Guilla, Ilma, Mina, Vilma* (Spanish)

Henka A popular Polish form of Harriet, "ruler of the house or home." See Harriet for other variations.

Hermina Czech form of Hermine, from the Greek, "child of the earth."
Herma, Mina

Hertha form of Eartha, "child of the earth." Hertha was the Teutonic goddess of fertility and peace.

Heta Hopi Indian: "race after a rabbit hunt." This nickname is a corruption of the word *yeta*, the traditional race to the village after a rabbit hunt. Used by the rabbit clan of the Hopis.

Hilary Latin: "cheerful" or "happy." Once a masculine name, now popular in the United States for girls.
Hillary

Hilda German: "battle maiden." This word is a source of many German names, including Hildegarde ("battle wind" or "battle fortress"), Hildemar ("battle celebrated"), and Hildreth ("battle counselor").
Hilde, Hildi, Hildie, Hildy

Hinda (HIN-dah) Yiddish: "a deer." Hinda was one of Muhammad's wives.

Hisa (hee-sah) Japanese: "long-lasting," with the connotation of longevity.
Hisae, Hisako, Hisayo (Japanese)

Hiti (HI-ti) Banti Eskimo: "hyena." Such totemic names, symbolizing a person's close identification with an animal, are common in many cultures.

Hoa Vietnamese: "flower" or "peace."

Hoku (HO-koo) Hawaiian: "star." Like most traditional Hawaiian names, this is used for both boys and girls.

Hola (HO-lah) Hopi Indian *mahola*: "seed-filled club," referring to the club used by dancers in Hopi religious ceremonies.

Holly Old English: "holy" or "holly tree." Traditionally, the holly is symbolic of foresight and defense and is the Oriental flower of December. Often bestowed on a girl born at Christmastime.
Holli, Hollie

Hoshi Japanese: "star." A traditional name in Japan.
Hoshie, Hoshiko, Hoshiyo

Huata (hoo-AH-tah) Miwok Indian: "carrying seeds in a burden basket."

Hulda Old German: "gracious" or "beloved"; or Hebrew: "weasel." Name of a Biblical prophetess.
Huldi, Huldie, Huldy

Humita (hoo-MEE-tah) Hopi Indian: "shelled corn."

Huso (HOO-so) Umbundu, Africa *ohuso yakai*: "the feigned sadness of a bride." The name is probably bestowed in Africa because the newborn baby is thought to resemble the bride in expression.

Huyana (hoo-YAH-nah) Miwok Indian: "rain falling."

MIWOK INDIAN SEED NAMES

Among the most colorful of all names in the world are those of the Miwok Indian. Often the meanings of these names are incredibly complex and refer to an incident that occurred at the time of the baby's birth or at some time during the mother's or father's life. Since seeds were a principal source of food and material for making jewelry in Miwok tribes, Miwok names frequently mention seeds and, in doing so, reveal much about Indian life. Here are some of these seed names and their elaborate hidden meanings.

HELKIMU—"hitting bushes with seed beater."
HOWOTMILA—"running hand down the branch of a shrub to find seeds for beads" (from *howotu*, "beads").
HUATAMA—"mashing seeds in mortar."
KANATU—"making mashed seeds into a hard lump."

I

Iantha (ee-AHN-thah) Greek: "violet-colored flower."

Ida Old German: "industrious one"; or Old English: "happy and prosperous." A true whole-world name, used not only in the United States, but also in France, Germany, Italy, Hungary, Portugal, Russia, and many other countries.
Idalia, Idaleene, Idalene, Idalina, Idaline, Idella, Idelle (English); *Iduska* (Czech); *Ide* (French); *Idette* (German); *Aida, Idalia* (Italian); *Itka* (Polish); *Ita* (Yiddish)

Idette (ee-DET-te or eye-DET) German form of Ida.

Ilana (ee-LAH-nah) Hebrew: "a tree." Popular especially in Israel.
Elana, Elanit, Ilanit

Ilia (eye-LEE-uh or ILL-ee-ah) Latin: "from Ilium (or Troy)" In Roman mythology Ilia was the mother of Romulus and Remus. The same name was also used by American Indians, but the Indian meaning has been lost.

Ilka Slavic *milka:* "flattering" or "ambitious." Used in many Slavic countries. Also a form of Helen.

Ilona Hungarian "beauty." Also a Hungarian form of Helen, "light," or "torch." See Helen for other variations.

Ima (EE-mah or EYE-mah) Japanese: "now."

Imala (ee-MAH-lah) North American Indian: "disciplinarian."

Imma (EEM-mah or EYE-mah) Akkadian: "One who pours water from a jug." Name for the constellation Aquarius, the water bearer.

Ines (ee-NAYS or eye-NEZ) Spanish form of Agnes, "pure."
   Inesita, Inez, Ynes, Ynesita, Ynez

Inessa (ee-NAY-sah) Russian development of Ines.

Ingrid Old Norse: "Ing's ride," or "hero's daughter." In Norse mythology Ing, the god of the harvest, fertility, peace, and prosperity, took an annual mythical ride on his golden boar whose tusks tore up the earth so men could plant seeds. This is one of the most popular names in Norway and is used throughout Scandinavia.
   Inga, Inge, Inger, Ingeberg, Ingebor, Ingmar

Inoa (i-NO-ah) Hawaiian: "name" or "name chant."

Irene Greek *Eirene:* "peace."
   Eirena, Eirene, Erena, Erene, Ireen, Iren, Irena, Irin, Irina, Irine, Rene (English); *Irenka, Irka* (Czech); *Eirene, Eirini, Ereni, Nitsa, Rena* (Greek); *Iren, Irenka* (Hungarian); *Ira, Irisha, Irka, Irusya* (Latvian); *Irini* (Rumanian); *Arina, Arinka, Ira, Irena, Irina, Irisha, Iryna, Jereni, Orina, Orya, Oryna, Rina, Yarina, Yaryna* (Russian); *Irenea* (Spanish)

Irisa (ee-REE-sah) Greek: "the iris flower." This is a Russian form of the name Iris. In Western astrology the iris is the "herb" of the moon, which governs the sign of Cancer. In Japan the iris is the emblem of the warrior and the flower of May. A similar name is also found in Greek mythology, where Iris is the goddess of the rainbow and a messenger of the gods.

Isabel Old Spanish: "dedicated to God." Popular Spanish form of Elizabeth.
Bella, Belle, Isa, Isabella, Isabelle, Issi, Issie, Issy (English); *Izabella* (Czech); *Belle, Isabeau* (French); *Bella, Izabel, Fako, Karszin* (Hungarian); *Iza, Izabel, Izabella* (Polish); *Bela, Bella, Izabela, Izabele, Izabella* (Russian); *Belia, Belica, Belicia, Belita, Chabela, Chabi, Chava, Elisa, Isabelita, Liseta, Ysabel* (Spanish)

Ishi (ee-shee) Japanese: "stone." One of the few material names in Japan.
Ishie, Ishiko, Ishiyo (Japanese)

Istas (EE-stahs) North American Indian: "snow."

Ituha (ee-TOO-hah) North American Indian: "the strong, sturdy oak."

Iuana (ew-AH-nah) North American Indian: "blowing backward as the wind blows over the waters of a bubbling stream."

Ivria (eev-REE-uh) Hebrew *Ivri*: "from the other side (of the Euphrates River)" or "from Abraham's land." Ivri was the term originally used for the Jewish people in the Bible.
Ivriah, Ivrit

Ivy Old English: "ivy vine." The ivy was considered sacred in classical Greek and Roman mythology.

Iwilla Afro-American: "I will arise again." Invented name used by Afro-Americans in the 1800s.

Iza (EE-sah) Modern Polish form of Louise, "famous warrior-maiden."

Izusa (ee-ZOO-sa) North American Indian: "white stone."

————————————— **J** —————————————

Jacinta (ha-SEEN-ta) Spanish: "hyacinth."
Jacinna, Jacinth, Jacynth

Jacqueline Hebrew *Ya'agob*: "the supplanter." A feminine form of Jacob.
Jacki, Jackie, Jacquelyn, Jacqueta, Jacquetta, Jaclyn

Jade Spanish: "the jade stone." In Burma and Tibet jade is considered a supernatural charm. When worn, the stone is said to strengthen weak hearts and divert lightning. When tossed into water, it causes mist, rain, and snow. And if poison is poured into a cup made of jade, legend has it the cup will crack.

Jael (ya-AYL) Hebrew: "wild she-goat," or "mountain goat." Used in Israel for both boys and girls. Also an astrological name for a child born under Capricorn, the symbol of which is the goat.

Jafit (ya-FEET) Hebrew: "beautiful" or "lovely."
Jaffa, Jaffice

Jamie, Jaime Hebrew: "the supplanter." A feminine form of James.
Jaimi, Jaimie, Jaimy, Jamee, Jami, Jamie, Jayme, Jaymee, Jaymi

Jamila (jah-MEE-lah) Arabic: "beautiful." A favorite among Moslems. The Prophet Muhammad taught that ugly names should be changed; hence he renamed a girl called Asiyah (or "rebel") Jamila.
Jamilah, Jamillah, Jamillia

Jane Hebrew: "God is gracious." This feminine form of John has literally hundreds of variations throughout the world.
Jan, Jana, Janae, Janeen, Janel, Janela, Janella, Janelle, Janean, Janessa, Janet, Janeta, Janetta, Janette, Janey, Janice, Janie, Janina, Janine, Janis, Janna, Jannell, Jany, Jayne, Jaynell, Jean, Jeanette, Jeani, Jeanie, Jeanne, Jeanine, Jenni, Jennie, Jenny, Jess, Jessi, Jessie, Jessy, Jinni, Jinnie, Jinny, Joan, Joana, Joanna, Joanne, Joeann, Johanna, Joni, Jonie, Jony (English); *Joana* (Brazilian); *Jana, Janka, Janica, Jenka, Johanka, Johanna* (Czech); *Jensine* (Danish); *Jeanne, Jeanette* (French); *Hanna, Hanne, Hannele, Hanni, Johanna, Jutta* (German); *Ioanna* (Greek); *Janka, Johanna, Zsanett* (Hungarian); *Sheena, Shena* (Irish); *Gianina, Giovanna* (Italian); *Jana, Janina, Zanna* (Latvian); *Janina, Janyte* (Lithuanian); *Jana, Janina, Jasia, Joanka, Joanna, Joasia, Zannz* (Polish); *Ivanna, Ioanna* (Russian); *Iva, Ivana, Ivanka* (Slavic); *Juana, Juanita, Nita* (Spanish)

Jardena (yar-DAY-na) Hebrew: "to flow downward." The masculine form of this name is Jordan.

Jarita (ja-REE-ta) Arabic: "an earthen water jug." In Hindu legend Jarita was a bird mother who risked her own life to save her four sons in a burning forest and as a result became human.

Jasmine Persian: "the jasmine blossom." The jasmine is considered symbolic of amiability and sweetness.
Jasmin, Jasmina, Jazmin, Jessamine, Jessamyn, Jessi, Jessie (English); *Yasiman, Yasmine* (Hindi)

Jayne Sanskrit: "victorious."

Jean French: "God is gracious." A Scottish form of Jane or Joan now used in many parts of the world. See Jane.
Jeane, Jeanette, Jeanie, Jeanine, Jeannette, Jennette, Jennica, Jennine (English); *Janne* (Finnish); *Jeanne* (French); *Kini* (Hawaiian); *Janka, Johanna* (Hungarian);

Giovanna, Vanna (Italian); *Jana* (Latvian); *Janina,
Janka, Janeska, Jasia, Jena, Nina* (Polish); *Ivana* (Slavic)

Jelena (yay-LAY-nah or juh-LAY-nah) Popular Russian form
of Helen, "light" or "a torch." See Helen.

Jemina (jay-MEE-nuh) Hebrew: "right-handed."
Jem, Jemi, Jemma, Jemmi, Jemmie, Jemmy

Jenica (zhye-NEE-ka or anglicized to jah-NEE-kah) Contemporary Rumanian form of Jane.

Jennifer Old Welsh: "white phantom," or "white wave."
One of the most popular names in the United States.
*Genn, Gennifer, Genny, Ginnifer, Jenifer, Jeniffer, Jenn,
Jenni, Jennie, Jenny, Jeny*

Jessica Hebrew: "wealthy."
Jess, Jessi, Jessie, Jessy, Jesseca, Jessalyn, Jesslyn
(English); *Janka* (Hungarian); *Gessica* (Italian)

Jillian Latin: "innocent, downy-haired one."
Gilli, Gillian, Gillie, Jill, Jilliana, Jillie

Jin Japanese: "super-excellent." This unusual name is seldom bestowed in Japan, possibly because of an Oriental superstition that a child who receives too demanding
a name will never live up to it.

Jina (JEE-na) Swahili: "name."

Joana One of the most common names in Brazil, Joana is a
form of Jane. See Jane.

Joby Hebrew: "afflicted" or "persecuted." Originally a
nickname for Jobina, but now gaining use in the United
States as an independent name.
Jobi, Jobie

Jodi Hebrew: "praised." Once a short form of Judith, this
has gained status as an independent name.
Jodie, Jody

Joella (jo-AYL-lah or jo-EL-ah) Hebrew: "the Lord is willing." The masculine form of this name is Joel. Popular in Israel.
Joela, Joelle, Joellen, Joellyn

Jolan (YO-lawn or jo-LAN) Greek: "violet blossom." Hungarian form of Yolanda. See Yolanda for other forms.

Joline Hebrew: "she will increase." Contemporary feminine form of Joseph used in the United States. Much more common today than the older Josephine.
Joleen, Jolene

Jonina (yo-NEE-nah or jo-NEE-nah) Hebrew: "dove," referring to the dove of peace.
Jona, Jonati, Jonit, Yona, Yonit, Yonita

Jora Hebrew: "autumn rain." Astrological name for a girl born under the autumnal water sign Scorpio.
Jorah

Joyita Spanish: "an inexpensive but beautiful jewel."
Joy, Joya

Juanita Spanish form of Jane, "God is gracious." See Jane.
Juana, Nita

Judith Hebrew: "of Judah" or "praised one."
Judi, Judie, Judy, Jodi, Jodie, Jody (English); *Judita* (Bulgarian); *Jitka* (Czech); *Judithe* (French); *Ioudith* (Greek); *Juci, Jucika, Judit, Jutka* (Hungarian); *Giulia* (Italian); *Judite* (Latvian, Portuguese); *Judita* (Lithuanian); *Yudif, Yudita* (Russian); *Judit* (Swedish, Norwegian)

Julia Latin: "youthful." A truly international name, Julia is popular in the United States, Poland, Portugal, Sweden, Norway, and Spanish-speaking countries.
Gillie, Juli, Julie, Juliet, Julietta, Julina, Juline, Julissa (English); *Jula, Julca, Juliana, Juliska, Julka* (Czech); *Juliane, Juliette* (French); *Juli, Julianna, Julinka, Juliska*

(Hungarian); *Sile* (Irish); *Jula, Julcia* (Polish); *Iulia* (Rumanian); *Yulinka, Yuliya, Yulka, Yulya* (Russian); *Sileas* (Scottish); *Jula, Juliana, Yula* (Serbian); *Juliana, Julieta, Julita* (Spanish)

Julie Popular in the United States, Czechoslovakia, Germany, France, and other countries, this contemporary name is a form of Julia.

Jun (joon) Chinese: "truth"; or Japanese: "obedient."

Junella A modern combination of June plus Ellen, with the meaning "born in June." Astrological name for a girl born under the sign of Gemini, the twins, or Cancer, the crab.

———————————— K ————————————

Kachina (ka-CHEE-na) North American Indian: "sacred dancer."

Kagami (ka-GA-mee) Japanese: "mirror," in the sense of clear and pure reflections.

Kai Hawaiian: "sea" or "seawater."

Kala (KAH-la) Hindi: "black" or "time." One of the 1,008 names for the Hindu god Siva. Also a boys' name.

Kalama (kuh-LAH-muh) Hawaiian: "the flaming torch." This was the name of the wife of Kamehameha III, who ruled Hawaii from 1837 to 1847.

Kalanit (ka-la-NEET) Hebrew: "the brightly colored kalanit flower." This flower name comes from Israel, where kalanit flowers are common in the countryside.

Kalere (ka-LAY-ra) African: "small woman." First used in the Niger Delta, this name predicts the baby will grow to be short in height.

Kali (ka-LEE or KAH-lee) Hindi: "black goddess" or "time, the destroyer." One of the many Indian names for the Hindu mother goddess Sakti. See Sakti for more information.

Kalila (ka-LEE-la) Arabic: "girlfriend" or "sweetheart." A term of endearment in Arabic countries.
Kaleela, Kalilla, Kaylee, Kaylil

Kalinda (ka-LIN-da or ka-LEEN-da) Hindi: "the sun." Hindu nature name borrowed from the mythical Kalinda Mountains, from which the sacred river Jumna, or Jamna, flows.
Kaleenda

Kalindi (ka-leen-dee) Hindi: "the Jumna River." Kalindi was the original name of the Jumna, one of the seven sacred rivers in India. While in ancient times nature names were considered lowly and even disgusting in India, today many Hindu girls are named after rivers and flowers.

Kaliska (ka-LEE-ska) Miwok Indian: "coyote chasing deer." According to one Miwok legend, the coyote created the world and all the animals and then held a conference on how he should build man. Each animal wanted man to be like him. The lion wanted him to have a loud roar, the bear wanted him to be silent and strong, and the beaver insisted he have a flat tail. But the coyote said he could think of something better than any one of these qualities, and that night while everyone slept, he stole the best ideas he had heard that day and created man.

Kalli Greek: "lark." Once a nickname for Calandra, this is now an independent name in the United States. Another possible source is Greek: "beautiful blossom."
Cal, Calli, Callie, Kal, Kallie, Kally

Kaluwa (ka-LOO-wa) Usenga, Africa: "the forgotten one." The African Usengas believe that spirits who can never be reincarnated because their names have been forgotten are wandering the earth, working evil. To appease these demons, children are sometimes given this name.

Kalyca (ka-LEE-ka) Greek: "rosebud."
Kali, Kalie, Kaly, Kalica, Kalika

Kama Hawaiian form of Thelma, "the nursling." Also Hindi: "love." According to mythology, the Hindu god Kama rides a parrot and shoots flower-tipped love arrows from a sugarcane bow with a bowstring of bees.

Kamali (KA-ma-lee or ka-MA-lee) Mashona, Southern Rhodesia: "spirit." Kamali is a spirit believed to protect newborn babies when there is illness in the village.

Kamaria (ka-ma-REE-ah) Swahili: "like the moon."

Kamata (ka-MA-ta) Miwok Indian: "throwing gambling bones on the ground in a hand game." This name reveals an unusual pastime among Miwok women.

Kameke (ka-MAY-ke) Umbundu, Africa *omeke*: "a blind person." Given to a child with small, squinty eyes.

Kameko (KA-may-ko) Japanese: "tortoise child," indicating a home for longevity. A variation is Kameyo, "generations of the tortoise."

Kamila (ka-MEE-la) Arabic: "the perfect one." Also a Hungarian, Latvian, and Polish form of Camille, "helper at a ceremonial sacrifice."
Kamilah, Kamilla, Kamillah

Kanani (kuh-NA-nee) Hawaiian: "the beauty."
Ani, Nani

Kane (KA-ne) Japanese *kaneru*: "the doubly accomplished." *Kaneru* literally means "to do two things at once." In Japanese the same sound is also used for a character which means "bronze."

Kanene (ka-NAY-ne) Umbundu, Africa: "a little thing in the eye is big." Popular proverb name.

Kanika (ka-NEE-ka) Mwera, Kenya: "black cloth."

Kanya (KAHN-ya) Hindi: "virgin." Hindu name for a child born under the astrological sign of Virgo. Kanya is also another name for the goddess Sakti.

Kapua (ka-POO-uh) Hawaiian: "blossom."

Kapuki (ka-POO-kee) Bari, Southern Sudan: "first-born daughter." Popular among the Bari living on the banks of the Upper Nile and gaining popularity in other parts of the world.

Karen Greek *Katharos*: "pure." Popular both in the United States and Russia.
Caren, Carin, Caron, Caryn, Kari, Karon, Karyn (English); *Kaarina* (Finnish); *Karina* (Latvian); *Karina, Karine, Karyna* (Russian); *Karin* (Swedish)

Kari Contemporary U.S. form of Caroline, "little womanly one."
Karee, Karie, Karry, Kary

Karida (KA-ree-da) Arabic: "untouched" or "virginal."

Karla German, Czech, and U.S. development of Charlotte. Interestingly, the same name was borne by an Australian aborigine man and meant "fire." This Australian culture has such a taboo against speaking a dead person's name that when Karla died, his name was extinguished from the language and a new word for fire was introduced. See Charlotte.

Karma Hindi: "action." Karma embodies the Hindu principle that all of one's actions morally affect this or a future life. Karma can also be interpreted as "fate" or "destiny."

Karmel Hebrew: "vineyard," "garden," or "farm." Modern Israeli name.
Carmel, Carmeli, Carmi, Carmia, Carmiel, Karmeli, Karmi, Karmia, Karmiel

Karolina Russian and Hungarian development of Caroline, "little womanly one." See Caroline.

Kasa (KAH-sha) Hopi Indian *patsip-qasa*: "fur-robe dress," a type of lizard with a tough hide. The name comes from the Hopi earth cult.
Kasha, Kahsha

Kasi (KA-shee) Hindi: "from the holy city." One of the most popular names among the Hindus of Madras, Kasi is the colloquial name for Banaras, one of the seven holy Hindu cities. The city was once the capital for the Kasi tribe.

Kasinda (ka-SEEN-duh or anglicized to ka-SIN-da) Umbundu, Africa *osinda*: "the earth that blocks the passage behind a burrowing animal." Used by the Ovimbundu of Africa for a child born into a family that already has twins.

Kassia Modern Polish form of Katherine, "pure." See Katherine.

Kate Popular form of Katherine, "pure."
Kati, Katie, Katy

Kateke (ka-TAY-ke) Umbundu, Africa: From the Ovimbundu proverb "*Kateke tueya tua lia palonga; kaliye kalo peya oku lila povilindo*," "The days we came, we ate off the dishes; now it comes to eating off wooden bowls." Loosely translated, the saying means "We have stayed too long and worn out our welcome." A name for someone who seems easy to handle at first but grows more difficult once you get to know her.

Katherine, Kathleen, Kathryn Greek *katharos*: "pure." With its many variations, this is one of the most popular names in the world and has been since the fourteenth century.
Caitlon, Caitrin, Cari, Cass, Cassi, Cassie, Cassy, Catarina, Caterina, Catharina, Catherine, Cathe, Cathelina, Cathi, Cathie, Kate, Kathryn, Kathi, Kathie,

Kathy, Kati, Katie, Katy, Kay, Kaye, Kit, Kitti, Kittie, Kitty (English); *Kata, Katarina, Katerina, Katica, Katka, Katuska* (Czech); *Katharina, Kati, Rina* (Estonian); *Catant, Catherine, Trinette* (French); *Katchen, Katharina, Kathe, Katrina, Trina, Trine, Trinchen* (German); *Kata, Katalin, Kati, Katica, Katinka, Kato, Katoka, Katus* (Hungarian); *Katrin* (Icelandic); *Caitlin, Caitria* (Irish); *Caterina, Cathe* (Italian); *Kofryna* (Lithuanian); *Karena, Karin, Katla* (Norwegian); *Kasia, Kasienka, Kasin, Kaska, Kasia, Kassia* (Polish); *Catarina* (Portuguese); *Katenka, Katerinka, Katinka, Katka, Katya, Katryna, Kateryna, Kisa, Kiska, Kitti, Kotinka, Yekaterina* (Russian); *Catalina* (Spanish); *Kajsa, Kolina* (Swedish)

Katura (KA-too-ra) Babudja, Southern Rhodesia, *ku tura*: "I feel better now," referring to the words a mother may speak after giving birth. Literally, the name means "to take a load from one's mind."

Katya (KAHT-ya) Popular Russian form of Katherine, "pure."

Kaula (KOW-luh) Hawaiian: "prophet."

Kaulana (kow-LA-nuh) Hawaiian: "famous one."

Kaveri (ka-VAIR-ee) Hindi: "the sacred Kaveri River." The seven sacred rivers play an important role in Hindu ceremonies, and it is believed that bathing in these rivers, particularly in the Ganges, washes away one's most evil sins. In ancient times a man of high caste was forbidden to marry a girl with a nature name because her name indicated she was inferior. Today, however, many girls are given such names.

Kavindra (ka-VEEN-dra) Hindi: "mighty poet." Often used as a name element to create other names.

Kaya (KA-ya) Hopi Indian *kaka-hoya*: "my elder little sister," implying that while the baby is small she is still wise; or Japanese: "a rush" or "a yew." Also a Ghanaian born-to-die name meaning "stay and don't go back."

Kayla Contemporary U.S. form of Kay or Katherine, "pure."

Kei (kay) Japanese: "rapture" or "reverence." A favorite in Japan, where a common variation is Keiko.

Keiki (ke-EE-kee or KAY-kee) Hawaiian: "child."

Kekona (ke-NO-nuh) Hawaiian: "second-born child."

Kelda Old Norse: "fountain" or "spring." Used in Scandinavia as well as the United States.
Keli, Kelie, Kelli, Kellie, Kelley, Kelly

Kelila (ke-LEE-la) Hebrew: "crown" or "laurel," a symbol of victory and beauty. A favorite in Israel.
Kaile, Kayle, Kelilah, Kelula, Kyla, Kyle (Yiddish)

Kelly Irish Gaelic: "warrior." Originally a boys' name, now commonly used for girls. Also a pet form of Kelda.
Keli, Kelia, Kellen, Kelley, Kelli, Kellia, Kellie, Kellina, Kellisa

Kelsi Irish Gaelic: "warrior;" or Scandinavian: "from the ship island." Gaining in popularity in the United States.
Kelci, Kelcie, Kelsy, Kelsie, Kelsy

Kenda "child of clear, cool water." Contemporary U.S. name. Also an astrological name for a girl born under one of the water signs: Cancer, Scorpio, or Pisces.
Kendi, Kendie, Kendy, Kennda, Kenndi, Kenndie, Kenndy

Kerani (ke-RA-nee) Sanskrit: "sacred bells." Popular among the Todas of India.
Kera, Keri, Kerie, Kery, Rani

Kesava (ke-SA-va) Hindi: "having much (or fine) hair." Another name for the Hindu god Vishnu, also known as Krishna.

Keshia Africa: "favorite one." Popular contemporary U.S. name. Made famous by child actress Keshia Knight Pulliam, who plays Rudy on *The Cosby Show*.

Kesi (KE-see) Swahili: "a child born when her father is in trouble."

Kessie Fanti or Ashanti, Ghana: "chubby one." For a child who is chubby at birth.

Ketzia (ket-ZEE-a) Hebrew: "cinnamonlike bark." Hence, this name has the connotation of fragrance.
Ketzi, Kezia, Kezi

Kichi (KEE-chee) Japanese: "the fortunate one."

Kiele (kee-EL-e) Hawaiian: "gardenia" or "fragrant blossom."

Kikilia (ke-ke-LEE-uh) Hawaiian from of Cecilia, "dim-sighted." See Cecilia for other forms.

Kiku (kee-KOO or KEE-koo) Japanese: "chrysanthemum." A favorite in Japan, this name refers to the Japanese flower of September. In the Orient the mum is a symbol of longevity; in Western astrology it's the flower of Scorpio.

Kim Old English: "ruler" or "chief." Also a nickname for Kimberly.

Kimama (ke-MA-ma) Shoshone Indian: "butterfly." According to one American Indian legend, the Creator took the form of a butterfly and flew all over the world, looking for the best place to create man.

Kimberly Old English: "from the royal-fortress meadow" or "from the brilliant one's meadow." Extremely popular modern U.S. name.
Kim, Kimberlee, Kimberli, Kimberlie, Kimmi, Kimmie, Kym

Kimi (KEE-mee) Japanese: "peerless" or "sovereign."
Kimie, Kimiko, Kimiyo (Japanese)

Kini (KEE-nee) Hawaiian form of Jean "God is gracious." Also a boy's name, meaning "king."

Kirima (ki-ri-ma) Banti Eskimo: "a hill."

Kirsi (KEER-see) Dravidian, India: "the flowering ama-
ranth." Popular among the Todas of India.

Kirsten Widely used in Scandinavia (particularly in Sweden
and Norway) as a form of Christina, "Christian." See
Christina for other forms.

Kisa (KEE-sa) Russian: "kitty" or "pussycat." A favorite
nickname in Russia.

Kishi (kee-shee) Japanese: "beach." Connotes longevity.

Kiska Favorite Russian form of Katherine, "pure." See
Katherine for other variations.

Kismet Contemporary American name meaning "fate" or
"destiny."

Kissa (kiss-SAY) Luganda, Uganda: "born after twins."

Kita (kee-ta) Japanese: "north." Refers to old Oriental
beliefs regarding direction and position.

Kiwa (kee-wah) Japanese: "born on a border."

Klarika Hungarian and Slavic form of Claire, "brilliant"
or "illustrious." See Claire for other forms.

Klesa (KLAY-sa) Hindi: "pain." The negative meaning is
purposely designed to ward evil spirits away from the
child.

Koko (KO-ko) Japanese: "stork." In Japan the stork is a
symbol of longevity.

Kolenya (ko-LAYN-ya) Miwok Indian *kole*: "to cough."
The unusual meaning is "fish coughing." According to
a Karok Indian legend, the fish was the first living
thing created. In the zodiac the fishes are the symbol of
Pisces.

Kolina (ko-LEE-na) Pretty Swedish form of Katherine,
"pure." See Katherine for other forms.

Kona (KO-na) Hindi: "angular." Kona is another name for Saturn, the black god in Hindu mythology. At one time, the name was given to a baby in the hope of appeasing this god. Also an occult name for a child born under Capricorn, which is ruled by the planet Saturn.

Konane (ko-NA-ne) Hawaiian: "bright as moonlight."

Kori Modern U.S. name derived from Cora, which in turn comes from Greek for "maiden."
Cori, Corie, Cory, Corri, Corrie, Corry, Korie, Kory, Korri, Korrie, Korry

Kostya (KO-stya) Popular Russian form of Constance, "firm" or "constant." See Constance for other forms.

Koto (KO-to) Japanese: "harp."

Krishna Hindi: "delightful." Once used primarily in India, now a popular contemporary U.S. name. Krishna is a Hindu incarnation of Vishnu, the god protecting all creation. It is believed that when some great evil has occurred, Vishnu comes down to earth in human form as either Krishna or another incarnation, Rama. See Devaki.

Kristin Popular Scandinavian form of Christina, "Christian." Now a favorite in the United States as well. See Christina.

Krysta Polish form of Christina.

Kuai Hua (kwigh hwa) Chinese: "mallow blossom." In China the mallow blossom is the flower of September and symbolic of the power of magic against evil spirits. The English equivalent is Melba.

Kulya (KOOL-ya) Miwok Indian: "sugar-pine nuts burned black." The name may indicate that at birth there was so much excitement, the pine nuts on the coals were ignored and thus burned.

Kumi (KOO-mee) Japanese: "braid." A popular Japanese variation of this name is Kumiko ("braid child").

Kumuda (kuh-MOO-da) Sanskrit: "lotus." This flower is revered by both Hindus and Buddhists. The Hindus associate it with the birth of Brahma, and many Hindu deities often sit enthroned upon its petals. In contrast, Buddhists believe in a heaven where souls lie enveloped in lotus buds upon the Sacred Lake of Lotuses until they are admitted to paradise on judgment day.

Kuni (KOO-nee) Japanese: "country-born." A popular Japanese variation is *Kuniko* ("country-born child").

Kuri (KOO-ree) Japanese: "chestnut." The chestnut tree occasionally appears in Oriental legends, including one story of a mythical tree so large its branches shaded several provinces, and so magical it could not be cut down.

Kusa (KOO-sah) Hindi: "the sacred kusa grass." Also called *darbha*, this sacred grass has long leaves tapering to needle points and allegedly came from the hair of the god Vishnu in his incarnation as a turtle. A ring of kusa worn during sacred rites is said to protect one against evil and purify one of sin. An annual kusa festival is held on the eighth day of the moon during the month of Bhadrapada (August-September), at which time an offering of the grass is believed to obtain immortality for ten of one's ancestors.

Kwanita (kwa-NEE-ta) Zuni Indian form of the Spanish Juanita, "God is gracious." The English equivalent is Jane.

Kyla Yiddish name meaning "crown" or "laurel." See Kelila. Also a form of Kyle (from the Irish Gaelic meaning either "good-looking" or "one who lives near the chapel").

Lacey Favorite contemporary U.S. form of Larissa, "cheerful."
Lacee, Lacie

Lahela (luh-HAY-luh) Hawaiian development of Rachel,
"ewe." See Rachel.

Laka (LA-kuh) Hawaiian: "attract" or "tame." Name for
the Hawaiian goddess of the hula.

Lakeisha (la-KAY-shuh) Contemporary American name, the
origin of which is unclear. Many recently invented
U.S. names use the *La-* prefix, followed by a more
familiar name. Examples include:
Lalisa, Larita, Larine, Latara, Latasha, Latonya

Lakya (LAHK-ya) Hindu *laksmanavaram*: "born on Thursday."

Lala Slavic name meaning "tulip."

Lalita (lah-LEE-tuh) Hindi: "charming." One of the more
than one thousand names for the Hindu goddess Sakti.
See Sakti.

Lana Hawaiian: "buoyant" or "to float." Also a popular
form of Helen

Lani (LAH-nee) Hawaiian: "sky" or "heavenly." See box
on page 114.

Lara Latin: "shining and famous." Also a popular pet
name in Russia from Larissa (Greek: "cheerful one").
See Larissa.

Lari Once a nickname for Laura "crowned with laurel," or
Lara, "shining" or "famous," Lari is used today in
the United States as an independent name. In astrology
the laurel is the plant of the sun, which governs the
sign Leo. See Laura.

Larissa (lah-REE-sah) Russian name from the Greek for
"cheerful one."
Lara, Larochka

Laura Latin *laures*: "crowned with laurel." The masculine
form of this name is Lawrence.
*Lari, Larilia, Laureen, Laurel, Laurella, Lauren,
Laurena, Laurene, Lauretta, Laurette, Lauri, Laurice,
Laurie, Lauriette, Lora, Loree, Loreen, Loren, Lorena,
Lorene, Loretta, Lorette, Lori, Lorinda, Lorita, Lorna,
Lorri, Lorrie, Lorry* (English); *Lora* (Bulgarian); *Laure,
Laurette* (French); *Lola* (Hawaiian); *Lorenza* (Italian);
Laurka (Polish); *Laurinda* (Portuguese); *Lavra* (Russian);
Laureana (Spanish)

Lauren Popular modern form of Laura. Well-known namesakes: model Lauren Hutton and actress Lauren Bacall.
Laurin, Lauryn, Lorin, Lorrin, Loryn, Lorynn, Lorynne

Lavinie (lah-VEEN-yuh) Latin: "purified" or "lady from
Latium." Modern French form of Lavinia.
Lavinia, Lavina (English)

Layla (LAH-ee-lah or anglicized to LAY-lah) Arabic: "born
at night." Popular Swahili name. See Leila.

HAWAIIAN SKY NAMES

Many traditional Hawaiian names speak of the sky.
These names frequently have a religious, heavenly connotation. Among them:

AHULANI (ah-hoo-LAH-nee) "heavenly shrine."
ALOHILANI (ah-loh-hee-LAH-nee) "bright sky."
HOKULANI (hoh-koo-LAH-nee) "star in the sky."
IWALANI (ee-wah-LAH-nee) "heavenly sea bird."
KAKAULANI (kah-cow-LAH-nee) "placed in the sky."
LEILANI (lay-LAH-nee) "heavenly flower."
MALULANI (mah-loo-LAH-nee) "under heaven's protection."
OKALANI (oh-kah-LAH-nee) "of the heavens."
PILILANI (pil-ee-LAH-nee) "close to heaven."

Lea Hebrew: "weary." Used in Hungary, Sweden, and the United States.
Leah, Lee, Leigh, Lia, Liah (English); *Lia* (French, Italian, Portuguese); *Lean* (German); *Leah* (Yiddish)

Leandra Latin: "like a lioness." Astrological name for a girl born under Leo.
Leodora, Leoine, Leoline, Leonanie, Leona, Leonelle, Leonette, Leonice, Leonissa

Ledah Hebrew: "birth"; also form of Letitia, "gladness."
Leda, Lida, Lidah

Lee Chinese: "plum"; Old English: "one who lives in the pasture meadow"; or Irish Gaelic: "poetic child." Also a short form of Lea, "weary."

Leeba Hebrew: "heart." Used today especially in Israel.

Leena Estonian form of Helen, "light" or "torch."
Elli, Hele, Lenni (Estonian)

Lehua (le-HOO-uh) Hawaiian: "sacred to the gods." Also the name of a native flower in Hawaii.

Leila (LIGH-lah or LAY-lah) Arabic: "born at night." In an ancient Persian legend, *Leila and Majnun*, Leila is the heroine. The name was also popular in the nineteenth century when Byron used it in *The Giaour*.
Laila, Layla, Leilia, Lela, Lila

Leilani (lay-lah-nee) Hawaiian: "heavenly flower." (See page 114 for other Hawaiian sky names.)

Lela (LEH-lah) Popular Spanish form of Adelle, "noble." See Adelle for other forms.

Lena Hebrew: "dwelling" or "lodging"; or Latin: "alluring one." Popular name in Israel. Also a nickname for the German Magdalene and the Russian Galina.
Lenah, Lina, Linah (English); *Liene* (Latvian)

Lenka (LEHN-kah) Czechoslovakian form of Helen, "light" or "torch." See Helen.

Lenora See Helen.

Leor Hebrew: "I have light." Modern Israeli name. Also used for boys.

Leotie (leh-oh-TEE-e or anglicized to lay-O-tee) North American Indian: "prairie flower."

Leska (LESH-kuh or LES-kah) In Czechoslovakia this is a pet form of Alexandra, "helper and defender of mankind." See Alexandra.

Leslie Scotch Gaelic: "one who lives in the gray fortress." Originally a Scottish place name, now extremely popular as a given name in the United States.
    Lesli, Lesley, Lesly, Lezli, Lezlie, Lezly

Lesya (LEHSH-yah) A favorite in Russia. See Alexandra.

Leta (LEH-tah) Swahili: "bring." This name may be combined with a second name to mean "bring happiness" or "bring luck." In the United States this is also a short form of Letitia ('gladness") and Latonia ("sacred to Latona"), a name identified with the Greek goddess Leto, mother of the moon and sun.

Letitia Latin: "gladness."
    Leda, Leta, Letti, Lettie, Letty, Tish (English); *Leticia* (Hungarian, Spanish, Portuguese); *Letizia* (Italian); *Letycia* (Polish)

Levana Latin: "the rising sun." Appropriate for a child born under the astrological sign of Leo, ruled by the sun.

Levia (leh-VEE-uh) Hebrew: "to join." The masculine form is Levi.

Lexa Popular Czech nickname. See Alexandra.

Lexie Used today as an independent name in the United States, Lexie was once a nickname for Alexandra, "helper and defender of mankind."

Leya (LEH-yah) Spanish name meaning "loyalty to the law." Also used by the Tamil of South India and Ceylon to designate the constellation and the astrological sign Leo.

Lia Modern name used in the United States, France, Greece, Portugal, and Italy either from the Greek ("one who brings good news") or from the Hebrew Leah ("weary"). See Lea.

Lian Chinese: "the graceful willow."

Liana French *liane*: "the liana vine," referring to a brilliantly blossomed tropical climbing plant.
Lean, Leana, Leane, Liane, Lianna, Lianne

Libby Popular modern U.S. form of Elizabeth.

Lida (LEE-dah) Popular Russian nickname. See Lidia.

Lidia Greek: "from Lydia," an ancient country in Asia Minor, or "happy." Lidia is used around the globe.
Lydia, Lydie (English); *Lidka* (Czech); *Lydie* (French); *Lidi* (Hungarian); *Lida, Lidka* (Polish); *Lida, Lidiya, Lidka, Lidochka* (Russian)

Lidiya (lee-DEE-uh) Introduced into Russia by the Greek Orthodox Church. See Lidia.

Lien Chinese: "lotus." The buds, blossoms, and seeds of the eight-petal lotus are all visible simultaneously, and hence in China the flower is considered a symbol of the past, present, and future. The lotus also symbolizes purity, and a familiar proverb in China is "The lotus springs from the mud." See Kumuda for Buddhist beliefs regarding the flower.

Liene (LI-e-ne) Latvian form of Lena.

Lien Hua (lay-ehn hwah) Chinese: "lotus flower." In China the lotus is the flower of summer and July. See Lien.

Li Hua (lee-hwah) Chinese: "pear blossom." In China the

pear blossom is the flower of August and a symbol of longevity.

Lila (LEE-luh) Hindi: "the free, playful will of god;" Persian: "lilac"; or a Polish nickname for Leopoldine, "bold defender of the people."

Lilia (lee-LEE-uh) Hawaiian: "the lily flower." A pretty Hawaiian variation is Lileana (le-lee-AH-nuh). See Lillian.

Liliha (lee-LEE-huh) Hawaiian: "disgust." The name of a woman governor of the Hawaiian isle of Oahu during the 1820s.

Lilith Arabic: "of the night." In Eastern mythology Lilith was Adam's first wife. She was created separately from Adam and was the first feminist, challenging Adam's authority as head of the household. When Adam refused to compromise, Lilith left him, and God then created Eve from Adam's rib so there would never be any question of Adam's (or man's) superiority. Lilith is said to have become a demon.

Lilka (LEL-kuh) Polish form of Louise, "famous warrior-maiden." See Louise for other forms.

Lillian Latin *lilium*: "the lily flower."
   Lil, Lila, Lili, Lilia, Lilian, Liliane, Lilla, Lilli, Lillie, Lilly, Lily (English); *Lilli* (Estonian); *Lilian, Lieschen, Liesel, Lilli, Lili, Lily, Lizzie* (German); *Lilika* (Greek); *Lilia, Lileana* (Hawaiian); *Boske, Bozsi, Lilike* (Hungarian); *Lilana* (Latvian); *Leka, Lelya, Lena, Lenka, Lili, Olena, Olenka* (Russian); *Liljana* (Serbian); *Lilia* (Spanish)

Liluye (lee-LOO-ye) Miwok Indian: "chicken hawk singing when soaring."

Lina (LEE-nah) Popular Russian diminutive of many names. See Angela, Adelle, and Caroline.

MIWOK INDIAN CHICKEN-HAWK NAMES

The chicken hawk appears in many Miwok Indian names, which are always quite colorful. Among these intriguing names:

NOKSU—"smell of a chicken hawk's nest."

PUTEPU—"chicken hawk walking back and forth on a limb."

TIWOLU—"chicken hawk turning its eggs with its bill while they are hatching."

TOLOISI—"chicken hawk tearing a gopher snake with its talons."

YUTKIYE—"chicken hawk lifting ground squirrel from the ground."

YUTTCISO—from *yutuk*: "stick on," and means "lice thick on a chicken hawk."

Linda Spanish: "pretty one."
Lindi, Lindie, Lindy, Lynda

Lindsey Old English: "from the isle of the serpents" or "from the linden-tree island." Traditionally a boys' name, Lindsey is gaining popularity in the United States as a girls' name. Popularized to some extent by actress Lindsay Wagner.
Lindsi, Lindsie, Lindsy, Lindsay, Linsey, Linsi, Linsie, Linsy

Linette Old French: "a linnet bird." Comes originally from a Latin word meaning "flax," the seeds on which the linnet bird feeds.
Lanette, Linet, Linetta, Linette, Linnet, Lynette, Lynnet, Lynnette

Liolya (lee-OHL-yah) A favorite Russian form of Helen.

Liona (lee-O-nuh) Hawaiian: "lion." The lion is the symbol of the sign Leo.

Lirit Hebrew: "poetic," "lyrical," or "musical." Modern Israeli name.

Lisa Popular modern U.S. form of Elizabeth, "dedicated to God." Also a Scandinavian favorite. See Elizabeth.

Liseli (lee-SEH-lee) Popular Zuni Indian name of unknown meaning.

Liseta (lee-SEH-tah) Contemporary Spanish form of Elizabeth. See Elizabeth for dozens of variations.

Lisette (lee-SET-te) German form of Elizabeth. Also a French form of Louise, "famous warrior-maiden."

Lissa Once an American nickname for Melissa ("honey" or "a bee") or Millicent ("honest" or "diligent"), this is now widely used as an independent name. The melissa plant is considered symbolic of sympathy and love and is an Arabic emblem of rejuvenation.

Lissilma (le-SEEL-mah) North American Indian: "be thou there." Because many old Indian names were sloppily recorded, the exact tribe from which this name comes has been lost.

Litonya (li-TOHN-yah) Miwok Indian *litanu*: "to dart down." Connotatively, the name means "hummingbird darting down after having flown straight up." In the occult world the hummingbird is considered a love charm to enchant members of the opposite sex.

Litsa Modern Greek form of Evangelia, which is a form of Angela, "angel" or "one who brings good news." See Angela and Evangelia.

Livana (lee-VAH-nuh) Hebrew: "white" or "the moon." In astrology the moon governs the sign of Cancer. *Levana, Leva, Liva*

Livanga (lee-VAHN-gah) Umbundu, Africa: From the Ovimbundu proverb "*Livanga oku soka ku livange oku lia,*" "Be first to think, but don't be first to eat." The proverb warns of the danger of being poisoned by rotten meat if one does not think first and check it for spoiling.

Liviya (li-VEE-yah) Hebrew: "lioness." The variations Livia and Levia also mean "crown."
Levia, Leviya, Livia

Livona (li-VO-nuh) Hebrew: "spice" or "incense."
Levona

Liza Form of Elizabeth ("dedicated to God") popular in both the United States and Russia. See Elizabeth.

Lizina (LI-zi-nah) Latvian form of Elizabeth.

Lokelani (loh-ke-LAH-nee) Hawaiian: "heavenly rose." Hawaiian sky-flower name.

Lola Popular modern U.S. form of Dolores and Charlotte. Also a Hawaiian development of Laura, "crowned with laurel."

Lolita Popular Spanish pet form of the Virgin Mary name Maria de los Dolores, "Mary of the Sorrows." See Dolores.

Lolotea (loh-loh-TEH-ah) Zuni Indian development (through the Spanish name Dorotea) of Dorothy, "God's gift."

Lomasi (lo-MAH-see) North American Indian: "pretty flower."

Loretta (lo-REH-tah) Spanish: "pure." The same name is also a form of Laura, "crowned with laurel."
Laret, Larette, Lauret, Laureta, Lauretta, Loret, Loreta, Lorette

Lota Hindi: "portable drinking cup." Hindus often name their children after inanimate objects. See Almira for an explanation of the custom.

Lotta (LO-tah) A favorite Swedish form of Caroline, "little womanly one."

Louise Old German: "famous warrior-maiden."
Alison, Alyson, Eloise, Lois, Lou, Louisa, Louisetta, Lu (English); *Aloyse, Lisette* (French); *Aloisa, Luise* (German); *Eloisia* (Greek); *Eloisa* (Italian, Swedish); *Lovisa* (Norwegian); *Iza, Lilka, Lodoiska, Ludka, Ludwika, Luisa* (Polish); *Louisa* (Rumanian); *Luiza, Luyiza* (Russian); *Eloisa, Luisa* (Spanish)

Lucita (loo-SEE-tah) Spanish name for Mary, mother of Jesus, shortened from Maria de la Luz, "Mary of the Light."
Lusita (Zuni Indian)

Lucy Latin *lucia*: "light," implying the child brings light. The masculine form of this name is Lucius or Luke.
Lou, Lu, Luce, Lucette, Luci, Luciana, Luciane, Lucida, Lucie, Lucile, Lucille (English); *Lucine* (Bulgarian); *Lucia, Lucie* (Czech); *Lucienne* (French); *Luzi, Luzie* (German); *Luke* (Hawaiian); *Luca, Lucia* (Hungarian); *Lugia* (Italian); *Lucija* (Latvian); *Lucya* (Polish); *Luzija* (Russian); *Luci, Lucika, Lucka* (Slavic); *Luciana, Lucila* (Spanish)

Lulani (loo-LAH-nee) Hawaiian: "the highest point in heaven." A lofty Hawaiian name for girls and boys.

Lulu North American Indian: "rabbit"; or Anglo-Saxon: "soothing influence."

Luna Spanish *luna*: "moon" or "satellite." Popular Zuni Indian name. In astrology the moon rules the sign of Cancer, whereas the tarot card of the moon corresponds to Pisces.

Lusa Finnish form of Elizabeth, "dedicated to God."

Lusela (loo-SAY-lah) Miwok Indian: "bear swinging its foot when licking it." Of all animals, the bear is probably the most popular in Miwok names.

Luyu (LOO-yoo) Miwok Indian *luyani*: literally, "to shake the head," with the connotation "dove shaking its head sideways."

Luz Spanish: "light." This popular Spanish name is a shortened form of Maria de la Luz, "Mary of the Light."

Lydia See Lidia.

Lynn Old English: "waterfall" or "pool below a waterfall." *Lin, Linell, Linelle, Linette, Linn, Linne, Linnette, Lyn, Lyndel, Lyndell, Lyndelle, Lynelle, Lynette, Lynna, Lynne, Lynnelle, Lynnette* (English); *Lina* (Spanish)

———————————— **M** ————————————

Machi (mah-chee) Japanese: "ten thousand." In Japan round numbers were once considered good omens.

Maddie Popular contemporary U.S. form of Madeline.

Madeline Greek: "of Magdala," the Palestinian city on the Sea of Galilee where Mary Magdalene once lived. *Lena, Lenna, Lina, Linn, Lynn, Lynne, Mada, Madalena, Madalyn, Maddi, Maddie, Maddy, Madelaine, Madeleine, Madelena, Madelina, Madge, Madlen, Madlin, Mady, Magda, Magdalena, Mala, Malena, Marleen, Marlena, Marlina, Marline* (English); *Magda, Magdelena* (Czech); *Marlene, Lena, Lene* (German); *Magdolna* (Hungarian); *Maddelina* (Italian); *Lena, Magdelina, Magda, Magia* (Polish); *Madelina, Magdalina, Magda, Mahda* (Russian); *Magaly, Magda, Magola, Lena* (Spanish)

Magara (MAH-gah-rah) Mashona, Southern Rhodesia: from the words *ku gara*, meaning "to sit" or "to stay." Often given by Southern Rhodesians to a baby who cries so much her parents don't know what to do. The name refers to the long hours the parents sit and cuddle the infant.

Magda (MAHG-duh) A true whole-world name, used not only in the United States, but also in Russia, Poland, Czechoslovakia, and Spanish-speaking countries, comes from the Greek and refers to Mary Magdalene. See Madeline.

Magena (mah-GEH-nah) North American Indian: "the coming moon."

Maggie See Margaret.

Mahala North American Indian: "woman"; or Hebrew: "tenderness." Famous namesake: singer Mahalia Jackson. *Mahalah, Mahalia, Mahela, Mahelia, Mahila, Mahilia*

Mahesa (mah-HEH-shah) Hindi: "great lord." One of the 1,008 names for the Hindu god Siva, also used for boys.
Maheesa, Mahisa (English)

Mahina (muh-HEE-nuh) Hawaiian: "moon." See Luna for the moon's astrological significance.

Mahira (mah-HEE-rah) Hebrew: "quick" or "energetic."
Mehira

Makadisa (mah-kah-DEE-sah) Baduma, Africa: "she was always selfish." Often bestowed as a nickname by the Baduma people in Africa.

Makana Hawaiian: "gift or present."

Makani (muh-KAH-nee) Hawaiian: "the wind." Also for boys.

Malia (muh-LEE-uh) Hawaiian form of Mary, "bitter." Also a Zuni Indian name derived from the Spanish Maria. See Mary.

Malila (muh-LEE-lah) Miwok Indian: "salmon going fast up a rippling stream."

Malina See Madeline. This name, from the Tabascan language, is also a favorite among Mexican Indians.

Malka Hebrew: "a queen."

"GIFT" NAMES

The idea of a child being a gift from God is evident in dozens of names throughout the world. Among the many "gift names," we find the Nigerian Aniweta ("the spirit Ani brought it"), the Ukrainian Bohdana ("given by God"), the English Dorothy and its many variations, including the German Dorlisa and the Russian Dasha ("God's gift"), the English Edith, with its many forms including the Czech Dita and the Hungarian Duci ("rich gift"), and the Swahili Zawadi ("gift").

Mallory Old French: "one who wears plate-mail"; or Old German: "an army counselor." Popular contemporary U.S. name also used for boys.
Mal, Mallorey, Mallorie, Malori, Malorie, Malory

Mana (MAH-nuh) Hawaiian: "supernatural power."

Manaba (mah-NAH-bah) Navaho Indian: "war returned with her coming." See Doba.

Manda (MAHN-dah) Spanish form of Armanda, "harmony" or "battle maiden." Also one of the Hindi names for Saturn, god of the occult.
Armanda, Mandi, Mandie, Mandy

Mandara (mahn-DAH-rah) Hindi: "the mythical mandara tree." It is said that in the shade of the mandara tree in the Hindu paradise, all worldly cares are forgotten. According to ancient tree-worship beliefs, plants were not only conscious but able to feel pain. Each tree was believed to contain a tree spirit who had to be given flowers and sweetmeats. In return, the tree could be consulted as an oracle and had the power to grant children fame and wealth. Before a tree was cut, the cutter prayed to the tree deity so that the god would find another tree and not be angry with him.

Mandisa (mahn-DEE-sah) Xhosa, South Africa: "sweet."

Mandy Originally a nickname for Amanda, "worthy of love," Mandy is now an independent contemporary name. See also Manda.
Mandi, Mandie

Mangena (mahn-GAY-nuh) Hebrew: "song" or "melody."
Mangina (Hebrew)

Mani From the prayer *om mani padme hum*, the first and greatest of all charms among Tibetan Buddhists. Though the meaning of these sacred words is unknown, repeating them is believed to thwart evil and impart all wisdom and knowledge.

Mansi Hopi Indian: "plucked flower."
Mancey, Manci, Mancie, Mansey, Mansie, Mansy (English)

Manya A popular Russian nickname. See Mary.

Mara A name popular around the world. Used in Russia, Serbia, Hungary, and other countries as a form of Mary, "bitter," and in Czechoslovakia as a short form of Tamara, "palm tree." See Mary.

Marci This modern American name was once a nickname for Marcia ("martial or warlike one"), but is used today as an independent name.
Marcie, Marcy, Marsi, Marsie, Marsy

Marcia Latin: "martial or warlike one," referring to the Roman god Mars. The masculine form is Marcus. See Marci above.
Marcella, Marcelia, Marci, Marcille, Marcy, Marquita, Marsha

Marganit (mahr-gah-NEET) Hebrew: "the marganit flower," referring to a flower with red, blue, and golden blossoms that's native to Israel.

Margaret Latin: "a pearl." Popular in many forms worldwide.
Daisy, Greta, Gretta, Madge, Mag, Maggi, Maggie,

Maggy, Marga, Marge, Margery, Marget, Margie, Margret, Marguerite, Margy, Marjorie, Marjory, Meg, Megan, Meggi, Meggie, Meggy, Meghan, Peg, Peggi, Peggie, Peggy, Rita (English); *Margarid* (Armenian); *Marketa* (Bulgarian); *Gita, Gitka, Gituska, Margita, Margareta, Marka, Marketa* (Czech); *Marga, Margarete, Mari, Meeri, Reet* (Estonian); *Marjatta* (Finnish); *Margot, Marguerite* (French); *Grete, Gretel, Gretchen, Margareta, Margarete, Margit, Margot, Margret* (German); *Margareta, Margaritis, Margaro* (Greek); *Gitta, Manci, Margit, Margita, Margo* (Hungarian); *Margarita* (Italian, Lithuanian); *Grieta, Margrieta* (Latvian); *Gita, Margita, Margisia, Rita* (Polish); *Margarida* (Portuguese); *Perla* (Slavic); *Margreta, Margrete* (Swedish, Norwegian); *Margarita, Marga, Margara, Rita, Tita* (Spanish)

Margaux (MAR-go) Modern U.S. invention, said to have come from Margaux champagne.

Mari Contemporary American name. See Mary.

Maria The popularity of the Virgin Mary's name in Spanish-speaking countries makes this the most common Spanish name in the world. See Mary.
Carmen, Dolores, Jesusa, Lucita, Luz (Spanish)

Marini (mah-REE-nee) Swahili: "fresh, healthy, and pretty."

Marisha (mah-REE-sha) Popular pet name in Russia. See Mary.

Marissa Latin: "of the sea."
Maris, Marisa, Mari, Meris, Merisa, Merissa

Marlene (mahr-LEH-ne) German form of Madeline popularized in the United States by actress Marlene Dietrich.

Marni Hebrew: "to rejoice." Pet form of Marnina, now used in the United States as an independent name.

Marta Popular form of Martha, used worldwide. Common today not only in the United States, but also Sweden,

Norway, Rumania, Lithuania, Italy, Hungary, Bulgaria, Czechoslovakia, Poland, Russia, the Ukraine, Serbia, and most Spanish-speaking countries. See Martha.

Martha Aramaic: "lady" or "mistress." See also Marta above.
Mart, Marti, Martie, Marty, Matti, Mattie, Matty, Pat, Patti, Patty (English); *Marticka* (Czech); *Marthe* (French); *Martus, Martuska* (Hungarian); *Macia, Masia* (Polish); *Martina, Maita* (Spanish)

Mary Hebrew: "bitter." One of the world's most popular names, Mary commemorates the mother of Jesus Christ and was once considered too sacred to be given to a child. But from the twelfth century on, the name became increasingly popular in nearly every country.
Mame, Mamie, Mara, Marabel, Marella, Maren, Mari, Maria, Mariam, Marian, Mariana, Marianna, Marice, Maridel, Marie, Marietta, Mariette, Marilee, Marilin, Marilyn, Marion, Marita, Marla, Marlo, Marya, Maryann, Maryanna, Maryanne, Marylin, Marylinn, Marylyn, Maura, Maure, Maureen, Maurene, May, Meri, Meriel, Merrill, Mimi, Minette, Minni, Minnie, Minny, Miriam, Mitzi, Molli, Mollie, Molly, Muriel, Muriell, Polli, Pollie, Polly (English); *Marca, Marenka, Marienka, Mariska, Maruska* (Czech); *Marye* (Estonian); *Maija, Maijii, Maikki, Marja* (Finnish); *Manette, Manon, Marie, Maryse* (French); *Marika, Maroula, Roula* (Greek); *Mara, Mari, Marika, Mariska, Marcsa* (Hungarian); *Maire, Maura, Maureen, Moira, Moire, Moya, Muire* (Irish); *Mare* (Latvian); *Marija* (Lithuanian); *Macia, Manka, Maryla, Maryna* (Polish); *Maricara* (Rumanian); *Maria, Mariya, Marya, Manka, Manya, Marinka, Marisha, Maruska, Masha, Mashenka, Mashka, Mura* (Russian); *Mairi, Moire, Muire* (Scottish); *Mari, Maria, Marita, Mariquita, Maruca, Maruja* (Spanish); *Mirjam* (Swedish, Norwegian); *Miriam* (Yiddish); *Meli* (Zuni Indian)

Masago (mah-SAH-go) Japanese: "sand," referring to the sand's eternal quality and expressing a hope for the child's long life.

Masha (MAH-shah) Classic Russian form of Mary, "bitter."

Masika (mah-SEE-kah) Swahili: "born during the rainy season."

Matana (mah-TAH-nah) Hebrew: "gift." Modern Israeli name referring to the baby as a gift from God. (See "Gift Names" on page 125.)

Matilda Old German: "battle maiden." This name is used in Estonia, Italy, Latvia, Lithuania, Rumania, Russia, Serbia, Sweden, Norway, the United States, and Spanish-speaking countries. In most of these countries, Tilda and Tilli are favorite pet forms.
Mat, Mathilda, Matti, Mattie, Matty, Maud, Maude, Tilda, Tildy, Tillie, Tilly (English); *Matylda, Tylda* (Czech); *Mahaut, Matilde* (French); *Maddy, Malkin, Mathilde, Matty, Patty* (German); *Matelda* (Italian); *Macia, Mala, Tila* (Polish); *Matilde, Matusha, Matuxa* (Spanish)

Matrika (mah-TREE-kah) Hindi: "mother." One of the many names for the Hindu goddess Sakti. See Sakti.

Matsu (MAHT-soo) Japanese: "pine." In the Orient the pine is the symbol of stability and firm old age, as well as the plant of January.

Maureen Irish Gaelic: "little Mary" or "little bitter one"; or Old French: "dark-skinned."
Maura, Maurene, Maurine, Moira, Mora, Moreen (English); *Morena* (Spanish)

Mausi (MAW-see or MAU-see) North American Indian: "plucking flowers."

Maya Hindi: "God's creative power." In the Hindu religion God's powers include His ability to act through man and to create life. According to sacred Hindu writings, "God resides in the heart of all beings, and by His maya moves them from within as if they were turned by a machine."

Meda (MAY-duh) North American Indian: "prophet," "priestess," or "edible root."

Mega (MEH-gah) Spanish: "gentle, mild, and peaceful."

Megan, Meghan Greek: "great and mighty." Also an Irish form of Margaret, "a pearl."
Meagan, Meaghen, Meg, Megen, Meghann

Mei (may) Hawaiian name from the Latin *maia*, "great one." The English equivalent is May.

Meira (meh-EE-rah) Hebrew *M'eeraw:* "light." Popularized in Israel by the late Israeli Prime Minister Golda Meir, who changed her name from Golda Meyerson, following the Israeli custom of choosing a Hebrew name.

Mel Portuguese: "honey."

Mela (MAY-lah) Hindi: "religious gathering." Also a Polish form of Melanie, "black" or "dark."

Melanie Greek: "black" or "dark." Melanie is probably derived from Melanesia, the name of a region northeast of Australia, where the people are predominantly dark-skinned. Melanesia literally means "black islands." This name is used not only in the United States, but also Czechoslovakia, France, and Germany. Another popular Czech, French, German, Italian, and Polish form of the name is Melania.
Melani, Melany, Melenia, Mel, Melli, Mellie, Melly, Meloni, Melonie, Melony (English); *Ela, Mela, Melka* (Polish); *Melana, Melaniya, Melanka, Melanya, Melashka, Melasya, Milya* (Russian); *Milena* (Slovenian)

Melantha Greek: "black flower." The name probably comes from the deep-purple lily that once grew along Mediterranean shores.

Melba Latin *malva*: "the mallow flower"; or Greek *malako*: "soft" or "slender." In China the mallow is considered a magic charm against evil; it's also the flower of September and the astrological sign of Virgo.
Malva, Melva

Melcia (MELT-shuh or anglicized to MEL-shuh) Polish form of Amelia, "industrious" or "flatterer." See Amelia.

Meli (MEH-lee) Zuni Indian form of Mary, "bitter." Also a Greek name meaning "honey."

Melia (meh-LEE-ah) Spanish form of Cornelia, "yellowish" or "cornel tree." See Cornelia.

Melinda Greek: "gentle and mild."
Linda, Lindi, Lynda, Malina, Malinda, Malinde, Mallie, Mally, Malina, Melina, Melynda, Melli, Mellie, Melly

THE MOST UNPOPULAR NAMES IN THIS COUNTRY

Lists of the most popular names abound. But what of the most *unpopular* names in the United States? According to Stephen Pile's *Book of Heroic Failures*, the following Christian names—all used between 1838 and 1900—have fallen into "spectacular neglect."

Abishag	Despair	Minniehaha
Amorous	Dozer	Murder
Babberley	Energetic	Salmon
Brained	Feather	Strongitharm
Bugless	Ham	Tram
Clapham	Lettuce	Uz

Melissa Greek: "honey" or "a bee."
Lissa, Melessa, Meli, Melie, Melisa, Melisse, Melita, Melitta, Melli, Mellie, Melly, Milli, Millie, Milly

Melka (MEL-kah) Polish form of Melanie, "black" or "dark." See Melanie for other forms.

Melosa (meh-LO-sah) Spanish: "honeylike, sweet, or gentle."

Menora (me-NOR-uh) Hebrew: "a candelabrum." Modern Israeli name.
Menorah (Hebrew)

Meredith Old Welsh: "a guardian from the sea."
Meri, Merideth, Merri, Merrie, Merry

Meri Finnish: "the sea." In Hebrew the same name means "rebellious," implying bitterness, and may come from Mary or Miriam.

Meriwa (me-RI-wuh) Banti Eskimo: "thorn." This may have been used originally as a magic name to ward off evil spirits, to trick them into believing that the child was unloved because she had a name with an unpleasant meaning.

Meryem (MAI-re-em) Turkish development of Miriam, "rebellious" or "bitter," or Mary, "bitter."

Mesha (MAY-shah) Hindi: "ram." Hindu astrological name for a child born under the sign of Aries, the ram.

Mia Modern U.S. and Israeli name from Michaela, "Who is like God?" Also a pet form of Maria. Popularized by actress Mia Farrow.

Michele, Michelle Hebrew *Mikhael*: "Who is like God?" Much more popular in the United States today than the older form Michaela. The masculine form of this name is Michael.
Mia, Michal, Michel, Micki, Mickie, Micky (English); *Michaelle* (Italian)

Michi (mee-chee) Japanese: "the righteous way." In Japanese another character associated with this sound means "three thousand," which expresses the hope that the family will extend for many generations.

Midori (mee-do-ree) Japanese: "green." At one time Japanese color names referred to human qualities; Midori implies a hope the child will be illustrious.

Migina (mee-GEE-nah) Omaha Indian: "moon returning." This name indicates the child was born during the new moon. In astrology the moon governs the sign of Cancer, the tarot card of the moon corresponds to Pisces.

Mika (MEE-kah) North American Indian: "the knowing raccoon"; Japanese *Mikazuki*: "the moon of the third night (of the old lunar month)," or "new moon." In Russia this is a pet form of Dominika, "belonging to the Lord" or "born on Sunday."

Miki Japanese: "stem." Possibly refers to the family tree. *Mikie, Mikiyo* (Japanese)

Mila (MEE-lah) Slavic: "loved by the people." Popular Czech name. The longer version is Ludmila.

Milada (mi-LAH-dah) Czech *mi-lada*: "my love." *Lada* refers to a goddess of youth, fertility, and love.

Milena (MI-leh-nuh or mi-LAY-nuh) Slavic form of Melanie.

Mili (MEE-lee or MIL-ee) Hebrew: "who is like me." Modern Israeli name. Also a short form of Millicent or Millie, "honest and diligent."

Milica (MI-lits-uh or anglicized to mi-LEE-kuh) Originally from the ancient Gothic *amal*, "hard work." Thus, this name means "industrious." Slavic form of Amelia.

Millicent Old German: "loyal and industrious."
Lissa, Mel, Mellicent, Melli, Mellie, Mellisent, Melly, Mili, Milli, Millie, Millisent, Milly

Mimi French form of Helmine, "unwavering protector." Also a short form of Miriam, "bitter" or "rebellious."

Mina (MEE-nah) Used by many cultures around the world. Czech short form of Hermina, "child of the earth"; German, Polish, and English short form of Helmine, "unwavering protector"; and a Hindu astrological name for a child born under Pisces, symbolized by the fishes.

Minal (mee-NAHL) North American Indian: "fruit."

Minda Hindi: "knowledge" or "wisdom."

Mindy Originally a nickname for Minna ("love"), now used as an independent name.
Mindi, Mindie

Mineko (mee-NE-ko) Japanese: "peak." Loosely translated, means "mountain child."

Minette French form of Helmine, "unwavering protector." For other variations, see Helmine.

Minna German form of Helmine.

Minowa (mi-NO-wah) North American Indian: "moving voice."

Mio (MEE-o) Japanese: "triple cord."

Miri (MEE-ree) English Gypsy: "mine." Also an Israeli form of Miriam.

Miriam Hebrew: "rebellious" or "bitter." Original Hebrew form of Mary.
Mimi, Minni, Minnie, Mitzi (English); *Miri* (English Gypsy); *Mirjam* (Finnish)

Mituna (mi-TOO-nah) Miwok Indian *mituye*: "to roll up." The connotation is "wrapping a salmon with willow stems and leaves after catching it."

Mitzi Form of Miriam, "rebellious" or "bitter."

Miwa (mee-wah) Japanese: "the far-seeing." The common Japanese variation Miwako means "far-seeing child."

Miya (mee-yah) Japanese: "temple" or "Shinto."

Miyo (mee-yo) Japanese: "beautiful generations," often varied to Miyoko, "beautiful generations child."

Miyuki (mee-YOO-kee) Japanese: "deep snow," connoting the peaceful silence following a heavy snowfall.

Molly Popular contemporary form of Mary.
Molli, Mollie

Mona Greek: "just"; Italian: "my lady"; or Miwok Indian: "gathering jimson-weed seed."

Mora Spanish: "little blueberry."

Morena Spanish form of Maureen, "little Mary" or "little bitter one." See Maureen.

Morgan Old Welsh: "seashore." In Arthurian legend Morgan Le Fay was King Arthur's sister. Popularized recently by actress Morgan Fairchild.
Morganne, Morgen

Moriah Hebrew: "God is my teacher."
Moria, Morice, Moriel, Morit

Mozelle (mo-ZEH-le or anglicized to mo-ZEL) Hebrew: "taken from the water." Feminine form of Moses.
Moselle

Mu Lan (moo-lahn) Chinese: "magnolia blossom." In China the magnolia is the flower of May and a symbol of sweetness.

Mulya (MOOL-yah) Miwok Indian: "knocking acorns off a tree with a long stick," from *mule*, "to beat or hit." Acorns and fish were the chief foods of many North American Indian tribes. According to one Indian legend, all the creatures loved the first-born man except the she-frog, who envied his beautiful legs. Determined to get rid of the man, the frog spit poison into the man's water, and he died. The first-born man had promised he would give the Indians their most valued possession, and from his ashes sprang the first oak, covered with acorns as large as apples.

Muna (MOO-nah) Hopi Indian: "freshet." Given to a child born during the season the streams rise. From the Hopi cloud cult.

Mura (moo-rah) Japanese: "village." The name may refer to the fact that a child or her parents came to the country from a village.

Mu Tan (moo-TAHN) Chinese: "tree peony blossom." In China the peony, called the king of flowers, is the flower of March and spring, and a symbol of love and affection.

--------------------------- **N** ---------------------------

Nadia (NAH-dee-uh) Slavic: "hope." Used especially in Russia. Made well known by Rumanian gymnast Nadia Comaneci.
Nadine (English); *Nadina* (Latvian); *Nata* (Polish); *Dusya, Nada, Nadenka, Nadina, Nadiya, Nadka, Nadya* (Russian)

Nagida (nah-GEE-duh) Hebrew: "wealthy" or "ruler."

Naida Latin: "a river or water nymph." Astrological name for a child born under one of the water signs.

Nani Hawaiian: "beautiful." Also a modern Greek form of Ann, "graceful."

Nara Japanese: "oak"; or Old English: "nearest one." Also a North American place name of unknown meaning. In Japan the oak is a symbol of steadfastness and stability. According to one prehistoric myth, man sprang from the oak, thus making it the most sacred of trees.

Nari Japanese: "thunderpeal." A Japanese variation is Nariko, "thunder child."

Narilla (nah-REE-luh) English Gypsy: the exact meaning of this name is obscure.
Narrila

Nashota (nah-SHO-tah) North American Indian: "twin." Appropriate for a girl born under the astrological sign of Gemini, the twins.

Nasnan Carrier Indian: "surrounded by a song."

Nasya (NAH-see-ah or anglicized to NAHS-yuh) Hebrew: "miracle of god." Modern Israeli name.
Nasia

Nata North American Indian: "speaker or creator"; Hindi: "rope dancer." Also a Polish form of Nadia, "hope," and a Russian and Polish form of Natalie.

Natalie Latin: "born on Christmas." Popular in Czechoslovakia, France, and Germany, as well as the United States.
Nat, Nati, Natie, Natti, Nattie, Natty, Netti, Nettie, Netty, Natala, Natalina, Nataline, Nathalia, Nathalie, Noel, Noelle, Novella (English); *Natalia, Natasa* (Czech); *Natalia* (German and Portuguese); *Natalia, Nata, Natka, Nacia* (Polish); *Nata, Natalka, Natalya, Natasha, Talya, Tasha, Tashka, Taska, Tasya, Tata, Tuska, Tusya* (Russian); *Natacha, Nati, Talia* (Spanish)

Natane (nah-TAH-ne) Arapaho Indian: "daughter."

Natasha Russian form of Natalie, "born on Christmas." For other forms, see Natalie.

Natesa (nah-TAY-shah or anglicized to nah-TE-sah) Hindi: "dance lord." One of the 1,008 names for the Hindu god Siva. Siva is usually pictured with either one or five faces, four arms, and a third eye which appeared in order to save the world from darkness when his wife playfully covered his two eyes with her hands. The third eye can allegedly turn men to ashes.

Natka (NAHT-kah) Popular Russian form of Nadia, "hope."

Navit (nah-VEET) Hebrew: "beautiful" or "pleasant."
Nava, Navice

Neci (NE-see) Latin: "intense and fiery," referring to one who lives intensely. Commonly bestowed in modern Hungary.

Neda (NEH-duh) Old English: "prosperous guardian." A feminine form of Edward. Also a Slavic form of Natalie, "born on Christmas."

Nediva (neh-DEE-vuh) Hebrew: "noble and generous."

Neely Irish Gaelic: "champion." Contemporary U.S. feminine form of Neal.
Nealie, Nealy, Neeli, Neelie

Neema (NEE-mah or in Swahili neh-EH-mah) Swahili: "born during a prosperous time."

Neka (NEH-kah or as the Indians would have pronounced it NAY-kah) North American Indian: "the wild goose." This may have been used by a proud father who, following an Indian tradition, named his daughter for a feat he had accomplished, in this case the shooting of many wild geese.

Nelia (NEH-lee-ah) Spanish form of Cornelia, "yellowish" or "cornel tree." See Cornelia.

Nelka (NEL-kuh) Latin: "rock." Modern Polish form of an old feminine form of Peter—Petronella.
Ela, Nela, Nelka, Petra (Polish); *Petra, Tona* (Spanish)

Nenet Egyptian: "the goddess Nenet." In the Egyptian *Book of the Dead*, the goddess Nenet personifies the inert, motionless character of the primeval waters in which the Creator is said to have lived.

Nepa (NEH-pah) Arabic: "walking backward." This is another name for the constellation Scorpio, the scorpion. Alchemists believed that iron could be turned to gold only when the sun was in this sign of the zodiac.

Nerissa Greek: "daughter of the sea." Astrological sign for a girl born under one of the water signs: Pisces, Cancer, or Scorpio.
Nerice, Nerine, Nerisse, Rissa

Nessa Russian pet form of Anastasia, "of the Resurrection." See Anastasia.

Netia (NEHT-ee-ah) Hebrew: "plant" or "shrub." Modern Israeli name.
Neta, Netta

Netis (NAY-tis) North American Indian: "trusted friend."

Neva (NEH-vah) Spanish *nieve*: "snowy" or "extremely white." Nevada, "white as snow," comes from the same source.

Neza (NEH-zhuh) Slavic form of Agnes, "pure." See Agnes.

Niabi (nee-AH-bee) North American Indian: "a fawn."

Nicole, Nichole Greek: "victorious army" or "victorious people." The masculine form is Nicholas.
Colette, Collette, Cosette, Nichol, Nicholle, Nicki, Nickie, Nicol, Nicola, Nicolette, Nicoli, Nicoleen, Nicoline, Nicolle, Nikki, Nikolette, Nikolia (English); *Niki* (Greek)

Nida (NEE-dah) Omaha Indian: "the Nida creature," referring to a mythical being or animal which, according to Omaha legend, crept elflike in and out of the earth. Also an Indian name referring to the bones of extinct mammals, such as the mastodon.

Nika Favorite Russian form of Dominique, "belonging to God."

Niki Modern Greek form of Nicole, "victorious army" or "victorious people."

Nili (NEE-lee) Hebrew: an abbreviation for the words meaning "the glory (or eternity) of Israel will not lie or repent" from 1 Samuel 15:29. During World War I a pro-British/anti-Turkish underground organization in Palestine was named Nili. Current Israeli name for both girls and boys.

Nina North American Indian: "mighty"; or Spanish: "girl." Also a familiar form of Ann.
Ninetta, Ninette, Ninnetta, Ninnette

Ninita (nee-NEE-tah) Spanish: "little girl." This name is popular among the Zuni Indians.

Nipa (NEE-pah) Todas, India: "stream."

Nirel (ni-RAYL) Hebrew: "God's light" or "planted field." Modern Israeli name.

Nirveli (neer-VAY-li) Todas, India: "water" or "water child."

Nishi (nee-shee) Japanese: "west." A Japanese proverb goes, "From the east the root, from the west the fruit."

Nisse (NIS-suh) Scandinavian: "friendly elf" or "friendly brownie."
Nissa

Nita (NEE-tah) Choctaw Indian: "bear." Also a Spanish form of Ann.

Nitara (ni-TAH-rah) Sanskrit: "deeply rooted."

Nitsa Popular modern Greek form of Helen, "light" or "torch." See Helen.

Nituna (nee-TOO-nah) North American Indian: "my daughter."

Nizana (nee-ZAH-nah) Hebrew: "bud." Hebrew flower name.
Nitza, Nitzana, Zana

Noga (NO-guh) Hebrew: "shining" or "morning light." Also used as a boys' name in Israel.

Nolcha (NOL-chah) North American Indian: "the sun."

Nona Latin: "nine." Implying "ninth-born child." Also a possible numerological name.

Nori (NOR-ee) Japanese: "precept" or "doctrine."

Noura (NO-rah) Arabic: "light," indicating a hope that the child's presence will bring illumination.

Nova Hopi Indian: "chasing (a butterfly)." From the Hopi badger cult. Also Latin: "young one."

Numa (NOO-mah) Arabic form of the Biblical Naomi, "beautiful and pleasant."

Nuna (NOO-nah) North American Indian: "land."

Nuria (noo-REE-ah) Hebrew: "fire of the Lord." Currently used in Israel as well as other countries. *Nuri, Nuriel* (Israeli)

Nurit (noo-REET) Hebrew: "little yellow flower." The plant from which this name comes blooms annually in Israel. *Nurice, Nurita* (Israeli)

Nusi (NOO-shi) Hungarian form of Hannah, "graceful." See Hannah.

———————————————— O ————————————————

Oba (oh-BAH) Yoruba, Nigeria: "ancient river goddess."

Odelia Hebrew: "I will praise God."

Odera (oh-DAY-ruh) Hebrew: "plough."

Ogin (oh-GEEN) North American Indian: "the wild rose."

Okalani (oh-kuh-LAH-nee) Hawaiian: "of the heavens" or "from heaven." See "Sky Names" box on page 114.

Oki (oh-kee) Japanese: "in the middle of the ocean." Possibly given originally to a child born at sea.

Olathe (o-LAH-tha) North American Indian: "beautiful."

Olena (o-LAY-nah) Popular Russian form of Helen, "light" or "torch." See Helen for other forms.

Olesia (o-LE-shuh) Polish form of Alexandra, "helper and defender of mankind." See Alexandra.

Olga Old Norse *helga*: "holy one." First popularized by Saint Olga, who spread Christianity in Russia during the tenth century. Still one of the most popular names in Russia today, Olga is now used around the world. *Elga, Helga, Olia, Olva* (English); *Olina, Olunka, Oluska* (Czech); *Olli, Olly* (Estonian); *Ola, Olenka* (Polish); *Lelya, Lesya, Olenka, Olesya, Olka, Olya, Olyusha* (Russian)

Oliana (o-le-AH-nuh) Hawaiian: "oleander." Refers to an evergreen with white or red blossoms.

Olisa (o-LEE-sah) Ibo, Africa: "God." Often in Africa, this name is used as part of a longer name. Belu Olisa, for example, implies that nothing is possible without God's help or approval.

Oma Arabic: "commander." The masculine form is Omar.

Omusa (o-MOO-sah) Miwok Indian *omusa*: "to miss with arrows," referring to a time the child's father tried to shoot a deer and missed.

Ona Lithuanian form of Hannah, "graceful." See Hannah for other variations.

Onatah (q-NAH-tah) Iroquois Indian: "corn spirit and daughter of the earth." According to Iroquois legend, the corn spirit was captured by the spirit of evil while looking for dew. She was imprisoned underground until the sun guided her back to her lost fields. She never again looked for dew.

Onawa (o-NAH-wah) North American Indian: "wide-awake one." For a child who never sleeps and keeps her parents awake or for a baby who is brightly alert.

Onella Hungarian equivalent of the English Nellie, from Greek for "light." See Helen for other forms.

Oni (OH-nee) Yoruba, Nigeria: "child born on holy ground"; or Beni, Nigeria: "desired."

Onida (oh-NEE-dah) North American Indian: "the looked-for one."

Orah Hebrew: "light."
Ora, Oralee, Orit, Orlice, Orly (Hebrew)

Orenda Iroquois Indian: "magic powers." This name refers to the power inherent in all things, from rocks to man. According to Iroquois belief, this force can affect and control others; therefore, owning an object or animal with great strength is said to increase one's inner potential. The Huron Indians called this same force Oki; the Sioux named it Wakanda.

Oriana Celtic: "golden"; or Latin: "dawning."
Oralia, Orelda, Orelle, Orlann, Orlene

Orino (o-REE-no) Japanese: "weaver's field."
Ori

Orlenda Russian *orlitza*: "female eagle." This name was first used by English Gypsies.

Ornice Hebrew: "fir" or "cedar tree."
Orna, Ornit (Hebrew)

Osen Japanese: "thousand." This unusual name from Japan is probably bestowed because of an old belief in the magical power of round numbers.

Oya Miwok Indian: "to name," the connotation being "naming or speaking of the kuiatawila bird (jacksnipe)."

----------------------------- P -----------------------------

Padma (PAHD-mah) Hindi: "lotus." The national flower of Hindu India, the padma opens by day and closes at night. In Hindu belief, the god Brahma sprang from a mystical lotus, which grew from the god Vishnu's navel.

Paka (PAH-kah) Swahili: "pussycat."

Palila (pah-LEE-luh) Hawaiian: "bird."

Paloma (pah-LO-mah) Spanish: "dove." A symbol for peace. The name is given to a baby who coos.

Pamela Greek: "all-honey." This name was actually invented in the sixteenth century by Sir Philip Sidney, the poet who also created the name Stella.
Pam, Pamella, Pamelina, Pammi, Pammie, Pammy

Pandita (pahn-DEE-tah) Hindi: "scholar."

Panya (PAHN-yah) A favorite Russian form of Stephanie, "crowned one." See Stephanie for other forms.

Papina (pah-PEE-nuh) Miwok Indian: "a vine growing on an oak tree."

Pasha Greek *Pelagos*: "from the sea." Very popular in Russia.
Palasha, Pashka, Pelageya (Russian)

Pati Miwok Indian: literally "to break by twisting," but connotes "twisting willows for carrying fish." In astrology the fishes are the symbol of Pisces.

Patia (pah-TEE-uh) Spanish Gypsy: "leaf." The name connotes the freshness of spring.

Patricia Latin: "noble." The masculine form is Patrick.
Pat, Patrice, Patsy, Patti, Patty, Tricia, Trish, Trisha

Paula Latin: "little." A familiar name in many countries, including the United States, Hungary, Latvia, Poland, and Spanish-speaking countries.
Pauletta, Paulette, Pauli, Paulie, Paulina, Pauline, Paulita, Pauly, Polli, Pollie, Polly (English); *Paulina* (Bulgarian); *Pavla, Pavlina* (Czech); *Paolina* (Italian); *Pawlina, Pola, Polcia* (Polish); *Pavla, Pavlina, Pavlinka* (Russian); *Paulita* (Spanish)

Pausha (PO-shah) Hindi: "born during the Hindu lunar month of Pausha," which corresponds to the astrological sign of Capricorn.

Pavla (PAHV-lah) Czech and Russian form of Paula, "little."

Pazia (pah-ZEE-uh) Hebrew: "golden."
Paz, Paza, Pazice, Pazit (Israeli)

Pedzi Babudja, Southern Rhodesia: from the Babudja verb *ku pedza*, "to finish." The name literally means "finisher" and is bestowed on the last child a mother plans to have.

Peke (PE-ke) Old German: "shining" or "glorious." A form of Bertha used in Hawaii, the name originally referred to an ancient German fertility goddess.

Pelipa (peh-LEE-pah) Greek: "lover of horses." A Zuni Indian form of Philippe. See Philippe for other forms.

Pemba (PEHM-bah) Bambara, Africa: "the force of present existence." Working with Faro (the force of the future), Pemba is said to make the world go around, move the stars, and direct the affairs of mankind.

Penda Swahili: "loved one."

Penelope Greek: "weaver." A true whole-world name, Penelope is used in Sweden, Norway, Spain, Portugal, Italy, France, and other countries, including the United States.
Pen, Penina, Penine, Penni, Penny (English); *Pinelopi, Pipitsa, Popi* (Greek); *Pela, Pelcia, Penelopa, Lopa* (Polish)

Peni Carrier Indian: "his mind." Once used by a Carrier prophet who is said to have communicated with the spirit world during cataleptic fits and could allegedly hear what people were thinking.

Penina (pay-NEE-nay) Hebrew: "coral" or "pearl."
Peninit, Penny

Pepita Spanish name from Hebrew: "addition" or "increase," implying the child will be fruitful. Pepita is a form of Josephine that became quite popular in Spanish countries after 1621, when the Pope named March 19 a festival day for Saint Joseph.

Perla (PER-luh) Slavic form of Margaret, "a pearl."

Philippe Greek: "lover of horses." The masculine form of
this name is Phillip.
Phil, Philipa, Philli, Phillie, Pippa, Pippy (English);
Fiipote, Philippine (French); *Filippa, Filippina, Pippa*
(Italian); *Filpina, Filipa, Ina, Inka* (Polish)

Pilar (pee-LAHR) Spanish: "pillar" or "fountain base."
A favorite in Spanish-speaking countries, this name
refers to the Virgin Mary, pillar of the Christian religion.

Pilisi (pi-LEE-see) Greek: "a green branch." This name
comes to us from Hawaii. The English equivalent is
Phyllis.

Pinga (PEEN-gah) Hindi: "dark" or "tawny." One of the
more than one thousand names for the Hindu goddess
Sakti. See Sakti.

Pita (PEE-tah) Bari, Southern Sudan: "fourth-born daughter."

Pollyam (poh-lee-YAHM) Hindi: "the goddess of the
plague." Among the Hindus of Madras this is a popular name for both sexes and is bestowed to appease the
plague spirit and to keep her from striking.

Poni (PO-nee) Bari, Southern Sudan: "second-born daughter."

Poppy Latin: "the poppy flower." The poppy is the Occidental flower of August and the Chinese flower of
December. In Occidental astrology the poppy is the
herb of the moon, which governs the sign Cancer.

Posala (po-SAH-lah) Miwok Indian: "to burst," with the
connotation of "pounding farewell-to-spring seed."

Pualani Hawaiian: "heavenly flower." This name probably
refers to the wild ginger blossom or the bird-of-paradise
in bloom.
Puni

MIWOK FAREWELL-TO-SPRING-SEED NAMES

As you've no doubt noticed while reading this book, the Miwok Indians (a people of central California and one of the largest groups of American Indians in California) have extremely colorful nature names, which reflect their partnership with the natural world around them. The Miwok, who speak a language known as Moquelumnan, always create names that mean more than they first appear to mean on the surface.

Among Miwok farewell-to-spring-seed names, for example, we have:

MALKUYU—"farewell-to-spring flowers drying."

MEMTBA—from *memttu*: "to taste" and means "tasting farewell-to-spring seed after it has been mashed with the pestle but while still in the mortar."

LOIYETU—"farewell-to-spring in bloom."

MULIYA—from *mule*: "to beat or hit," with the connotation "hitting farewell-to-spring seed with a stick as the seed hangs on the bush."

----------------------------Q----------------------------

Querida (keh-REE-dah) Spanish: "beloved."

Questa French: "one who searches."

Queta (KAY-tah) Short form of Spanish name Enriqueta, which in turn is a form of Henrietta, "ruler of the household."

Quinette Latin: "fifth-born."
*Quin, Quinci, Quincie, Quincy, Quinetta, Quintessa,
Quintina, Tess, Tessa, Tessi, Tessie, Tina*

-----------------------------**R**-----------------------------

Rabi (rah-BEE) Arabic: "breeze." The name has the connotation of a pleasant, fragrant scent.
Rabiah

Rachel Hebrew: "an ewe." In the Bible, Rachel was Leah's
sister and a rival for their husband Jacob's affection.
Rachele, Rachelle, Rae (English); *Rahil* (Bulgarian);
Rachelle (French); *Rahel* (German); *Lahela, Rahela*
(Hawaiian); *Raquel* (Spanish, Portuguese); *Rakhil,
Rakhila, Rashel* (Russian); *Rakel* (Swedish and Nor-
wegian); *Rachel, Ruchel* (Yiddish)

Radinka (RAH-den-kuh) Slavic: "energetic" or "active."

Radmilla (RAHD-mel-luh) Slavic: "worker for the people."

Raizel (RAY-zel) Yiddish: "rose flower."
Rayzil, Razil

Rakel A favorite in Sweden. See Rachel.

Ramla (RAHM-lah) Swahili: "fortune-teller."

Ramona (rah-MO-nuh) Spanish: "mighty protector" or "wise
protector."

Randi Old English: "shield-wolf." Popular today as a
modern feminine form of Randolph. The name possibly refers to a war shield that made its owner invincible.
Randee, Randie, Randy

Rane (RAH-neh) Latin: "queen" or "pure." Popular today in Norway. In Iceland the same name is used for
boys. See Regina.

Rani (RAH-nee) Hindi: "queen."

Ranita (rah-NEE-tah) Hebrew: "song" or "joy." Modern Israeli name.
Ranice, Ranit (Israeli)

Raquel Spanish form of Rachel, "an ewe." See Rachel.

Rashida (rah-SHEE-dah) Swahili: "righteous."

Rasia (RAH-see-uh) Greek: "rose."

Ratri (rah-TREE) Hindi: "night." One of the many names for the revered Hindu goddess Sakti. See Sakti.

Rawnie (RAW-nee) English Gypsy: "lady."

Razilee (rah-zi-LEE) Hebrew: "my secret."
Razili

Rea Greek: "poppy." Modern flower name. Rea can also be translated as "a stream," making it an appropriate astrological name for a child born under one of the water signs of the zodiac.

Rebecca Hebrew: "bound." In the Bible Rebekah was Isaac's wife.
Becca, Becki, Beckie, Becky, Bekka, Bekki, Bekkie, Reba, Rebeka (English); *Reveka* (Bulgarian, Greek); *Rebeka* (Czech, Hungarian, Polish); *Rebeque* (French); *Rebekka, Rebekke* (German); *Rebeca* (Portuguese, Spanish); *Reveca* (Rumanian); *Revekka* (Russian); *Becky, Rebekah, Rifka* (Yiddish)

Regina Latin *regina:* "queen."
Gina, Raina, Regan, Regi, Regie, Reggi, Reggie, Reggy, Regine, Reyna, Rina (English); *Reine, Reinette* (French); *Gina, Regine* (German); *Reina* (Italian, Spanish); *Rane* (Norwegian); *Ina, Rega, Renia* (Polish)

Ren Japanese: "water lily" or "lotus." The lotus is the Buddhist symbol of purity, because the flower grows from muddy water and remains unstained, and of perfection, because its fruit is ripe when the flower blooms and thus embodies the oneness of Buddhist teaching and knowledge. The Buddhist paradise contains a pond filled with ambrosia and multicolored lotus blossoms, and the flower is said to have sprung from the graves of devout Buddhists.

Rena (RAY-nah) Modern Greek form of Irene, "peace." See Irene.

Renee A French form of Renata, meaning "reborn." Especially popular today in the United States.
Rene, Renelle, Reni, Renie, Renni, Rennie

Renia (REN-yah) Polish form of Regina, "queen." See Regina for other Polish forms.

Reseda Latin: "the fragrant mignonette blossom."

Resi (REH-see) German form of Theresa, "reaper." For other forms, see Theresa.

Reva (RAY-vah) Hindi: "the sacred Narmada River." One of the seven sacred Hindu rivers in India.

Rez Hungarian: "copper." For a girl with copper-colored hair.

Rhea Latin: "the poppy flower"; or Greek: "a flowing stream." In the Egyptian *Book of the Dead* Rhea is also another name for the goddess Nut, a deity with a serpent's head and human body who personified the primeval waters in which the Creator first lived.

Rhoda Greek: "rose." Popular modern flower name.

Ria Spanish: "the mouth of a river." Spanish nature name.

Rida (REH-dah) Arabic: "favor." The name implies the child is in God's favor. Also a boys' name.

Rihana (ree-HAH-nuh) "sweet basil." This name is frequently used by Moslems in the Middle East. In Western myth the basil is an emblem of poverty and hate.

Rimona (ri-MO-nuh) Hebrew: "pomegranate." Popular in Israel.

Rin Japanese: "park." Originally a place name now bestowed on baby girls.

Risa Latin: "laughter." Gaining popularity in the United States.

Risha (REE-shah) Hindi: "born during the solar month of Vrishabha." On the Hindu calendar Vrishabha corresponds to the sign of Taurus, the bull.

Rita A popular form of Margarita, a Spanish form of Margaret, meaning "a pearl." Also a Hindu name referring to the concept of the underlying natural and moral order present in the universe.

Ritsa (REET-sah) Popular modern Greek form of Alexandra, "helper and defender of mankind." See Alexandra for other forms.

Riza Hungarian form of Theresa.

Roberta Old English: "one who shines with fame."
Bobbet, Bobbette, Bobbi, Bobbie, Bobby, Robbi, Robbie, Robby, Robin, Robina, Robinia, Robinette (English); *Berta, Bobina, Roba* (Czech); *Robine* (French); *Berta, Erta* (Polish); *Berta, Bertha, Bertunga, Ruperta* (Spanish)

Rohana (roh-HAH-nah) Hindi: "sandalwood."

Ronli Hebrew: "joy is mine."
Rona, Roni, Ronia, Ronice, Ronit

Rosaleen Irish diminutive of Rose, meaning "love." Dark Rosaleen is a symbolic name for Ireland.

Rose Greek: "a rose." The rose is the flower of Gemini and a symbol of romantic love.
Rhoda, Rosalia, Rosalie, Rosella, Roselle, Rosetta, Rosette, Rosi, Rosie, Rozy, Zita (English); *Ruza, Ruzena, Ruzenka* (Czech); *Roza, Rozalia, Rozsi, Ruzsa* (Hungarian); *Rosa, Rosetta* (Italian); *Roze, Rozele, Rozyte* (Lithuanian); *Roza, Rozalia* (Polish); *Ruza, Ruzha* (Russian); *Chalina, Chara, Charo, Rosa, Rosalia, Rosana, Rosita, Shaba, Zita* (Spanish)

Roselani (ro-se-LAH-nee) English-Hawaiian rose + *lani*: "heavenly rose." This name refers to a small red rose that grows on Hawaii.

Rozene (ro-ZAY-nuh) North American Indian form of Rose, "a rose flower."

Ruana (roo-AH-nah) Hindi: "the ruana instrument," referring to a musical instrument used in India which resembles a viol. See Almira for an explanation of inanimate-object names.

Ruchi (ROO-chee) Hindi: "a love growing into a wish to please and shine before the beloved."

Rudra (ROO-drah) Hindi: "rudraksha-plant child." Among the Hindus the berries of the sacred rudraksha plant are used for making rosaries. The god Siva, as he contemplates the destruction of the world, is said to shed rudraksha-seed tears. The seeds nearly always have several "faces," and it is believed that anyone finding a one-faced seed will have his or her every wish and a life of wealth, luxury, and power.

Ruri (roo-REE) Japanese: "emerald." Naming children after precious stones dates back to an ancient belief that gems protect one from evil spirits. In the West the emerald is the birthstone of May and Taurus, the bull.

Rusalka (ROO-sahl-kah) Czechoslovakian: "wood nymph." A favorite in Czechoslovakia.

Ryba (REE-bah) Czech: "fish." In astrology the fishes are the symbol of Pisces.

———————————— S ————————————

Sabina Latin: "woman from the Sabine country." This name is used today in Bulgaria, Czechoslovakia, Finland, Italy, Poland, Russia, the Ukraine, Spanish-speaking countries, and the United States.

Sabia, Sabin (English); *Bina* (Czech); *Sabine* (German, Finnish, Latvian); *Sabcia, Sabinka, Sabka* (Polish); *Savina* (Russian)

Sabra (SAH-bruh) Hebrew: "thorny cactus." Refers to a prickly but edible fruit native to the coastal plains of Israel. The name for a native-born Israeli.
Sabrina

Sachi (SAH-chee) Japanese: "bliss."

Sada (SAH-dah) Japanese: "the chaste."

Sadira Persian: "the lotus tree." For the significance of the lotus in Hindu and Buddhist beliefs, see Kumuda and Ren.

Sadzi (sahd-ZEE) Carrier Indian: "sun heart," referring to a clock.

Sagara (sah-GAH-rah) Hindi: "ocean."

Sakari (sah-KAH-ree) Todas, India: "sweet one."

Saki (SAH-kee) Japanese: "cape." The same Japanese word also refers to a strong Oriental liquor.

Sakti (SAHK-tee) Hindi: "energy." One of the major Hindu goddesses, Sakti embodies both virginal innocence and bloodthirsty destruction. As the eternal virgin, she is sometimes represented as a young girl of about fifteen. The Sakti of illicit love, in contrast, is associated with incest and adultery. As a goddess of terror, she is worshiped by death cults, and it is said that the blood of the sacrifices before her image never dries.

Sakuna (sah-KOO-nah) East Indian: "bird."

Sakura (sah-KOO-rah) Japanese: "cherry blossom." In Japan the cherry blossom is the national flower, the flower of March, and a symbol of wealth and prosperity. In China it is the flower of April and a symbol of a good education.

Sala (SAH-lah) Hindi: "the sacred sala tree." The sala is said to contain a spirit who, if worshiped, brings rainfall; it is also believed that Buddha died under the sala's branches. One beam of this tree is said to bring blessings and peace to a home.

Salome Hebrew: "peace." In the New Testament of the Bible, Salome was the daughter of Herodias.
Sal, Saloma, Salomi (English); *Salama* (Arabic); *Salomé* (French)

Samantha Aramaic: "one who listens."
Sam, Sammi, Sammie, Sammy

Samara (sah-MAH-rah) Hebrew: "a guardian," or "guarded by God."

Sameh (SAM-eh) Arabic: "forgiver." Common among Moslem Arabs, this name refers to one of the ninety-nine qualities of God listed in the Koran. Strictly orthodox Moslems believe a name should come from the Koran or Muhammad's immediate family.

Sanura (sah-NOO-rah) Swahili: "like a kitten."

Sanuye (sah-NOO-ye) Miwok Indian: "red cloud coming with sundown."

Sanya (SAHN-yah) East Indian: "born on Saturday," from the Indian word *Sanivaram*, meaning "Saturday."

Sapata (sah-PAH-tah) Miwok Indian: "bear dancing with forefeet around a tree" or "bear hugging tree." From the Miwok word *sapatu*, "to hug."

Sara, Sarah Hebrew: "princess" or "one who laughs." As Abraham's wife and Isaac's mother, Sara is an important figure in the Bible and has inspired names all over the world. The form Sara is popular around the globe, from the United States to Bulgaria, France, Germany, Hungary, Italy, Portugal, Rumania, Russia, Sweden, Norway, and Spanish-speaking countries.
Sadie, Sadye, Saida, Sally, Sari, Sarene, Sareen, Sarine,

MIWOK INDIAN BEAR NAMES

Of all the animals, the bear is the most popular and most frequently mentioned in Miwok Indian names. Such names often refer to an event that occurred in the mother's or father's life. Among the many colorful "bear names" are:

ETUMU—from *etumu*: "to sun oneself," and means "bear warming itself in the sunlight."

ETUMUYE—from *etumü*: "to climb a hill," meaning "bear climbing a hill."

HAUSU—from *hausus*: "to yawn," and means "bear yawning as it awakes."

HELTU—"bear barely touching people as it reaches for them."

KUTATTOA—from *kutatcnani*: "to discard unwanted garbage," with the disagreeable meaning "bear scattering intestines of a person as it eats him."

KUTCUYAK—from *kutci*: "good," and means "bear with good hair."

LIPETU—from *lile*: "up," or in this case "up over" or "on top of," and means "bear going over a man hiding between rocks."

MOEMU—from *mo'ani*: "to meet," and *moeye*: "to join," and means "bears sitting down to look at each other."

NOTAKU—from *notcaku*: "to growl" and means "growling of a bear as someone passes by."

Sarina, Sarette, Saretta, Sadella, Zara, Zarah, Zaria (English); *Sarotte, Zaidee* (French); *Sari, Sarika, Sarolta, Sasa* (Hungarian); *Sala, Salcia* (Polish); *Sarka, Sarra* (Russian); *Chara, Charita, Sarita* (Spanish)

Saril (shuh-RIL) Turkish: "the sound of running water."

Sarolta (SHAW-rohl-tah) Hungarian form of Charlotte, "little womanly one." Also a Hungarian form of Sara, "princess" or "one who laughs."

Sasha Favorite Russian form of Alexandra, "helper and defender of mankind." See Alexandra for many other forms.

Satinka (sah-TEEN-kah) North American Indian: "magic dancer."

Saura (SOW-rah) Hindi: "sun worshipers." Refers to a Hindu sect devoted exclusively to the worship of the sun. Hence, appropriate for a child born under Leo, which is ruled by the sun.

Sawa (SAH-wah) Japanese: "marsh"; or Miwok Indian: "rock," implying "rock on the edge of a river." The Indians believed that many spirits dwelled in rocks, an idea perhaps suggested by the many tools made from rock or the fire sparked from flint.

Seda Armenian: "echo through the woods."

Sedna (SED-nah) Eskimo: "the goddess of food." According to Eskimo legend, Sedna lives in the sea and, if her taboos are violated, she causes a storm to keep seals, polar bears, and whales from leaving their homes. These animals were said to have been created from sections of her fingers, which her father cut off.

Seki Japanese: "great." The name is an unusual one to come from Japan because of an old Oriental superstition that a child with too ambitious a name will never live up to it. Seki can also mean "barrier," in the sense of a city or toll gate, or "stone."

Selima (se-LEE-mah) Hebrew: "peace."

Selina Greek: "sprig of parsley" or "the moon." In astrology the moon is the ruler of the sign Cancer, the crab.

Cela, Celene, Celina, Celinda, Celine, Sela, Selena,
Selene, Selia, Selinda, Seline, Sena

Selinka Popular Russian form of Celeste, "heavenly."

Selma Arabic: "secure"; also a shortened form of Anselma, from Old Norse meaning "divinely protected."

Sema Greek: "a sign from the heavens."

Sen Japanese: "wood fairy." This name refers to an ancient Japanese hermit believed to live in the mountains and said to possess magical powers. The sen or sennin hermit, usually pictured as a wrinkled old man with a flowing white beard, is said to live for thousands of years; hence the name expresses a hope for longevity. Also used for boys.

Shada (SHAH-dah) North American Indian: "pelican." No explanation for this unusual meaning could be found.

Shahar (shah-HAHR) Arabic: "the moon." In astrology the moon governs the sign Cancer.

Shaina (SHAY-nah) Yiddish: "beautiful."

Shaka Contemporary American name meaning "warrior."

Shammara (SHAH-mah-rah) Arabic: "He girded his loins."

Shani (SHAH-nee) Swahili: "marvelous."

Shanna Popular modern U.S. name. Probably a form of Shannon.

Shannon Irish Gaelic: "small, old, wise one."
Shana, Shani, Shanon, Shannah, Shannan, Shannen,
Shauna, Shawna, Shawni

Shappa (SHAH-pah) North American Indian: "red thunder." Given by the Indians to a child born during a violent storm.

Sharai (shah-RIGH) Hebrew: "a princess." This is the original Hebrew name from which the English Sharon is derived.

"SEXY" NAMES:
DRAWBACKS IN THE CORPORATE WORLD?

Far away as it seems now, your baby girl will one day grow up. And when she does, her name may be perceived as "sexy" or "unsexy." If she has a sexy name, she may have more dates as a young woman, but she may also have more trouble scaling the corporate ladder. Such are the findings of a study done by Deborah Linville at Rensselaer Polytechnic Institute (a popular training ground for Fortune 500 company managers).

Linville asked seniors and graduate students at RPI to rate 250 women's names on a scale from 1 (nonsexy) to 7 (sexy). She then asked students in another group to play boss and decide—on the basis of only their first names—which women they'd hire and promote. Male students promoted women with "unsexy" names like Edna and Elvira much faster and more readily than they did those with names that were considered sexy, such as Cheryl and Michelle. Linville's conclusion: When choosing women for jobs, men are prejudiced by the sexiness of the women's first names.

Names considered sexiest? You have to remember that such names will change over the years. But in this study the sexy names were: Alicia, Andrea, Adrienne, Candace, Christine (ranked number one), Dawn, Gail, Heather, Holly, Jacqueline, Jennifer, Julia, Kathy, Maria, Marilyn, Melanie, Renee, Susan, Tamara, and Tina. Names with the least sex appeal were: Alma, Cornelia, Doris, Edna, Elvira, Esther, Ethel, Florence, Magdalena, Myrtle, Rosalind, Silvana, and Zelda.

Sharissa Modern U.S. invention, possibly a combination of Sharon ("princess") plus Melissa ("honey" or "a bee"). Hence, the connotation is "honey-sweet princess." *Shari, Sharie, Sharice, Sharine, Sheri, Sherie, Sherice, Sherine, Sherissa, Rissa*

Sharma Gaining popularity in the United States, Sharma appears to be an American creation from Sharon ("princess") plus Mary ("bitter"). *Sharmine*

Shawna A modern U.S. form of Sean, which in turn is an Irish form of John, "God is gracious." Also a variation of Shannon, "small, old, wise one." *Sean, Shana, Shanna, Shauna, Shawn, Shawni, Shawnee*

Sheena An Irish form of Jane, "God is gracious." *Shena*

Shika (shee-kah) Japanese: "deer." This name implies docility and gentleness rather than grace and beauty.

Shina (SHEE-nah) Japanese: "goods," in the sense of possessions. Can also mean "virtue."

Shino (SHEE-no) Japanese: "slender bamboo," a symbol of fidelity.

Shiri (SHEE-ree) Hebrew: "my song." *Shira, Shirah*

Shizu (SHEE-zoo) Japanese: "quiet" or "clear." Especially popular in Japan. *Shizue, Shizuka, Shizuko, Shizuyo* (Japanese)

Shoushan (shoo-SHAHN) Armenian development of Susan, "lily."

Shumana (SHOO-mah-nah) Hopi Indian: "rattlesnake girl." Used by the Hopis of the rattlesnake cult. *Chuma, Chumana, Shuma*

Shura (SHOO-rah) Contemporary Russian form of Alexandra, "helper and defender of mankind." See Alexandra for other forms.

Shuri (SHOO-ree) English Gypsy: the exact meaning is unclear.

Sidra Latin: "related to a constellation" or "related to the stars." Astrological name for a child born under any sign.

Signe Old Norse: "beautiful, victorious counselor"; or Latin: "a singer." Popular today in Norway, possibly as a form of Sigrid.

Sigrid Old Norse: "beautiful, victorious counselor" or "beautiful victory." Popular modern Scandinavian name now used in many parts of the world.

Sihu (SEE-hoo) North American Indian: "a flower" or "a bush."

Siko (SEE-ko) Mashona, Southern Rhodesia: "crier." Given in Africa to a baby girl who cries a lot the first day.

Silivia (see-lee-VEE-uh) Hawaiian development of the Latin Silva, "from the forest."

Sipeta (see-PAY-tah) Miwok Indian: from *sipe*, "to pull out." The connotation is "pulling white sucker fish from under a flat rock."

Sisika (si-SEE-kah) North American Indian: "swallow" or "thrush."

Sissy Modern U.S. Originally a nickname for "sister" and popularized by actress Sissy Spacek.

Sita (SEE-tah) Hindi: "furrow"; or Spanish *zita*: "rose." In Hindi this name refers to a mother earth goddess and the wife of the god Rama. The Spanish form of the name comes from the Zuni Indians.

Siti (SEE-tee) Swahili: "lady."

Sofia Greek: "wisdom." Commonly spelled Sophia in the United States, this name is also used around the world, in Russia, Italy, and Spanish-speaking countries. *Sophia, Sophie, Sophy, Sunya* (English); *Zofia, Zofie,*

Zofka (Czech); *Sofi, Sophron* (Greek); *Sonja* (Norwegian); *Zocha, Zofia, Zosia, Zosha* (Polish); *Sofya, Sofka, Sonia, Sonya* (Russian); *Chofa, Chofi, Fifi, Sofi, Soficita* (Spanish); *Sofi* (Swedish); *Sofya* (Turkish); *Zofia* (Ukrainian)

Solana (so-LAH-nah) Spanish: "sunshine."

Soma (SO-mah) Hindi: "moon." Hindu name given to a child born on *Somavara*, Monday, in the solar month Karka, under the sign of Cancer, which is ruled by the moon.

Sonya Popular Russian and Scandinavian form of Sofia, "wisdom."

Sora (SO-rah) North American Indian: "a warbling song bird."

Soso (SO-so) Miwok Indian: "tree squirrel biting a tiny hole in a pine nut."

Stacy, Stacey Modern U.S. name created from either Anastasia ("of the Resurrection") or Eustacia ("peaceful" or "fruitful"). See Anastasia.
Staci, Stacia, Stacie (English); *Stasa, Staska* (Czech); *Stasya, Tasenka, Taska, Tasya* (Latvian, Lithuanian, Russian); *Tasia* (Spanish)

Stephanie Greek *stephanos*: "crowned." The masculine form is Stephen.
Stef, Stefa, Steffi, Steffie, Stepha, Stepania, Stepanie, Stephana, Stevena, Teena (English); *Stefania, Stefka* (Czech); *Stefanie, Trinnette* (French); *Stefani, Stephanine* (German); *Stamatios* (Greek); *Stefa, Stefania, Stefcia, Stefka* (Polish); *Panya, Stefania, Stepanida, Stepanyda, Stesha, Steshka, Stepa* (Russian)

Stesha Favorite Russian name. See Stephanie above.

Stina German short form of Christel, "Christian."

Sue Ellen Popular modern combination of Sue ("lily") plus Ellen ("light" or "torch").

Suela (soo-EL-ah) Spanish short form of Consuela, "consolation."
Chela, Suelita

Sugi (SOO-gee) Japanese: "cedar." A giant sugi or a group of such trees is often associated with a Shinto shrine, and hence the tree has become almost symbolic of the shaded mystery of such sanctuaries. In Japan the cedar is also an emblem of moral rectitude.

Suke (SOO-ke) Hawaiian development of Susan, "lily." See Susan.

Suki (SOO-kee) Japanese: "beloved"; Miwok Indian: "chicken hawk with a long tail"; also an eighteenth-century form of Susan, often spelled *Sukey*.

Sula (SOO-luh) Icelandic: "the gannet" (referring to a large sea bird); also a short form of Ursula, "little she-bear."

Suletu (soo-LEH-too) Miwok Indian: from *sulete*, "to fly around." The connotation is "California jay flying out of a tree." The jay appears in Indian creation legends as a mischief-maker who was doomed to become a lesser creature on earth. In most myths the poor jay's tragic flaw is false pride.

Sumi (SOO-mee) Japanese: "the clear" or "the refined."

Suni (SOO-nee) Zuni Indian: "a Zuni Indian."

Sunki (SHOON-kee or anglicized to SOON-kee) Hopi Indian: "overtake." The name may refer to a proud feat in the father's life: the chasing and overtaking of wild game or an enemy. Used by members of the Hopi horn cult.

Surata (soo-RAH-tah) Hindi: "blessed joy." The name refers to a mystical experience achieved through love-making.

Suri (SOO-ree) Todas, India: "knife." A nickname from the Todas for a child with a sharp nose. Once a name is used among the Todas, it cannot be bestowed again for four generations, and if by chance two people have the same name, one of them picks another.

Surya (SOOR-yah) Hindi: "the sun god." In Hindu mythology the sun god Surya is pictured with a dwarfish, burnished-copper body and red eyes. Hindu astrological name for a child born under Leo, which is ruled by the sun.

Susan Hebrew *shoshannah*: "lily" or "graceful lily." With all its forms, this name is one of the most popular in the world. A modern Israeli meaning is "rose."
Sue, Suka, Sukee, Sukey, Suki, Sukie, Suky, Susanna, Susannah, Susanne, Susetta, Susette, Susi, Susie, Susy, Suzanna, Suzannah, Suzanne, Suze, Suzetta, Suzette, Suzi, Suzie, Suzy (English); *Shoushan* (Armenian); *Suzana* (Bulgarian); *Suzan, Zuza, Zuzana, Zuzanka, Zuzka* (Czech); *Susanne, Susetta, Suzanne, Suzette* (French); *Susanne, Suse* (German); *Suke, Suse* (Hawaiian); *Sonel* (Hebrew); *Zsa Zsa* (Hungarian); *Sosanna* (Irish); *Susanna* (Italian); *Zuza, Zuzanna, Zuzia, Zuska* (Polish); *Suzana* (Rumanian); *Susanka* (Russian); *Siusan* (Scottish); *Chana, Sudi, Susana* (Spanish)

Sutki (SHOOT-kee or anglicized to SOOT-kee) Hopi Indian: "a broken coil of potter's clay." Used originally by Hopis in the cloud cult, this name may refer either to an event in the father's or mother's life or the first thing one of the parents saw after their baby was born.

Suzamni (soo-ZAHM-nee) Carrier Indian name of French origin, this is a combination of Susan ("lily") plus Annie ("graceful").

Suzu (SOO-zoo) Japanese: "little bell." A favorite in Japan, this name refers to the suzu, a tiny metal bell often placed in a silk charm bag and attached to a child's girdle so that a pretty tinkling is heard whenever she moves. Originally it was thought the sound would frighten demons; more recently it was believed the amulet would keep the child from falling. Japanese variations: Suzue ("branch of little bells"), Suzuki ("bell tree"), and Suzuko ("bell child").

Sydney Old French: "from the city of St. Denis, France." The masculine form is Sidney.
Sy, Syd, Sydny

————————————— **T** —————————————

Tabia (tah-BEE-ah) Swahili: "talents."

Tabitha Greek: "gazelle."
Tab, Tabatha, Tabbi, Tabbie, Tabbitha, Tabby

Taci (TAH-shee) Zuni Indian: "washtub." Probably originally bestowed because a washtub was the first object the parent saw after the baby was born.

Tadita (tah-DEE-tah) Omaha Indian *tothito*: "to the wind!" or more loosely "a runner." The name refers to the running of pipe bearers in a Hedewachi ceremony.
Tadeta

Taima (tah-EE-mah) North American Indian: "crash of thunder." Used by various Indian tribes for a girl or boy born during a thunderstorm.

Taipa (tah-EE-pah) Miwok Indian: "to spread wings." The more elaborate connotation is "valley quail spreading its wings as it alights."

Taka (TAH-kah) Japanese: "tall," "honorable," or "a falcon."

Takala (TAH-kah-lah) Hopi Indian: "corn tassel." From the cloud cult.

Takara (tah-KAH-rah) Japanese: "treasure" or "precious object."

Takenya (tah-KEHN-yah) Miwok Indian: "falcon swooping and knocking down its prey with its wings."

Taki (TAH-kee) Japanese: "a plunging waterfall."

Takuhi (tak-koo-HEE) Armenian: "queen."
Takoohi (Armenian)

Tala (TAH-lah) North American Indian: "wolf." The name implies intelligence and good luck.

Talasi (TAH-lah-shee or anglicized to tah-LAH-see) Hopi Indian: "corn tassel flower." Used by Hopis in the cloud cult.

Talia (tah-LEE-uh) Hebrew: "heaven's dew." The variations Talor and Talora mean "dew of the morning." Also a Spanish form of Natalie, "born on Sunday."
Tal, Talya

Talula (tah-LOO-lah) Choctaw Indian: "leaping water." Made famous by actress Tallulah Bankhead.
Talli, Tallie, Tallulah, Tally

Tama (TAH-mah) North American Indian: "thunderbolt"; Japanese: "jewel."

Tamaki (TAH-mah-kee or anglicized to tah-MAH-kee) Japanese: "armlet" or "bracelet."
Tamako, Tamayo

Tamara Hebrew: "a palm tree." Popular in the United States, Czechoslovakia, Latvia, Russia, the Ukraine, and Spanish-speaking countries.
Tamar, Tami, Tamie, Tammi, Tammie, Tammara, Tammy (English); *Mara* (Czech); *Tama, Tamarka, Tomochka* (Russian)

Tami (TAH-mee) Japanese for "people."

Tamika (TAH-mee-kah or anglicized to tah-MEE-kah) Japanese: "people child." Popular modern U.S. name.
Tami, Tamike, Tamiko, Tamiyo

Tanaka (tah-NAH-kah) Japanese: "dweller in or near a rice swamp."

Tani (TAH-nee) Japanese: "valley."

Tanisha Hausa, Africa: "born on Monday." Popular modern U.S. name.

Tansy Hopi Indian: "the tansy flower." Used by the Indians belonging to the tansy-mustard clan.

Tanya Popular Russian form of Tatiana, "a fairy queen."
Tania, Tanka, Tata, Tanka, Tuska, Tusya

Tao Chinese: "peach." The peach is one of the three sacred Buddhist fruits and a symbol of longevity and immortality. A similar name is Tao Hua, "peach blossom." The peach is called the tree of the fairy fruit because of the peach tree of the gods which grew in the mythical gardens of the Royal Lady of the West. The tree was said to have bloomed only once in three thousand years and exactly three thousand years later yielded the Fruits of Immortality. It is said these peaches were eaten by the Eight Taoist Immortals. In Taoist philosophy, Tao means "the way," referring to the ultimate truth of the universe.

Tara Irish Gaelic: "rocky pinnacle." Also the name of the ancient capital of Ireland. The same name is used in India as the name of a Buddhist savior goddess. Currently popular in the United States.
Tarra, Tera, Terra

Tasarla (tah-SAHR-luh) English Gypsy: "morning" or "evening," referring to a time when the sun is low on the horizon.

Tasha Popular Russian form of Natasha, which in turn is a form of Natalie, "born on Christmas." See Natalie.

Tasida (tah-SEE-dah) Sarcee Indian: "a rider." The literal meaning is "on-top-(of a horse)-he sits." Also used for boys.

Tassos (TAH-sohs) Modern Greek form of Theresa, "reaper." See Theresa.

Tasya (TAHS-yah) A diminutive used in Russia and Spain as well as the United States. See Anastasia.

Tatum Middle English: "to be cheerful." Popularized by actress Tatum O'Neal.
Tate

Tawia (tah-WEE-ah) Fanti or Ashanti, Africa: "born after twins." Also a Polish form of Octavia, "eighth."

Tawnie (TAW-nee) English Gypsy: "little one." The masculine form is Tawno.

Tazu (tah-zoo) Japanese: "rice-field stork." The stork is a symbol of longevity. Japanese children are occasionally named after an animal, fish, or bird, perhaps because the parents hope the child will develop some admirable quality associated with that animal.

Temira (teh-MEE-ruh) Hebrew: "tall." This name expresses the hope a child will grow tall.
Timora

Tempestt French: "stormy" or "tempestuous one."
Tempest

Tereza A great favorite in Brazil, Tereza is a Portuguese form of Theresa, "reaper." See Theresa for other forms.

Tesia (TE-shuh) Polish form of Theophila, "loved by God," or Hortense, "gardener."

Tess A modern U.S. form of Tessa ("fourth child") or Theresa ("reaper").

Tetsu (TET-suh) Japanese: "iron." The odd meaning for this name stems from an ancient Oriental belief that demons and evil spirits were born during the Stone Age and therefore dreaded the influence of metals. Iron has been considered especially potent and magical in many cultures. Among the Kachin people of Upper Burma, for example, iron knives are brandished over a mother and her newborn, and old rags are burned in the hopes that the iron and the stench will drive demons away. In another part of Burma, on the Irrawaddy River, iron pyrites are believed to frighten alligators.

Thelma Greek: "the nursling."
Kama (Hawaiian)

Thema (TAY-mah) Akan, Ghana: "queen."
  Tayma

Theresa Greek: "reaper." This name gained great popularity worldwide in the 1600s when parents began naming their babies after Saint Theresa of Avila in Castile, a mystic and nun who performed many miracles.
  Tera, Terese, Teressa, Teri, Terie, Terri, Terrie, Terry, Tery, Tess, Tessa, Tessi, Tessie, Tessy, Trace, Tracey, Traci, Tracie, Tracy, Zita (English); *Tereza* (Bulgarian, Portuguese); *Terezia, Terezie, Terezka, Reza, Rezka* (Czech); *Tereson, Therese* (French); *Resel, Resi, Therese, Theresia, Tresa, Trescha* (German); *Tassos* (Greek); *Rezi, Riza, Rizus, Teca, Tercsa, Terez, Tereza, Terezia, Terike, Teruska, Treszka* (Hungarian); *Teresina, Tersa* (Italian); *Terese* (Norwegian); *Renia, Tesa, Tesia, Terenia, Tereska* (Polish); *Terezilya, Zilya* (Russian); *Techa, Tere, Teresita, Tete* (Spanish)

Thordis (THOR-des) Old Norse: "dedicated to Thor," the Norse god of thunder. A favorite in Norway.
  Thora, Tora

Tiffany Greek *theo-phaneia*: "appearance or manifestation of God." Originally a form of Theophania, now popular as a given name in the United States. Because of the close connection with the New York jeweler Tiffany, the name has some connotations of wealth and class.
  Tiffani, Tiffanie, Tiff, Tiffy

Tilda Estonian variation of Matilda, "battle maiden."

Timmi Originally a nickname for Timothea, "honoring God," Timmi is gaining use in the United States as an independent name.
  Timi, Timie, Timmie

Tina Short form of many names ending in *-tine* or *-tina* throughout the world, including the English Christina, the Russian Valentina, the Polish Khristina, and the Greek Constantina.

Tiponya (ti-POHN-yah) Miwok Indian: "great horned owl sticking her head under her body and poking an egg that is hatching," from the word *tipe*, "to poke." The owl appears frequently in Indian lore. According to a Kiowa legend, when the medicine man dies he becomes an owl, and when the owl dies he turns into a cricket. The Eastern Cherokees say the cry of the screech owl portends illness or death; the Penobscot people say that if a man mocks a screech owl, the bird with burn him up; and the Pawnees believe the owl is a protector from night evils.

Tirtha (TEER-tuh) Hindi: "ford."

Tirza (TEER-zah) Hebrew: "cypress tree" or "desirable."

Tisa (TEE-sah) Swahili: "ninth-born."

Tivona (tee-VO-nuh) Hebrew: "lover of nature." Especially popular in Israel.

Tiwa Zuni Indian: "onions." Bestowed because the first object the father or mother saw after the baby was born was an onion.

Tobit (to-BEET) Hebrew: "good." Used today in Israel for both boys and girls.
Tova, Tovah

Toby Hebrew: "God is good." The masculine form of this name is Tobias.
Tobi, Tobie

Toki Japanese: "time of opportunity."

Tokiwa (to-KEE-wah)—Japanese: "eternally constant." The name implies constancy as everlasting as the rocks.

Tolikna (toh-LEEK-nah) Miwok Indian: "coyote's long ears flapping." In many Indian legends the coyote created the world (see Kaliska). One story says the adventurous beast once went to the edge of the world and sat on the hole where the sun comes up; he then rode the sun across the sky.

Tomo Japanese: "knowledge" or "intelligence."

Tonya (TOHN-yah) Russian pet form of Antonina, "inestimable" or "priceless."

Tora Japanese: "tiger."

Tori Japanese: "bird." Still another example of a totem name (see box).

Toshi (TOH-shee) Japanese: "year."
Toshie, Toshiko, Toshiyo

Tosia (TO-shuh) Polish nickname for Antonina, "inestimable" or "priceless."

Toski (TOSH-kee) Hopi Indian: "a squashbug." Originally used by people in the cloud cult.

Tosya (TOS-yah) Popular Russian nickname of Antonia, "inestimable" or "priceless." See Antonia.

Totsi (TOHT-see) Hopi Indian: "moccasins." Used by the horn cult.

Trava (TRAH-vah) Czech: "grass," implying the freshness of spring.

JAPANESE ANIMAL NAMES

Nearly all people of the world name their children after animals. In our country, we have the common Lionel ("young lion"), for example. The Japanese also have such totemic names, which were once bestowed with the hopes the child might develop an admirable trait of that animal. Examples of such Japanese names: Chidori ("sanderling"), Kuma ("bear"), Taka ("hawk"), Tatsu ("dragon"), and Washi ("eagle").

Trella Spanish: "little star." A short form of Estrella, "star," used today not only in the United States but also in many Spanish-speaking countries.

Tresa German form of Theresa, "reaper." For other forms, see Theresa.

Trina (TREE-nah) Hindi: "piercing," referring to the sacred kusa grass; also a German form of Katherine. See Kusa and Katherine for further information.

Trinette French form of Katherine, "pure." See Katherine.

Trisha Hindi: "thirst," one of the 350 Hindu classifications of love; also a diminutive of Patricia, "noble."

Truda Old German: "battle maiden" or "spear strength." A Polish form of Gertrude.
Trude, Trudey, Trudi, Trudie, Trudy

Tula (TOO-lah) Hindi: "born under the astrological sign of Libra."

Tulsi (TOOL-see) Hindi: "the sacred tulasi plant," referring to an Indian form of basil. The plant is said to resemble the hair of the goddess Vrinda. Because her spirit enters the plant each night, one is forbidden to pick the tulasi leaves after dark.

Tusa (TOO-suh) Zuni Indian: "prairie dog."

Tuwa (TOO-wah) Hopi Indian: "earth."

Tyna (TEE-nah) A nickname for many Czech names, including Kristyne ("Christian") and Celestyna ("heavenly"). Also modern U.S. spelling of Tina.

--------------------------------- U ---------------------------------

Ulani (oo-LAH-nee) Hawaiian: "cheerful."

Uma (OO-mah) Hindi: "mother." One of the more than one thousand names for the Hindu goddess Sakti. See Sakti.

Umeko (oo-ME-ko) Japanese: "plum-blossom child." In Japan the plum blossom is a symbol of perseverance and patience and the emblem of the samurai.
Ume, Umeyo

Una (OO-nah) Hopi Indian: "remember." The coyote is implied in the name because he is said to remember food he has buried.

Ursula Latin: "little she-bear." This currently popular name is used in Bulgaria, Russia, Germany, Estonia, the United States, and Spanish-speaking countries.
Orsa, Orsel, Orsola, Ursa, Urse, Ursel, Ursie, Ursley, Ursola, Ursuline, Ursy (English); *Vorsila* (Czech); *Sula, Ulli, Urmi* (Estonian); *Ursule* (French); *Ulla, Ursel* (German); *Urzula* (Latvian); *Ursule* (Rumanian); *Ursulina* (Spanish)

Ushi (oo-SHEE) Chinese: "the ox." In ancient Chinese astrology, not only the months but also the hours, days, and years are named after signs of the zodiac. There is an hour of the ox, a day of the ox, a month of the ox, and even a year of the ox.

Utina (oo-TEE-nah) North American Indian: "(woman of) my country."

———————————— V ————————————

Valda Old Norse: "ruler" or "governor." Popular name in Scandinavia.

Valerie Old French: "strong one."
Val, Valaree, Valaria, Valeria, Valerey, Valery, Valerye, Valli, Vallie, Vally, Valry (English); *Wala, Waleria* (Polish); *Lera, Lerka, Valka, Valya* (Russian); *Valeriana* (Spanish)

Valma Modern Finnish form of Wilhelmina, "unwavering protector." See Wilhelmina.

Vanda (VAHN-dah) Popular Slavic form of Wanda, "wanderer." See Wanda.

Vanessa Greek: "butterflies." Some say this name was invented by author Jonathan Swift and only later came to be associated with a butterfly.
Ness, Nessa, Nessi, Nessie, Nessy, Van, Vana, Vania, Vanna, Vanni, Vannie, Vanny, Vanya

Vanya (VAHN-yah) Russian form of Jane, "gracious gift of God." Also a U.S. form of Vanessa.

Vardis (vahr-DEES) Hebrew: "rose." Most common today in modern Israel.
Varda, Vardia, Vardice, Vardina, Vardit

Varina A popular Slavic form of Barbara, "a stranger" or "foreigner." See Barbara.

Vatusia (vah-TOO-see-ah) Umbundu, Africa: From the Ovimbundu proverb *"Va tu sia,"* "They leave us behind." In other words, the dead are gone and we are left to mourn. An Ovimbundu woman may give this name to herself if she has suffered great anguish.

Veda Sanskrit: "sacred understanding." This name refers to the sacred Hindu writings which are believed to be uncreated and eternal.

Vera Latin: "true"; or Russian *vjera*: "faithful." A favorite in Russia, also used today in the United States, Czechoslovakia, Latvia, Serbia, and Spanish-speaking countries.
Vere, Verena, Verene, Verina, Verine, Verla (English); *Verka, Viera* (Czech); *Wera, Wiera, Wierka, Wiercia* (Polish); *Verasha, Verinka, Verka, Verunka, Verusya* (Russian); *Wera* (Swedish)

Veronica Greek: "forerunner of victory."
Berenice, Bernice, Nika, Roni, Ronnie, Ronny, Veronika (English); *Verona, Veronika, Veronka* (Czech); *Verenice, Verone, Veronique* (French); *Veronike* (German); *Berenike* (Greek)

Vickie Popular contemporary U.S. name, originally a short form of Victoria, "victory."
Vicki, Vicky, Viki, Vikie, Viky

Victoria Latin: "victory." This name became popular during Queen Victoria's reign in England.
Vicki, Vickie, Vicky, Viki, Vikie, Viky (English); *Viktoria* (Bulgarian); *Viktorie, Viktorka* (Czech); *Victoire* (French); *Nike* (Greek); *Vittoria* (Italian); *Vitoria* (Portuguese); *Tora, Vika, Viktoria* (Russian); *Vika, Viki* (Serbian); *Victoriana, Victorina, Vitoria* (Spanish); *Viktoria* (Swedish, Norwegian)

Vida Hebrew: "beloved." A feminine form of the Hebrew Dawid, or David.

Virginia Latin: "maidenly."
Ginger, Ginney, Ginni, Ginnie, Ginny, Jinny, Vergie, Virgy (English); *Virginie* (French); *Vegenia* (Hawaiian); *Gina, Ginata, Ginia* (Spanish)

Virida Spanish: "green," connoting the freshness of spring.

Visolela (vee-so-LAY-lah) Umbundu, Africa: from the Ovimbundu proverb "longings are of waterfalls, but these you pick over are of the drying trays." The saying means it is easy to use your judgment about the ordinary things of life, such as maize to be sorted in drying trays, but there are also desires of the heart which are as uncontrollable as waterfalls.

Vivian Latin: "alive."
Viv, Vivie, Viviana, Vivien, Vivienne, Vivyan (English); *Vivienne* (French); *Viviana* (Hawaiian, Italian)

----------------------**W**----------------------

Wakanda (wah-KAHN-dah) Sioux Indian: "inner magical power." See Orenda for a fuller explanation.
Kanda, Kenda, Wakenda

Wanda Old German: "wandering one."
Wandi, Wandie, Wandis, Wenda, Wendi, Wendie, Wendy, Wendeline (English); *Vanda* (Czech, Portuguese, Russian); *Wandzia* (Polish); *Wanja* (Swedish)

Waneta (wah-NAY-tah) North American Indian: "the charger"; also a short form of Wannetta, "little pale one."

Wenona (weh-NO-nah) North American Indian: "first-born daughter."

Wilhelmina Old German: "unwavering protector." See Helmine.
Billi, Billie, Helma, Helmine, Min, Mina, Minna, Minni, Minnie, Minny, Valma, Velma, Wilhelmine, Willamina, Wiletta, Wilette, Willi, Willie, Wilma, Wilmette, Wylma (English); *Valma* (Finnish); *Vilma* (Russian, Czech, Swedish)

Willow Middle English: "the willow tree" or "freedom." In Rumania, among the Gypsies of Transylvania, the willow was believed to have the power to grant mothers easy delivery and to give the sick and old renewed vitality.

Winda (WEEN-dah or anglicized to WIN-dah) Swahili: "hunt."

Winema (wee-NEH-mah) Miwok Indian: "woman chief."

Wisia (VEE-shuh or anglicized to WI-shuh) Polish form of Victoria, "victory."

Wyanet (wee-AH-net) North American Indian: "beautiful."

Wynne Old Welsh: "fair one."
Winne, Winnie, Winny, Wyn, Wynn

---------------------- **X** ----------------------

Xanthe Greek: "golden yellow."

Xavier Arabic: "brilliant"; or Spanish Basque: "one who

owns a new house." A boys' name now gaining popularity in this country for girls.
Xaviera, Javier

Xenia Greek: "hospitable."
Xena (English, Modern Greek); *Chimene* (French)

——————————————— **Y** ———————————————

Yachi (YAH-chee) Japanese: "eight thousand." Round numbers were once considered a good-luck charm in Japan and although the superstition has virtually vanished, many number names remain.
Yachiko, Yachiyo

Yachne (YAHK-ne) A favorite among Lithuanian and Polish Jews, this name comes from Hebrew and means "gracious."

Yaluta (yah-LOO-tah) Miwok Indian: "women out on a flat telling one another there is a lot of farewell-to-spring seed."

Yamka (YAHM-kah) Hopi Indian: "flower budding."

Yanaba (yah-NAH-bah) Navaho Indian: "she meets the enemy."

Yarkona (yahr-KO-nuh) Hebrew: "green." The name may refer to the yarkona bird, with its greenish-gold feathers, found in the southern part of Israel.

Yarmilla (YAHR-mil-luh) Slavic *yarmarka*: "trader in the marketplace."

Yasmeen (YAS-meen) Arabic: "the jasmine flower."
Jasmin, Jasmeen, Jasmine, Yasiman, Yasmine

Yasu (YAH-soo) Japanese: "the peaceful" or "the tranquil."
Yasuko, Yasuyo

Yelena (ye-LAY-nah) Russian form of Helen, "a torch" or "light." See Helen.

Yemina (ye-MEE-nuh) Hebrew: "right hand." The name connotes strength.

Yenene (yeh-NAY-neh) Miwok Indian: "wizard pressing his fingers on a sleeping person to 'poison' him."

Yepa (YAY-pah) North American Indian: "the snow maiden."

Yeva (YEH-vah) Russian form of Eva, "life-giving." See Eva.

Yoki North American Indian: "bluebird on the mesa."

Yoko Japanese: "positive child," "ocean child" or "female." The latter implies the dualism of the Oriental concept of the universe. According to Oriental belief, in the beginning the female principle Yo co-existed with the male principle In. Yo and In lay dormant in the chaotic egg until it eventually split into heaven and earth. This name was popularized in the West by singer Yoko Ono.

Yolanda Greek: "the violet flower." The violet is the flower of Aquarius and the month of February.
Eolanda, Eolande, Iolanda, Iolande, Iolanthe, Yolande, Yolane (English); *Jolan, Jolanka, Joli* (Hungarian); *Jola, Jolanta* (Polish); *Yola, Yoli* (Spanish)

Yoluta (yo-LOO-tah) North American Indian: "the farewell-to-spring seed."

Yonina (yo-NEE-nuh) Hebrew: "dove." Feminine form of Jonas.
Jona, Jonati, Jonina, Yona, Yonit, Yonita

Yori Japanese: "the trustworthy."

Yoshi Japanese: "the good" or "the respectful."
Yoshie, Yoshiko, Yoshiyo

Yoshino (yo-shee-no) Japanese: "good field" or "fertile field." The suffix *-no*, meaning "field," is often attached to Japanese names. Other examples: Kikuno ("chrysanthemum field"), Kurano ("storehouse field"), Orino ("weaver's field"), Umeno ("plum-tree field"), and Urano ("shore field").

Yovela (yo-VAY-luh) Hebrew: "rejoicing."

Yuki (YOO-kee) Japanese: "snow" or "lucky."
Yukie, Yukiko, Yukiyo

Yvette Old French: "yew bow." Modern U.S. development of the older name Yvonne.
Iwona, Iwonka (Polish); *Ivone* (Portuguese); *Ivona* (Russian)

———————————— **Z** ————————————

Zada (ZA-dah) Arabic: "lucky one." Popular in Syria.
Zaida, Zayda

Zahra (ZAH-rah) Swahili: "flower."

Zaltana (zahl-TAH-nuh) North American Indian: "high mountain."

Zanna (ZAH-nuh) Contemporary Latvian form of Jane, "gracious gift of God." See Jane.

Zara Arabic: "princess"; or Hebrew: "the brightness of dawn."

Zarifa (zah-REE-fah) Arabic: "graceful."

Zayit (zigh-EET) Hebrew: "olive." Also used in Israel as a boys' name.
Zeta, Zetana

Zea (ZAY-uh) Latin: "grain." This harvest name is appropriate for a girl born under one of the earth signs: Capricorn, Taurus, or Virgo.

Zel Persian: "a cymbal"; Turkish: "a bell."

Zelda Modern U.S. development of Griselda, "a gray battle maiden."

Zelenka (ZE-layn-kah) Czech: "little green one." This Czechoslovakian name implies the child is innocent and fresh.

Zera (ZAY-rah) Hebrew *zera'im*: "seeds."

Zerdali (zair-dah-LI) Turkish: "wild apricot."

Zerlinda Modern U.S. invention from Hebrew and Spanish: "beautiful dawn."

Zigana (ZEE-gaw-nah) Hungarian: "gypsy girl."

Zihna (ZHEE-nah) Hopi Indian *zynanta*: "spinning." Given by the Hopis to a child fond of whipping tops.

Zina (ZEE-nah) Nsenga, Africa: "name." Zina refers to a child's secret spirit name, known only to her family.

Zita Popular Spanish form of Rosita and means "little rose." See Rose.

Zizi (ZEE-zee) Modern Hungarian form of Elizabeth, "dedicated to God." See Elizabeth.

Zoë Greek: "life."

Zofia Czech, Polish, and Ukrainian form of Sophia, "wisdom."

Zoheret (zo-HAIR-et) Hebrew: "she shines."

Zohra (ZOH-rah) Arabic: "the blooming." Also a name for the planet Venus, which governs Taurus, the bull.

Zora Slavic: "aurora" or "dawn."

Zorina (SAW-re-nuh or anglicized to zo-REE-nuh) Slavic: "golden."
Zora, Zorana, Zori, Zorie, Zory

Zuri (ZOO-ree) Swahili: "beautiful."

Zuza (ZOO-zah) Czech form of Susan, "lily."

Zytka (ZET-kuh) Polish name used as a short form of many girls' names ending in *-ita*, including Rosita, Brigita, and Margarita.
Zyta

CHAPTER 6

Boys' Names

—————————————— A ——————————————

Aaron Hebrew: "lofty" or "exalted." A popular variation—
Aron—is used in the United States and other English-
speaking countries as well as in Germany, Poland,
Czechoslovakia, Hungary, Rumania, Norway, Sweden,
France, Russia, and Israel. Aaron was the brother of
Moses, and this is one of the most popular names in
the world.
Haroun, Harun (Arabic); *Aronne* (German); *Aharon*
(Hebrew); *Aranne, Aronne* (Italian); *Arek, Aronek* (Pol-
ish); *Aarao* (Portuguese); *Aronos* (Russian)

Abasi (ah-BAH-see) Swahili: "stern." In India the equivalent is Abbas, "stern of countenance," referring to one
of the ninety-nine attributes of God listed in the Koran.
Both forms are popular among Moslems.

Abdul (ahb-DOOL) Arabic: "servant of," implying the
child is a servant of God. A favorite among Moslems,
Abdul is used as an element in many names. Examples:
Abdul Karim, "servant of the generous One," and
Abdel Nasser, "servant of the victorious One."
Abdel, Abdullah (Arabic); *Abdalla* (Swahili)

Abi Turkish: "elder brother." Given to a first child when the parents plan to have other children.

Abraham Hebrew: "father of a mighty nation" or "father of the multitude."
Abe, Abi, Abie (English); *Ibrahim* (Arabic); *Avram* (Bulgarian, Greek, Rumanian); *Bram* (Dutch); *Abrahamo, Abramo* (Italian); *Abrao* (Portuguese); *Abrahan, Abran* (Spanish); *Arram* (Swedish); *Avram, Avrum* (Yiddish)

Abram Hebrew: "the lofty One is the Father." Popular shortened form of Abraham used in the United States, Poland, Russia, France, and Spanish-speaking countries.

Acar (uh-KUHR) Turkish: "bright."

Ace Latin: "unity."

Adair Scotch Gaelic: "one from the oak-tree ford."

Adal German: "noble."

Adam Hebrew: "man of the red earth." As the first man God created, Adam is a name popular in all Christian countries of the world.
Ad, Ade (English); *Adamec, Adamek, Adamik, Adamko, Adamok, Damek* (Czech); *Adi, Adrien* (Hungarian); *Adamo, Adan* (Italian); *Adomas* (Lithuanian); *Adas, Adamek, Adok* (Polish); *Adao* (Portuguese); *Adamka, Adas* (Russian); *Adhamh, Keady, Keddie, Keddy* (Scottish); *Adan* (Spanish); *Adem* (Turkish); *Adi* (Yiddish)

Adan Yoruba, Nigeria: "a large bat," from the proverb "If you do not have a large bat, you sacrifice a small one." In other words, you simply do your best. The same name is also a Spanish form of Adam.

Adar Syrian: "ruler" or "prince." Derived from the twelfth month of the Babylonian calendar. Also Hebrew: "fire," from the sixth month of the Jewish calendar.

Addison Old English: "Adam's son." Originally a last name, now used also as a first name.

Adeben (ah-deh-BEHN) Akan, Ghana: "twelfth-born son."

Adel Teutonic: "noble." Adel is used as an element in many names, including Adelar, "noble eagle," Adelard, "nobly resolute," Adelbern, "noble bear," and Adelhart, "nobly firm."

Adir (ah-DEER) Hebrew: "majestic" or "noble."

Adiv (ah-DEEV) Hebrew: "pleasant" or "gentle."

Adler Old English: "eagle."

Adli (ahd-LEE) Turkish: "just."

Admon (ahd-MOHN) Israeli: "a red peony flower." Refers to a flower that grows in the upper Galilee.

Adom (ah-DOHM) Akan, Ghana: "help from God."

Adri (AH-dree) Hindi: "rock." Adri was a minor god in Hindu mythology who protected mankind and once rescued the sun from evil spirits who tried to extinguish it.

Adrian Latin: "dark one." Popular today in the United States and Spanish-speaking countries.
Hadrian (English); *Adrien* (French); *Adorjan, Adi* (Hungarian); *Adriano* (Italian, Spanish); *Andreian, Adrik, Andrian, Andreyan, Andriyan, Andri* (Russian); *Hadrian* (Swedish)

Adriel Hebrew: "God's majesty" or "belonging to God's congregation."
Adri, Adrial

Agni (AHG-nee) Hindi: "god of fire." In Hindu lore Agni is depicted with three heads, either four or seven arms, and seven tongues (each with its own name) for lapping up the butter offered during sacrifices. He often has a ram at his side and rides in a glorious chariot driven by a red-limbed, golden-haired charioteer. The chariot's wheels are the seven winds.

Agu (ah-GOO) Ibo, Nigeria: "leopard."

Agustin (ah-goo-STEEN) Latin: "belonging to Augustus,

the exalted one." Commonly used in Spanish-speaking countries. The English equivalent is Augustus.

Ahanu (ah-HAH-noo) North American Indian: "he laughs.

Aharon Hebrew form of Aaron, "exalted" or "lofty." See Aaron.

Ahdik (AH-dik) North American Indian: "caribou" or "reindeer."

Ahir (uh-HEER) Turkish: "end" or "last." For the last child a mother intends to bear.

Ahmed (AH-med) Arabic: "the most praised." This name was occasionally used by Muhammad and is one of the more than five hundred names for the Prophet. An old Moslem saying holds that angels pray in every house where an Ahmad or Muhammad lives.
Ahmad

Ahmik (AH-mik) North American Indian: "the beaver." In Indian legend the beaver epitomizes skill.

Ahren Old German: "eagle." In astrology the eagle is one of the symbols of Scorpio.

Akando (ah-KAHN-do) North American Indian: "ambush." The name was possibly bestowed to commemorate a great feat the child's father performed.

Akar (ah-KAHR) Turkish: "flowing" or "running," referring to water.

Akil (ah-KEEL) Arabic: "intelligent," "thoughtful," or "one who uses reason."
Ahkeel, Akeel

Akim (ah-KEEM) Russian form of the Hebrew *Jehoiakım*, "God will establish."

Akin (ah-KEEN) Yoruba, Nigeria: "brave" or "heroic."
Ahkeen, Akeen

Akio (AH-kee-o) Japanese: "bright boy."
Akira

HIDDEN MEANINGS IN OUR OWN NAMES

People who don't understand Indian naming customs may make fun of American Indians when their names translate into English as "ambush," "sweaty blanket," "running bear," or "rain-in-the-face." But before feeling smug, they should investigate what their *own* names really mean. Here are some famous names from past and present and their less-than-glittering hidden meanings:

Calvin Klein—"young, small, bald man."
Mary Tyler Moore—"bitter, dark-skinned roofer."
Cecil B. De Mille—"The miller's dim-sighted son."
Claude Debussy—"lame son from the thicket of brush."
Barbara Walters—"foreign army ruler."
Woody Allen—"fierce forest warden."
John Fitzgerald Kennedy—"big-headed gracious gift of God, bastard son of the ruler with a spear."

Akron Ochi, Ga, Africa: "ninth-born son."
　　Akon

Akule (ah-KOOL) North American Indian: "he looks up." Possibly indicates one of the first things the baby did after birth.

Ala (ah-LAH) Arabic: "glorious."

Alain Popular French form of Allen, "handsome" or "cheerful." See Allen.

Alan See Allen.

Alastair Greek: "one who avenges." Also a Scottish form of Alexander, "helper and defender of mankind."
　　Al, Alaster, Allaster, Alister, Allister

Alben Latin: "blond, fair one."
　　Al, Alban, Albin, Alby (English); *Albin, Albinek, Binek*

(Czech); *Aubin* (French); *Albins* (Latvian); *Albek*, *Albinek*, *Binek* (Polish); *Albino* (Italian, Spanish, Portuguese)

Albert Old English: "noble and brilliant." This name became extremely popular after Queen Victoria married Prince Albert of Germany in 1840. Albert Einstein and Albert Schweitzer kept the name in the limelight in this century.
Adelbert, *Al*, *Albie*, *Bert*, *Berty*, *Elbert* (English); *Albertik*, *Ales*, *Berco*, *Berti*, *Berty*, *Bertik* (Czech); *Aubert* (French); *Albrecht*, *Bechtel*, *Bertchen* (German); *Alvertos* (Greek); *Alberto*, *Berto* (Italian, Portuguese, Spanish); *Alberts* (Latvian); *Albek*, *Bertek* (Polish)

Albie Contemporary American creation from Albert, "noble and brilliant."

Albin Russian form of Alvin, "everyone's friend."

Alder Old English: "from the alder tree." Commonly used today in Germany.

Aldrich Old English: "an old and wise ruler."
Al, *Aldric*, *Aldridge*, *Eldridge*, *Elric*, *Rich*, *Richie*, *Richy* (English); *Audric* (French)

Alein (ah-LIGHN) Yiddish: "alone."

Alex Popular short form of Alexander, "helper and defender of mankind."
Alec, *Alek*, *Alik*, *Alix*

Alexander Greek: "helper and defender of mankind."
Alec, *Alek*, *Aleks*, *Alex*, *Alexis*, *Alik*, *Aliks*, *Alix*, *Sande*, *Sander*, *Sandy*, *Saunders*, *Sawnie* (English); *Aleksandur*, *Alekko*, *Sander* (Bulgarian); *Ales*, *Leksik*, *Lekso* (Czech); *Aleksander*, *Leks* (Estonian); *Alexandre* (French); *Alik*, *Axel* (German); *Alexandros*, *Alekos* (Greek); *Elek*, *Sandor*, *Sanyi* (Hungarian); *Alsandair* (Irish); *Alessandro* (Italian); *Aleksander*, *Olek*, *Oles* (Polish); *Alexio* (Portuguese); *Alek*, *Aleksandr*, *Aleksei*, *Alexandr*, *Alexei*, *Les*, *Oles*, *Olesko*, *Oleksandr*, *Sanya*, *Sasha*, *Sashenka*, *Sushka*, *Shura*, *Shurik*, *Shurka* (Russian); *Alasdair*, *Alastair*,

Alister (Scottish); *Alejandro, Alejo, Jandino, Jando* (Spanish); *Aleksander* (Yiddish)

Alf Old Norse: "elfin." A favorite in Norway. See Alvin.
Alv

Ali Arabic: "Jehovah," "the highest," or "the greatest." Popular among Moslems in Turkey, Egypt, Persia, Jordan, India, and Arabia, as well as in the United States. Ali was a son-in-law of the Prophet, married to his daughter Fatimah.

Alim (ah-LEEM) Arabic: "wise" or "learned."
Alem, Aleem

Alister Popular Scottish form of Alexander, "helper and defender of mankind." See Alexander.

Allen Irish Gaelic: "handsome" or "cheerful."
Alan, Aland, Allan, Allyn (English); *Alain, Allain* (French); *Ailin* (Irish); *Alao* (Portuguese); *Ailean* (Scottish); *Alano* (Spanish, Italian)

Almiron (AHL-mee-ruhn) Hindi: "clothes basket." Naming children after common household objects is traditional in India because the Hindus believe God is manifested in everything. Hence, each time you say the child's name, you are pronouncing the name of God, which is considered a step toward salvation. The feminine equivalent is Almira.
Miron

Almon (ahl-MOHN) Hebrew: "forsaken" or "a widower."

Alon Hebrew: "oak tree." Nature name from Israel.

Alrik Old German: "ruler of all." Popular in Sweden.

Alroy Spanish: "the king."

Altair Arabic: "the flying eagle." Also refers to a first-magnitude star in the constellation Lyra.

Alton Old English: "one who lives in the old town or estate."
Alten, Altin

Alvin Old German: "everyone's friend" or "noble friend."
Al, Alvan, Alvie, Alwin, Alwyn, Elvin (English); *Aloin,
Aluin* (French); *Alvino* (Italian); *Albin* (Polish, Russian);
Alwin (Portuguese, German); *Aluino* (Spanish)

Alvis (AHL-vees) Scandinavian: "all-knowing."

Amado (ah-MAH-do) Latin: "loving deity" or "lover of
the divine." Popular in Spanish countries.
Amadeo, Amando

Ameer (ah-MEER) Arabic: "prince."
Amir

Amiel (ah-mee-AYL) Hebrew: "Lord of my people."
Currently popular in Israel.
Ami

Amin (AH-min) East Indian: "faithful."
Ameen, Amitan, Amnon

Amon (AY-muhn) Hebrew: "related to the sun." Appropriate for a boy born under Leo, ruled by the sun.

Amory Old German: "divine, famous ruler."
Amor, Amery

Anders Popular Scandinavian form of Andrew, "strong and
manly."

André French form of Andrew. Currently popular in the
United States as well as France.

Andrew Greek *andreas*: "strong and manly."
Andi, Andie, Andy, Drew (English); *Andrei, Andres,
Andrey* (Bulgarian); *Andrej, Bandi, Ondro* (Czech);
Anders (Danish, Norwegian, Swedish); *André* (French);
Andreas (German); *Andreas, Evagelos* (Greek); *Andi,
Andor, Andras, Andris, Bandi, Endre* (Hungarian);
Andrius (Lithuanian); *Aniol, Jedrek, Jedrus* (Polish);
Andrei, Dela (Rumanian); *Andrey, Andreyka, Andrik*
(Russian); *Aindreas* (Scottish, Irish); *Andi, Andres,
Necho, Nesho* (Spanish)

Andy Short form of Andrew very popular as a full given
name today in the United States.

Anka Turkish: "the legendary phoenix" or "will-o'-the-wisp."

Annan (ah-NAHN) Ochi and Ga, Africa: "fourth-born son."

Anoki (ah-NO-kee) North American Indian: "actor."

Ansel Old French: "connected with or related to a nobleman."
Ancel, Ancell, Ansell, Ansil, Ansill

Ansis Latvian form of John, "gracious gift of God." See John.

Anthony Latin: "inestimable" or "priceless." A favorite variation—*Anton*—is used today in the United States, Bulgaria, Czechoslovakia, Russia, Germany, Rumania, Serbia, Sweden, and Norway.
Antony, Tony (English); *Antek, Antonin, Tonda, Tonik* (Czech); *Antoine* (French); *Andonios, Andonis, Tonis* (Greek); *Akoni* (Hawaiian); *Antal, Anti, Toni* (Hungarian); *Anntoin* (Irish); *Antonio* (Italian, Spanish, Portuguese); *Antons* (Latvian); *Antavas* (Lithuanian); *Antek, Antoni, Antonin, Antos, Tolek, Tonek* (Polish); *Antin, Antinko, Tosya, Tusya* (Russian), *Anders* (Scandinavian)

Archer Old English: "a bowman or archer."

Archibald Old German *ercanbald*: "genuine, simple, and bold."
Arch, Archie (English); *Archaimbaud, Archambault* (French); *Archibaldo* (Spanish)

Ardon (ahr-DOHN) Hebrew: "bronze."

Arel (ah-RAYL) Hebrew: "lion of God." The lion is the symbol of Leo.
Areli

Aren "eagle" or "rule." Popular in Norway and Denmark.

Ari Hebrew: "lion." Also a short form of Aristotle, "seeking the positive (or best) results."
Arie, Arri

Aric Old English: "a holy ruler." An older form of Richard coming back into vogue.
Arek, Areck, Arick, Ric, Rick, Ricky

Arif (ah-RIF) Turkish: "wise and intelligent."
Areef

Aristotle Greek: "seeking the positive (or best) results."
Ari, Arie, Arri

Arkin Norwegian: "the eternal king's son."

Arlen Irish Gaelic: "a pledge."
Arlan, Arland, Arlend, Arlin, Arlind

Arley Old English: "the bowman or hunter" or "from the rabbit meadow." Appropriate name for a boy born under Sagittarius, the archer.

Arlo Spanish: "barberry." Made well known by singer Arlo Guthrie.

Armand Old German: "armed" or "army man."
Arman, Armin, Armon, Armond, Ormond (English); *Armando* (Italian, Spanish); *Armands* (Latvian); *Arek, Mandek* (Polish); *Arman, Armen* (Russian)

Armon (ahr-MOHN) Hebrew: "castle" or "place."
Armoni

Armstrong Old English: "man with a strong arm in battle."

Arne (AHR-ne) Old German: "eagle." One of the most popular names in Norway, also used in Sweden and Denmark. A favorite form in Iceland is Arni.
Arni, Arnie, Arney

Arnon (ahr-NOHN) Hebrew: "rushing stream," implying the child is energetic.

Aron Popular form of Aaron used in Czechoslovakia, Hungary, Poland, Rumania, Scandinavia, Russia, and the United States. See Aaron.

Arpiar (ahr-pee-AHR) Armenian: "sunny" or "of sunshine."

Arri Modern Greek and American form of Aristotle, "seeking the positive (or best) results."

Arrio Spanish: "warlike."

Arslan (uhr-SLUN) Turkish: "lion." The lion is the symbol of Leo.

Art Popular short form of Arthur and Artemus.

Artemus Greek: "belonging to Artemis." Saint Artemis was a disciple of Saint Paul.
Art, Artie, Artimas, Artimis, Tim

Arthur Celtic *artos*: "a bear"; or Welsh: "noble one."
Art, Arte, Artie, Arty (English); *Atur* (used in many countries, including Russia, Bulgaria, Ireland, Hungary, Estonia, Poland, Rumania, Norway, and Sweden); *Artis* (Czech); *Athanasios, Thanasis, Thanos* (Greek); *Arto* (Finnish); *Arturo* (Italian, Spanish); *Artek* (Polish); *Artair* (Scottish)

Arve (AHR-ve) "inheritor of property" or "heir." One of the most popular names in Norway.

Arvid "man of the people." Popular in Sweden and Norway.

Asad (ah-SAHD) Arabic: "lion." Used to designate the constellation and astrological sign of Leo, the lion.
Alasid, Aleser, Asid, Assid

Asadel (A-sa-del) Arabic: "most prosperous one."

Ash Popular short form of Ashley, Asher, and other male names that start with *Ash*. According to an old superstition, the ash brings good luck. One old legend had it that a sprig of ash worn on the breast would give one prophetic dreams, and ash sap given to a newborn would frighten away evil spirits. Another superstition was that if the first parings of a child's nails were buried beneath an ash tree, he'd become a fine singer.

Asher Hebrew: "lucky," "blessed," or "happy."
Ash, Ashur

Ashley Old English: "one from the ash-tree meadow."
Ash

Ashlin Old English: "from the pool surrounded by ash

trees." Astrological name for a boy born under one of
the water signs: Pisces, Scorpio, or Cancer.
Ash, Ashlen

Ashon (ah-SHON) Ochi and Ga, Africa: "seventh-born
son."

Ashur Swahili: "born during the Moslem month of Ashur."
Also East Semitic: "warlike," and a form of Asher,
"lucky," "blessed," or "happy."
Ash

Asiel (ah-see-AYL) Hebrew: "God has created him."

Asim (ah-SEEM) Arabic: "protector" or "defender."
Aseem

Asker Turkish: "soldier."

Aswad (ahss-WAHD) Arabic: "black."

Atman (AHT-muhn) Hindi: "the self."

Atuanya (ah-TOO-ahn-yah) Ibo, Nigeria: "we throw the
eyes." Loosely translated, the name means "unexpect-
ed" and is given to a son born when a daughter was
expected.

Aubin French form of Albin, "blond, fair one."

Audric A French form of Aldrich, "an old and wise ruler."

Audun (OW-doon) Scandinavian: "deserted" or "desolate."
Currently popular in Norway. The feminine form is
Aud.

Aurek (AW-rek) Latin: "golden-haired." This is a modern
Polish form of an older name seldom used today—
Aurelius.
Aurel (Czech); *Aurele* (French); *Aurelius* (German);
Aurelio (Italian); *Aureli, Elek* (Polish); *Aurelian* (Ru-
manian); *Avreliy, Avrel* (Russian)

Avel Modern Greek: "breath." This name connotes the
mortality of man.

Averil Middle English: "born in the month of April." Averil is an ancient Anglo-Saxon word for April.
Averel, Averell, Averill, Avrel, Avril

Avery Old English: "elfin ruler."

Avi (ah-VEE) Hebrew: "father," referring to God.

Aviv (ah-VEEV) Hebrew: "spring," "freshness," or "youth." Used in modern Israel.

Awan (AH-wahn) North American Indian: "somebody."

Axel Scandinavian: "divine reward." Also a Scandinavian form of Absalom, meaning "father of peace." This name is commonly used in Sweden and Norway.
Axell

Azad (uh-ZUHD) Turkish: "free" or "born free."

Azi (ah-ZEE) Nigerian: "the youth," implying energy.

Azim (ah-ZEEM) Arabic: "defender," referring to one of God's ninety-nine qualities in the Koran.
Azeem

Azriel (ahz-ree-AYL) Hebrew: "God is my help."

ISRAELI HOLY NAMES

Many modern Israeli names contain references to religion or God. The name element *Avi-* frequently appears in such names. Examples include: Avidan ("God is just" or "Father of justice"), Avidor ("Father of a generation"), Aviel ("God is my Father"), Avital ("Father of dew"), Avner ("Father of light"), and Avniel ("My Father is my rock" or "My Father is my strength".)

--------------------------------- **B** ---------------------------------

Bailey Old French: "a steward or bailiff."
Bail, Bailie, Baillie, Baily, Bayley

Bainbridge Old English: "a bridge over a rapids." Probably originally bestowed on a child born near a bridge over white waters.
Bain, Bridger

Baird Irish Gaelic: "a bard" or "a traveling ballad singer."
Bard

Bal Tibetan-Sanskrit *bal-bala*: "wool-hair." English Gypsy name for a child born with lots of hair.

Balder Old Norse: "god of light" or "white god." In Norse mythology Balder was the son of the god Odin and was killed when touched by a sprig of mistletoe. His astrological sign corresponds to Gemini, the twins.
Baldur (Norse); *Baudier* (French)

Baldwin Old German: "bold friend" or "bold protector."

Balin (BAH-lin) Hindi: "mighty soldier." In Hindu mythology Balin is a monkey king. A notorious tyrant, he is said to have the power to extract half the strength from anyone who challenges him.
Bali, Valin

Bane Hawaiian form of Barney, "son of prophecy or consolation." Given to a child after much praying and waiting by parents. See Barney.

Baram Modern Israeli: "son of a nation." Derived originally from Abraham, "father of a nation."

Barney Hebrew and Greek: "son of prophecy or consolation." Modern U.S. form of the older name Barnabas.
Barn, Barnaby, Barnie, Barny (English); *Barnabe* (French); *Bane* (Hawaiian); *Barna* (Hungarian); *Barnebas, Bernabe* (Spanish)

Baron Old English: "a warrior or baron."

Barret Old German: "mighty as a bear."
Barrett

Barry Irish Gaelic: "pointed or like a spear"; Old French: "a form of barrier." Also a popular short form of Bernard.
Barri, Barrie

Barth Hebrew: "a farmer" or "son of the earth." Modern U.S. form of Bartholomew.
Bart, Bartel, Bat (English); *Bartek, Barto, Bartz* (Czech); *Bardo* (Danish); *Barthelmy, Bartholomieu, Bartholome* (French); *Bartel, Barthel, Bartol, Bertel* (German); *Barta, Bertalan, Berti* (Hungarian); *Barnaby, Bartek, Bartos* (Polish); *Parlan* (Scottish); *Jerney* (Slovenian); *Balta, Barto, Bartoli, Bartolo, Bartolome, Toli* (Spanish); *Barthelemy* (Swedish)

Baruch Modern Greek: "doer of good."

Basil Latin: "kingly" or "magnificent."
Bas, Vas, Vasily (English); *Vasil* (Bulgarian); *Bazil, Vasil* (Czech); *Basile, Bale* (French); *Basle* (German); *Vasilis* (Greek); *Bazel, Vazul* (Hungarian); *Basilio* (Italian, Portuguese, Spanish); *Bazek* (Polish); *Vasile* (Rumanian); *Vas, Vasili, Vasilek, Vassily, Vasya, Vasyl* (Russian); *Basilius, Basle* (Swedish)

Basir (buh-SEER) Turkish: "intelligent and discerning."

Baul (bal) English Gypsy: "snail."

Bavol (BAH-vohl) English Gypsy: "wind" or "air."

Bay Vietnamese: "seventh-born child." Also given to a child born on Saturday or in July, the seventh lunar month.

Beck Middle English: "a brook." Commonly used as a surname in Switzerland.

Bedrich (BED-rik) Czech form of Frederick, "peaceful leader."

Beldon Old English: "child of the unspoiled, beautiful glen."
Belden, Beldin

Belen Greek: "an arrow." May be given to a boy born under the sign of Sagittarius, the Archer.

Bello Fultani, Africa, *ballawo bini*: "the helper (or promoter) of the Islamic religion."

Bem Tiv, Nigeria: "peace."

Ben Arabic and Hebrew: "son" or "son of." This name is frequently used as part of longer Arabic names. Also short form of Benjamin, "son of my right hand."

Benedict Latin: "blessed."
Ben, Benedick, Bendix, Bennet, Bennett, Bennie, Benny, Dick (English); *Benedikt* (Bulgarian, Czech, German); *Benoit, Benoist* (French); *Benedik, Benedek, Benci, Benke, Bence* (Hungarian); *Benedetto, Betto* (Italian); *Bendik* (Norwegian); *Bendek, Benek* (Polish); *Venedict, Venedikt, Venka, Venya, Benedikt, Benedo* (Russian); *Benedicto, Beni, Benito, Benitin* (Spanish); *Bengt* (Swedish)

Benjamin Hebrew: "son of my right hand." Used in the United States, France, Germany, Hungary, Sweden, Norway, and Spanish-speaking countries. In the Bible Benjamin was Jacob's youngest son.
Ben, Benjy, Bennie, Benn, Benny (English); *Beni, Beno* (Hungarian); *Beniamino* (Italian); *Benek, Beniamin* (Polish); *Beatham* (Scottish); *Benja, Mincho* (Spanish); *Binyamin* (Yiddish)

Benzi Hebrew *Ben Zion*: "excellent son."

Berdy (BAIR-dee) Russian and Slavic form of Hubert, "brilliant mind" or "brilliant spirit."

Berg German: "mountain," for a child from the mountains. Used in Germany, Holland, Sweden, Israel, and the United States.

Berger French: "mountain dweller" or "shepherd." Common surname in Austria, now used as a first name in the United States and other countries.

Berk Turkish: "solid, firm, or rugged." Also a variant spelling of Burke, "from the fortress or stronghold."

Bernard Old German: "brave as a bear." A truly international name, Bernard is used in the United States, Bulgaria, Czechoslovakia, Poland, Russia, Rumania, and Norway. Two saints have had this name.
Barn, Barney, Barnie, Barny, Bern, Bernarr, Bernie, Berny, Burnard, Burnie, Burny (English); *Bernek, Berno* (Czech); *Bernardin* (French); *Beno, Berend* (German); *Vernados* (Greek); *Bernat* (Hungarian); *Bernard, Bernardino* (Italian); *Bernhards, Berngards* (Latvian); *Bernardas* (Lithuanian); *Benek, Bernardyn* (Polish); *Berngards* (Russian); *Björn* (Scandinavian); *Bearnard* (Scottish, Irish); *Bernal, Bernardel, Bernardo, Nardo* (Spanish)

Bersh English Gypsy: "one year."
Besh

Bertin Spanish: "distinguished friend." Made popular by Saint Bertin.

Berto (BAIR-to) Spanish short form of Alberto, "noble and brilliant." See Albert.

Berty Czech development of Albert, "noble and brilliant." Also a U.S. nickname for Albert.

Berwin Middle English: "friend of the harvest." Earth name for a child born under an earth sign: Taurus, Capricorn, or Virgo.

Beval (BAY-vahl) English Gypsy: "like the wind."

Birk Old English: "at the birch tree"; or North English: "from the island of birch trees." Once a nickname for a number of names, such as Birkett and Birkey, Birk is commonly used today as an independent name.

Björn (b.yern) A popular Scandinavian form of Bernard,

"brave as a bear," currently one of the most common names in Norway and Iceland. See Bernard.

Blair Irish Gaelic: "child of the fields." Earth name for a child born under one of the earth signs: Capricorn, Taurus, or Virgo.

Blaise See Blaze.

Blake Old English: "blond, fair-skinned one" or "dark."

Blane Irish Gaelic: "thin and lean."
Blain, Blaine, Blayne

Blaz Serbo-Croatian form of William, "unwavering protector." See William.

Blaze Latin: "stammerer." May have originated as a nickname for an older child who stuttered.
Blaise, Blase (English); *Blaise, Blaisot* (French); *Blasi, Blasius* (German); *Ballas* (Hungarian); *Biagio* (Italian); *Blazek* (Polish); *Vlas* (Russian); *Blas* (Spanish)

Boaz (BO-ahz) Hebrew: "swift and strong."

Bobby Popular form of Robert, "shining with fame," now used as an independent name.

Bodil (BO-del) Norwegian and Danish name meaning "commanding."

Bodua (bo-DOO-ah) Akan, Ghana: "an animal's tail." Bodua is the ruling spirit of the Akan day corresponding to our Sunday, and the name is given to a child born on that day.

Bohdan Favorite Ukrainian form of Donald, "world ruler." In the Ukraine Bohdan was popularized by the seventeenth-century Cossack leader Bohdan Chmelnyckyj. See Donald.
Bogdan, Bogdashka, Danya

Bond Old English: "tiller of the soil." Popular in the United States and Iceland.
Bonde, Bondon, Bonds

Borg Norse: "one who lives in a castle." Popular in Scandinavia.

Boris Slavic: "battler" or "stranger." A favorite in Hungary, Russia, and most Slavic countries.

Botan (bo-TAHN) Japanese: "peony." In Japan the peony is the flower of June.

Bour (BO-oor) Ghanaian: "rock."
Obo, Obour (African)

Bowen Gaelic: "small, victorious one"; or Old Welsh: "the well-born or youthful one's son."
Bow, Bowie

Boyce Old French: "son of the forest."

Brad Old English: "a broad or wide place." Frequently used as an independent name or as a short form of Bradford ("from the wide river crossing"), Braden ("from the wide valley"), Bradley ("from the wide meadow"), or Brady ("from the wide island").

Bradburn Old English: "from the broad brook."

Bradley Old English: "from the wide or broad meadow."
Brad, Brady, Lee

Bradshaw Old English: "large virginal forest."

Bram Dutch form of Abraham, "father of a mighty nation." See Abraham.

Brandeis "dweller on a burned clearing" or "one who comes from Brandeis," the name of three different places in Bohemia, a province of Czechoslovakia. This name is popular today in Czechoslovakia and Germany.
Brand, Brandt, Brandy, Brant

Brandon Old English: "one from the beacon hill."
Bran, Brand, Brandan, Branden, Brandy, Brandun, Brannon

Brede (BREH-deh) Scandinavian: "glacier." Modern Norwegian and Danish favorite.

Brencis Latvian form of Lawrence, "crowned with laurel." See Lawrence.

Brendan Irish Gaelic: "little raven" or "brave and bold, even in youth"; or German: "aflame."
Bren, Brenden, Brendin, Brendon, Brennan, Brennen

Brent Old English: "from the steep hill."

Brett Celtic: "from Brittania."
Bret

Brian, Bryan Celtic: "strong, virtuous, and honorable." Brian Boru was the most famous of all the Irish kings and defeated a Danish force in the eleventh century. Extremely popular today in Ireland and the United States.
Briant, Brien, Brion, Bryant, Bryon (English); *Briano* (Italian)

Brishen (BREE-shen) English Gypsy: "born during a rain."

Brodny Slavic: "one who lives near a shallow stream crossing."

Brody "man with an unusual beard," "man from the barony of Brodie," "man from the muddy place," "man from Brody in Russia," or "a ditch." This is an example of how over the centuries a name can come from many sources and take on many meanings.
Brodi, Brodie

Bron Afrikaans: "source."

Bruns German: "dark" or "brown-haired one."

Burke Old French: "one who lives at the stronghold or fortress."
Berk, Berke, Birk, Birke, Burk

Burr Scandinavian: "youth."

Burt Old English: "shining and glorious." Also a short form of Albert and Herbert.
Bert, Berty, Burty

---------------------------------- C ----------------------------------

Cadao (kad-YAW) South Vietnamese: "folk song" or "ballad."

Caesar Latin: "hairy or long-haired one." Over time the name has taken on the meaning of "emperor."
Cesar, Cesare (English); *Casar, Cezar, Kaiser* (Bulgarian); *Arek, Cezar, Cezary, Cezek* (Polish); *Kesar* (Russian); *Cesar, Cesareo, Cesario, Checha, Sarito* (Spanish)

Cahil (kah-HIL) Turkish: "young, inexperienced, and naïve."

Caldwell Old English: "cool, clear spring."
Cal, Calder

Caleb Hebrew *Kaleb*: "bold and impetuous" or "a dog." In the Bible Caleb, the long-lived son of Jephunneh, was with Moses as he and his people wandered in the wilderness. Popular among Puritans in the seventeenth century, Caleb has had a revival of popularity and is currently a fashionable modern U.S. name.
Cal, Cale, Kale, Kaleb (English); *Kalb* (Arabic)

Cam (kahm) English Gypsy: "beloved." The name actually refers to the sun, which governs the sign of Leo.

Camlo (KAHM-lo) English Gypsy: "lovely" or "amiable"; or Vietnamese: "sweet dew." One dark-skinned Gypsy band uses this as part of their tribal name—Kaulo Camloes—which translates as "the beautiful blacks."

Cappi (KAHP-pee) English Gypsy: "good fortune" or "profit."

Carey Old Welsh: "one who lives at the castle"; or Latin: "dear, costly." Popularized in the United States by actor Cary Grant.
Cary

Carl Short form of Charles, "strong and manly" and names starting with "Carl."
Carl, Carling

Carlisle Old English: "from the castle tower."
Carl, Carlyle

Carlos Spanish form of Charles, "strong and manly." See Charles.

Carney Irish Gaelic: "victorious one."
Car, Carny, Karney, Karny, Kearney

Carr Old Norse: "from the marsh."
Karr, Kerr

Carswell Old English: "child from the watercress spring." Astrological name for a boy born under a water sign: Pisces, Cancer, or Scorpio.

Carter Old English: "a cart driver." Originally a surname and now commonly given as a first name to a boy, especially if the mother's maiden name is Carter.

Carvel Manx: "a song"; or Old French: "from the marshy estate."
Carvell

Cary Popular form of Carey, "one who lives at the castle" or "dear, costly."

Casey Irish Gaelic: "brave, valorous, and watchful." Originally an Irish family name, Casey has been popular in the United States as a first name for nearly a century.
Case

Casimir Old Slavic: "he announces or commands peace." Popular in Poland because of Casimir the Pacific, Poland's renowned eleventh-century monarch.
Castimer (English); *Kazimir* (Bulgarian, Czech, German, Russian); *Kazmer* (Hungarian); *Kazek, Kazik, Kazio* (Polish); *Casimiro, Cachi, Cashi* (Spanish)

Casper Persian: "master of the treasure."
Caspar, Cas, Cass, Gaspar, Gasper, Jasper (English); *Kaspar* (Czech, German); *Jasper, Gaspard* (French); *Gaspar* (Hungarian, Portuguese, Russian, Spanish)

Cass Modern form of Casper, "master of the treasure."

Castel (kah-STEHL) Latin: "belonging to a castle." Most often used in Spanish-speaking countries.

Caton (kah-TOHN) Latin: "knowledgeable, wise." Used in Spain, Latin America, and South America.
Cato (English)

Cemal (ke-MAHL) Arabic: "beauty." Also a popular Turkish name.

Chad Old English *cadda*: "warlike one," or "related to Mars."
Chadd

Chaim (k[h]ighm, to rhyme with *time*) Hebrew: "life."
Hyam (Hebrew); *Chaimek, Haim* (Polish); *Khaim* (Russian)

Chal (chahl) English Gypsy: "lad," "boy," or "son."

Chalmers Scottish: "the head of the household."
Chalmer

Cham Vietnamese: "hard worker."

Chance Middle English: "good fortune."

Chandler Old French: "candlemaker."
Chan, Chane

Chane (CHAH-neh or anglicized to chain) Swahili: "weaving leaf." This name refers to either a strip or tough leaf used for weaving mats or a bundle. Hence, Chane connotes sturdy dependability.

Chaney (CHAH-ney) Old French: "oak wood."
Cheney

Chanoch (k[h]ah-NOHK[H]) Hebrew form of Clark, "clergyman" or "learned man." See Clark.

Charles Latin *carolus*, "strong and manly." This name has been popular around the globe for centuries. One of the most famous bearers of this name was Charlemagne (Charles the Great), who was crowned Holy Roman Emperor on Christmas Day in 800 A.D.

Carl, Cary, Chad, Charley, Charlie, Charlton, Chas,
Chick, Chip, Chuck (English); *Karl* (Bulgarian, Ger-
man, Russian); *Karel, Karlik, Karol* (Czech); *Kalle*
(Finnish, Swedish); *Charlot* (French); *Karal* (German);
Kalman, Kari, Karoly (Hungarian); *Carlino, Carlo,*
Carolo (Italian); *Karlen, Karlens, Karlis* (Latvian);
Karol, Karolek (Polish); *Karl, Karlen, Karlin* (Russian);
Carlo, Carlos (Spanish)

Charlton Old English: "from Charles's home" or a form
of Charles, "strong and manly." Another source: Old
English, "farmers' town."
Carleton, Carlton, Charleton

Chase Old French: "hunter." Appropriate for a boy born
under Sagittarius, the archer.

Chauncey Middle English: "a church official" or "chan-
cellor."
Chan, Chance, Chancey, Chaunce, Chauncy

Che (chay) Colloquial Spanish pet form of Joseph, "he
will increase." See Joseph.

Chen Chinese: "vast" or "great." One story is told of a
boy who was about to receive a fate name when his
father dreamed that a god appeared and wrote the
character Chen, proclaiming, "Give him this name."
The boy, Chang Chen (surname first), grew up to
become a minister of state. Fate names, once kept
secret, are now used freely in China, particularly by the
better educated.

Cheslav (ches-LAHF) Russian form of Chester, "living at
a fortified army camp." See Chester.

Chesmu (CHEHS-moo) North American Indian: "gritty."

Chester Old English: "living at a fortified army camp."
Ches, Cheston, Chet

Chet Popular contemporary U.S. form of Chester, originally a nickname now given as a full name.

Chevalier French: "knight."
Chev, Chevi, Chevy

Chi (chee or anglicized to KIGH) Ibo, Nigeria: "God." In Nigeria this name refers to a kind of personal guardian angel.

Chik English Gypsy: "earth."

Chim (kim) Vietnamese: "bird."

Christian Greek: "believer in Christ, the anointed one." Ten Danish kings have been called Christian, and the name has dozens of variations around the world.
Chris, Christy, Christen, Kris, Kristian (English); *Jaan, Kristian, Kristjan, Krists* (Estonian); *Christophe* (French); *Krischan* (German); *Christianos, Kristos* (Greek); *Kerestel* (Hungarian); *Christinao* (Italian); *Krists* (Latvian); *Krist* (Norwegian); *Chrystian, Crystek, Krystek, Krys, Krystian* (Polish); *Cristao, Cristiano* (Portuguese)

Christopher Greek *Christoforos*: "Christ-bearer." A third-century martyr, Saint Christopher is the patron saint of ferrymen and travelers.
Chris, Cris, Kit, Kris, Kriss (English); *Christofer, Kristof* (Czech); *Christoffer* (Danish); *Risto* (Finnish); *Christophe* (French); *Christoforus, Christoph, Kriss,*

NIGERIAN "CHI" NAMES

In Nigeria the god Chi plays an important role in naming babies. An individual's Chi, a personal god, is believed to come into being when one is born, to follow one throughout life, and to cause both misfortune and success. Among the many Chi names there are: Cinese ("Chi is protecting"), Chileogu ("Chi is our protector" or "Chi is our defender"), Cis (another spelling of Chi), Chioke ("gift of Chi"), Chinelo ("thought of Chi") Chike ("power of Chi"), and Chinua ("Chi's own blessing").

Stoffel (German); *Kristof* (Hungarian); *Christoforo* (Italian); *Kriss, Krisus* (Latvian); *Cristovao* (Portuguese); *Christof, Christofer* (Russian); *Cris, Cristobal, Tobal, Tobalito* (Spanish); *Kristofor, Kristoffer* (Swedish)

Ciceron Spanish form of Cicero, "chickpea."

Cilombo (chee-LOHM-bo) Umbundu, Angola: "roadside camp," a welcome sight to weary travelers in Africa. Hence, the implied meaning is "a sight for sore eyes." The name is a great favorite in Africa and is often given to girls as well as boys.

Ciro (SEE-ro) Spanish form of Cyrus, "the sun," which governs the sign Leo.

Clark Old French: "a scholar."
Clarke

Clay Old English: "mortal" or "of the earth." Also a short form of Clayton.

Clayton Old English: "dweller at the farm built on clay" or "mortal."
Clay, Clayten, Claytin

Clement Latin: "gentle" or "kind."
Clem, Clemens, Clemmie, Clemmy, Clemmons (English); *Kliment* (Bulgarian); *Klema, Klement, Klemo* (Czech); *Clemens* (Danish); *Klemens, Menz* (German); *Kelemen* (Hungarian); *Clemente, Clemenza* (Italian); *Klemens, Klimek* (Polish); *Klemet, Klim, Kliment, Klimka, Klyment* (Russian); *Cleme, Clemen, Clemente, Clemento* (Spanish)

Cody Old English: "a cushion."
Codi, Codie

Colin Irish Gaelic: "young and manly."
Colan, Cole, Collin (English); *Cailean* (Scottish)

Colman Icelandic: "head man" or "charcoal maker"; or Irish Gaelic: "little dove."
Cole, Colemun

Coman (ko-MAHN) Arabic: "noble."

Conrad Old German: "bold counselor." Spelled *Konrad*,
   this name is used in many countries, including the
   United States, Czechoslovakia, Germany, Hungary,
   Russia, and Sweden.
   Con, Conn, Conni, Connie, Cort, Curt, Kurt (English); *Conrade* (French); *Conny, Konni, Kurt* (German); *Conrado* (Italian, Portuguese, Spanish)

Corey Irish and Scottish: "he lives by a hollow (or misty)
   pool." Also used today for girls.
   Cori, Correy, Cory, Korey, Kory

Cornel Latin: "horn-colored" or "like a horn"; or Greek:
   "the cornel tree."
   Cornall, Cornell

Cowan Irish Gaelic: "a twin" or "hillside hollow." Appropriate for a boy born under Gemini, the twins.

Craig Scotch Gaelic: "from the crag."

Crispus Latin: "curly-haired one." Famous namesake: Crispus
   Attucks, a black seaman and probably a runaway slave,
   who was the first American to die in the Boston
   Massacre.
   Cris, Crispin (English); *Krispin* (Czech, German,
   Hungarian); *Crepin* (French); *Crispino* (Italian); *Crispo*
   (Spanish)

Curt Popular short form of Curtis ("courteous") and Conrad
   ("bold counselor").
   Kurt

Curtis Old French: "courteous."
   Curt, Kurt, Kurtis (English); *Curcio* (Spanish)

Cy A popular short form of Cyril and Cyrus, now used in
   the United States as an independent name.

Cyril Greek: "lordly."
   Cy, Cyrill (English); *Kiril* (Bulgarian); *Cyrille* (French);
   Cirillo (Italian); *Kirill, Kiryl* (Russian); *Cirilo, Ciro*
   (Spanish)

Cyrus Old Persian: "the sun." Appropriate for a boy born under the sign of Leo, ruled by the sun.
  Cy, Russ (English); *Kir* (Bulgarian); *Ciro* (Spanish, Italian)

---------------------------------- **D** ----------------------------------

Dabir (dah-BEER) Algerian, Egyptian: "secretary" or "teacher."

Dacey Irish Gaelic: "a Southerner." Also used for girls.
  Dace, Dacy

Dag Old Norse: "day" or "brightness." A favorite today in Norway because of its distinctively Norse sound. The feminine form is Dagny. Popularized around the world by former United Nations Secretary General Dag Hammarskjöld.

Dagan Hebrew: "corn" or "grain"; or East Semitic: "earth." May be given to a boy born under one of the earth signs: Capricorn, Taurus, or Virgo. The name can also refer to a Babylonian god of agriculture and fish, in which case it means "little fish."
  Dagon

Dalal (dah-LAHL) Sanskrit: "a broker." An East Indian name denoting the bearer's or father's occupation.

Dale Old English: "one who lives in the valley."
  Dal, Daley, Daly (English); *Dalibor* (Czech)

Damek Czech form of Adam, "earth" or "man of the red earth." See Adam.

Damien Greek: "a tamer of men" or "gentle." Used worldwide.
  Damian, Damon (English); *Damek, Damjan* (Hungarian); *Damiano* (Italian); *Damian, Damyan, Dema, Demyan* (Russian)

Damon A form of Damien used in the United States, England, Greece, and Portugal.

Dan Popular familiar form of Daniel ("God is my judge") now bestowed in the United States as a full name. Dan means "judge."

Dana Hebrew: form of Daniel, "God is my judge"; or Old English: "one from Denmark." See also Daniel.

Dane Old English: "a Dane" or "one from Denmark." Also a Dutch and Lithuanian form of Daniel.
Dana, Dain

Dani (DAH-nee or anglicized to DA-nee) Modern Israeli and Slavic development of Dan, "judge." Also popular in Hungary.

Daniel Hebrew: "God is my judge." Popular in the United States, Germany, Spain, Sweden, Norway, Rumania, Israel, and many other countries.
Dan, Dannie, Danny (English); *Danil* (Bulgarian); *Dano, Danko* (Czech); *Dane* (Dutch); *Taneli* (Finnish); *Donois* (French); *Dacso, Daneil, Dani* (Hungarian); *Daniele* (Italian); *Daniels* (Latvian); *Dane, Danukas* (Lithuanian); *Danek* (Polish); *Daniela, Danila, Danilka, Danya, Danylets, Danylo* (Russian); *Dusan* (Serbian, Croatian); *Dani* (Slovenian); *Danilo, Nelo* (Spanish)

Danior (DAH-nee-or) English Gypsy: "born with teeth."

Danladi (dahn-LAH-dee) Hausa, Nigeria: "born on Sunday."

Danny Popular modern form of Daniel ("God is my judge") now occasionally used as a full given name.

Danya (DAHN-yah) Russian form of Daniel.

Dar Hebrew: "pearl" or "mother-of-pearl."

Darby Old Norse: "one from the deer estate"; or Irish Gaelic: "a free man."
Dar, Darb, Derby

Darcy Irish Gaelic: "a dark man"; or Old French: "dweller in the fortress."
Dar, Darce, Darcey, Darse, Darsey, Darsy

Daren Hausa, Nigeria: "born at night." Also a modern U.S. form of Darren, "small great one" or "wealthy."

Darnell Old English: "from the hidden or secret nook." *Dar, Darnal, Darnall, Darnel*

Darren Irish Gaelic: "small great one"; or Greek: "wealthy." *Dare, Daren, Darin, Daron, Darrin, Darron* (English); *Dario* (Italian, Portuguese, Spanish)

Darryl Old French: "small, dear, or beloved." *Darel, Darrel, Darrell, Daryl*

Darwin Old English: "a beloved friend." *Dar, Derwin*

Dasan (DAH-sahn) Pomo Indian: "leader." In Pomo Indian creation legend, Dasan and his father were leaders of a bird clan who brought civilization with them from the waters.

Daudi (dah-OO-dee) Swahili: "beloved one."

Dave Short form of David, "beloved."

David Hebrew: "beloved." This all-time, worldwide favorite is used in virtually every European country and Russia. *Dave, Davie, Davy* (English); *Davidek* (Czech); *Davidde, Davide* (Italian); *Dovidas* (Lithuanian); *Dawid* (Polish); *Davi* (Portuguese); *Danya, Daveed, Dodya* (Russian); *Dawid, Dowid* (Yiddish)

Davin (DAH-vin) Old Scandinavian: "brightness of the Finns," who were once thought to be the most intelligent people of the North. Popular in Scandinavia.

Dekel (DAY-kel) Arabic: "palm tree" or "date palm." Popular today in Israel.

Del English Gypsy: "he gives." Also a short form of names beginning with *Del-*.

Delaney Irish Gaelic: "the challenger's descendent." *Del, Delan, Delainey*

WHERE MIDDLE NAMES BEGAN

The origins of many naming customs have been lost in antiquity. The very first names ever bestowed in primitive societies could have been a growl, a grunt, a howl, a click, a whistle, or even a purr. But we are able to trace the European custom of giving a child a middle name.

The Spanish were giving middle monikers as early as 1000 A.D. About the time Columbus discovered America, the Germans picked up on the custom. The British, however, considered the practice of giving a child two baptismal names almost sacrilegious. After British nobleman Sir Edward Cook declared a person should never have two Christian names, the British passed a law banning middle names. Rebellious though they were, not one Pilgrim on the *Mayflower* had a middle name.

The first recorded middle name in America belonged to Edwin Maria Wingfield, a male member of the Jamestown Colony. But the idea of giving a baby three names didn't really catch on here until the mid-1800s, possibly because by then many Germans with three names had immigrated to this country and were influencing their friends and neighbors.

The most unusual middle name ever bestowed? In his marvelous *Treasury of Name Lore*, Elsdon C. Smith tells of the liberal parents who decided to let each of their children choose her own middle name. In 1965, at the age of thirteen, their daughter Mary fell in love with the folk song, "Don't Ya Weep, Don't Ya Mourn" and insisted upon naming herself Mary Dontyaweepdontyamourn Schulz. So if you're thinking about letting your child choose her own middle name, you may want to reconsider.

Delano Irish Gaelic: "healthy black man"; or Old French: "from the nut-tree place."

Delbert Old English: "bright day" or "sunny day."
Bert, Bertie, Berty, Del

Delmar Latin *del-mar*: "of the sea." Especially popular in Spanish-speaking countries.
Del, Delmer

Delsin North American Indian: "he is so."
Del, Delsie, Delsy

Demothi (deh-MO-tee) North American Indian: "talks walking." Probably originally bestowed on a child who talked as he walked.

Deniz (de-NIZ) Turkish: "sea," implying huge waves or a storm. Common in Turkey.

Dennis Greek: "the god of wine." A popular modern form of Dionysus, the god of wine and vegetation.
Den, Denis, Denney, Denny, Deon, Dion (English); *Denis, Denys, Dione* (French); *Dionysus* (German); *Denes, Dennes* (Hungarian); *Denis* (Irish); *Dionigi, Dionisio* (Italian); *Denis, Denys, Denka, Denya* (Russian); *Dionis, Dionisio, Nicho* (Spanish)

Der Short form of Derek, "ruler of the people."

Derek Old German *dietrich*: "ruler of the people." See Theodoric.
Darik, Darrik, Der, Derk, Derrick, Derrik, Dirk

Deror (deh-ROHR) Hebrew: "freedom," "free-flowing," or "a swallow."
Dare, Darrie, Derori (Israeli)

Derry Irish Gaelic: "red-haired."

Devlin Irish Gaelic: "brave; one of fierce valor."
Dev, Devland, Devlen, Devlyn

Dewey Old Welsh: "beloved." Originally a Welsh form of David.

Dichali (dee-CHAH-lee) North American Indian: "he speaks often."

Didi (DEE-dee) Israeli diminutive of the older name Jedidiah, "loved by the Lord."
Deedee

Diego (dee-EH-go) Spanish form of Jacob, "the supplanter."
   See Jacob.

Dillon Irish Gaelic: "faithful."

Dima (DEE-mah) Russian nickname for Vladimir, which is
   a form of Walter, "powerful warrior" or "army ruler."
   See Walter.

Dimitri Greek: "belonging to Demeter," the goddess of
   fertility. Popular in both Russia and the United States.
   Demeter, Demetrius, Dimitry (English); *Dimitr* (Bul-
   garian); *Demetre* (French); *Demetrois, Dimitrios, Dimos,
   Mimis, Mitsos, Takis* (Greek); *Demeter, Domotor*
   (Hungarian); *Demetrio* (Italian, Spanish); *Dymek, Dymitry,
   Dyzek* (Polish); *Dima, Dimitre, Dmitri, Dmitrik* (Russian)

Dinos Latin: "firm and constant." Originally a Greek form
   of Constantinos, this name has surpassed its longer
   form in popularity. Dinos and Kostas are among the
   most popular boys' names in Greece today.
   *Costa, Gus, Konstandinos, Konstantinos, Kostas, Kostis,
   Kotsos* (Greek)

Dion Popular modern U.S. form of Dennis, "god of wine."
   Deon (English); *Dione* (French)

Dirk A short form of Derik, "ruler of the people," which
   is a form of Theodoric.

Dobry (DO-bree) Polish: "good."

Dohosan (do-HO-suhn) North American Indian: "a small
   bluff."

Domingo (do-MEEN-go) Spanish and Italian form of Dominick, "belonging to the Lord" or "born on Sunday."

Dominick Latin: "belonging to the Lord" or "born on
   Sunday."
   Dom, Domenic, Nick, Nickie, Nicky (English); *Dominik,
   Domek, Dumin* (Czech); *Dominique* (French); *Deco,
   Dome, Domo, Domokos, Domonkos* (Hungarian);
   Domenico, Domingo, Menico (Italian); *Dominik, Donek,*

Niki (Polish); *Domingos* (Portuguese); *Chuma, Chumin, Chuminga, Domicio, Domingo, Mingo* (Spanish)

Donahue Irish Gaelic: "dark warrior."
Don, Donnie, Donny, Donohue

Donald Irish Gaelic: "world ruler."
Don, Donal, Donnie, Donny (English); *Tauno* (Finnish); *Donaldo* (Italian); *Donalt* (Norwegian); *Pascual* (Spanish); *Bogdan, Bohdan, Danya* (Ukrainian)

Donato Latin: "a gift," implying the child is a gift from God. See Donot.
Donat, Donatus (English); *Donati, Donatello, Donato* (Italian); *Dodek, Donat* (Polish)

Donnelly Celtic: "brave dark or black man."

Donot Form of Donato ("a gift") used in many countries, including the United States, France, Hungary, Poland, and Russia.

Donovan Celtic: "dark warrior."
Don, Donavon, Donnie, Donny, Dunavan, Van

Dor Hebrew: "a generation" or "a home."

Doran Greek: "a gift."
Dorran, Dorren

Dorek (DOH-rek) Polish form of Theodore, "gift of God."

Dorian Greek *dorios*: "child of the sea." Appropriate for a boy born under one of the water signs: Pisces, Cancer, or Scorpio.

Doron Hebrew: "a gift," implying the child is a gift of God.

Dotan (do-TAHN) Hebrew: "law." Used today in Israel and the United States.
Dothan

Doug Popular short form of Douglas.

Douglas Scottish: "from the dark or black water." Famous Scottish clan name.
Doug, Douglass, Dugald

Dovev (dó-VAYV) Hebrew: "to whisper" or "to speak quietly."

Doyle Celtic: "black stranger" or "dark stranger."

Drake Middle English: "one who owns the 'Sign of the Dragon' Inn." Once an occupation name referring to a common trademark (the dragon) often used on hostelries or shops.

Dreng Norwegian: "hired farmhand" or "brave man."

Drew Short, popular form of Andrew, "strong and manly." See Andrew.

Duane Irish Gaelic: "small and dark."
Dwain, Dwane, Dwayne

Dudley Old English: "one from the people's meadow." Made famous in recent times by actor Dudley Moore.
Dudd, Dudly

Duff Celtic: "dark-faced."

Duke Old French: "a leader." Also a short form of Dukker.

Dukker (DOOK-kuhr) English Gypsy: "to bewitch" or "to tell fortunes."
Duke

Dumaka (doo-MAH-kah) Ibo, Nigeria: "help me with hands." This short-sentence name from Africa expresses the father's plan to put the boy to work.

Duman Turkish: "smoke" or "mist."

Duncan Scotch Gaelic: "a swarthy chief" or "dark-skinned warrior."
Dun, Dune, Dunn

Dunham Celtic: "dark or black man."
Dun, Dunam

Dur Hebrew: "to pile up" or "to encircle."

Durriken (DOO-ree-ken) English Gypsy: "a fortune-teller."

Durril (DOO-reel) English Gypsy: "the gooseberry."
Dur, Durrill

Dusan Serbo-Croatian form of Daniel, "God is my judge." See Daniel.

Dustin Old German: "a fighter." Dustin has become popular in the United States in recent years, possibly because of actor Dustin Hoffman.
Dust, Dustie, Dusty

Dwight Old Dutch: "blond or white."

Dyami (dee-AH-mee) North American Indian: "an eagle."

Dylan Old Welsh: "son of the wave" or "of the sea." In Welsh mythology Dylan the Dark was the son of the sea. Famous namesakes: poet Dylan Thomas; singer Bob Dylan.

Dyre (DEE-re or anglicized to dire) Norse: "dear" or "precious." Very popular in Norway.

------------------ E ------------------

Edan Celtic: "fire." Might be used for a boy born under one of the fire signs: Aries, Leo, or Sagittarius.

Eddy Scandinavian: "unresting." Also a short form of Edward, "wealthy guardian," or Edgar, "wealthy spearman."

Edgar Old English: "wealthy spearman."
Ed, Eddie, Eddy, Ned, Neddy, Ted, Teddy (English); *Edko, Edus* (Czech); *Edgard* (French, Hungarian, Russian); *Edgardo* (Italian, Spanish); *Edgars* (Latvian); *Edek, Garek* (Polish)

Edik Russian form of Edward, "wealthy guardian."

Edison Old English: "Edward's son."
   Ed, Eddie, Eddy, Edisen, Edson

Edmond Old English: "wealthy protector." Used in Germany,
   France, Poland, Rumania, Russia, and the United States.
   Ed, Eddie, Eddy, Edmon, Ned, Neddy, Ted, Teddy
   (English); *Esmond* (French); *Odi, Odon* (Hungarian);
   Eamon (Irish); *Edmondo* (Italian); *Edmunds* (Latvian);
   Mundek (Polish); *Edmon, Edmond* (Russian); *Edmundo,
   Mundo* (Spanish)

Edward Old English: "wealthy guardian." The most popu-
   lar form of this name in the world is Eduard, used in
   Czechoslovakia, Germany, Estonia, Poland, Rumania,
   Russia, Holland, Canada, England, and the United
   States.
   Ed, Eddie, Eddy, Ned, Neddy, Ted, Teddy (English);
   Edko, Edus, Edo, Edvard (Czech); *Edouard* (French);
   Edvard (Hungarian); *Edoardo, Eduards* (Italian); *Ed,
   Edek, Edzio* (Polish); *Eduardo, Duarte* (Portuguese);
   Edgard (Rumanian); *Edvard* (Swedish, Danish)

Einar Old Norse: "individualist" or "nonconformist." One
   of the most popular names in Norway and Iceland.
   Inar (English); *Ejnar* (Danish)

Elan (EH-lahn) North American Indian: "friendly."

Eldridge German: "mature counselor"; or Anglo-Saxon:
   "fearful and terrible."

Elek Short Hungarian form of Alexander, "helper and
   defender of mankind." Also a Polish variation of
   Aurek, "golden-haired."

Eli Hebrew: "Jehovah" or "the highest One."
   Eloy, Ely

Elia Zuni Indian form of Elijah, "Jehovah is my God."
   See also Ellis.

Elkan Hebrew: "he belongs to God."

Elki (EL-kee) Miwok Indian *elkini*: "to hang over" or "to
   hang on top of." The connotation is "bear hanging

intestines of people on top of bushes or rocks." The meaning may refer to an event in the father's or mother's past.

Ellery Middle English: "from the island of the elder trees."
Ellary, Ellerey

Elliott Hebrew and French: "Jehovah is my God."
Eliot, Elliot

Ellis Hebrew: "Jehovah is my God." Popular modern form of the older name Elijah.
Elias, Elis (English); *Elias, Elya, Ilja* (Czech); *Elie, Elihu* (French); *Elias* (German, Hungarian, Dutch, Portuguese, Spanish); *Elek, Eliasz* (Polish); *Elihu* (Swedish); *Eli, Elias, Elija, Elihu* (Yiddish)

Ellison Old English: "the son of Ellis."
Elison, Elson

Elman German: "like an elm tree."
Elmen

Elrad (AHL-rahd) Hebrew: "God rules."
Rad, Radd

Elsu (EHL-soo) Miwok Indian: "falcon flying" as in "falcon circling in the air."

Elton Old English: "from the old estate" or "from the old town." Popular today, possibly because of singer Elton John.

Eman (EH-mahn) Czech form of Manuel, "God be with us." See Manuel.

Emery Old German: "hardworking ruler."
Emerson, Emmery, Emory (English); *Imrich* (Czech); *Imrus* (Hungarian)

Emil Gothic: "industrious"; or Latin: "flatterer." Used in many countries, including Germany, Hungary, Poland, Sweden, Norway, England, Canada, and the United States.
Emilek, Milko, Milo (Czech); *Emile* (French); *Amal*

(German) *Emilio* (Italian, Portuguese, Spanish); *Emils* (Latvian); *Emilian* (Polish)

Eneas (eh-NEH-uhs) Spanish form of the Greek *Aeneas*, "the praised one."

Engelbert Old German: "as bright as an angel."
Bert, Bertie, Berty, Englebert, Ingelbert, Inglebert

Enli (EHN-lee) Dene Indian: "here below dog" and implies "that dog over there." The name originally may have referred to a dog the father or mother spotted shortly after the child was born.

Enoch (ay-NOHK) Hebrew: "educated" or "dedicated."

Enric Rumanian form of Harold.

Erik Old Norse: "ever powerful" or "eternal ruler." One of the most popular names in Denmark, Sweden, and the United States. Also used in Russia.
Erek, Eric, Erick, Ric, Ricki, Ricky (English); *Erich* (Czech, German); *Erico* (Italian, Portuguese); *Eriks* (Latvian, Russian)

Erwin Old English: "friend of the sea" or "white river."
Ervin (Czech); *Ervins* (Latvian); *Erwinek, Inek* (Polish)

Essien (eh-see-EHN) Ochi and Ga, Africa: "sixth-born son."

Ethan Hebrew: "firm and strong."
Etan

Etu (AY-too) North American Indian: "the sun." In astrology the sun governs Leo, the lion.

Eugene Greek: "noble" or "born of good family."
Gene (English); *Eugen, Zenda* (Czech); *Eugen, Eugenius, Eugenios, Evgenios* (German); *Jano, Jenci, Jensi, Jenoe* (Hungarian); *Genek, Genio* (Polish); *Eugeni, Genka, Genya, Yevgeniy, Zheka, Zhenka* (Russian); *Eugenio, Gencho* (Spanish); *Egen* (Swedish, Norwegian)

Evan Old Welsh: "young warrior" or "young bowman." Also a Welsh form of John, "gracious gift of God."
Ev, Evin, Ewan, Owen

Ezra Hebrew: "help." Many Biblical names are derived from this source, including Azrikam, Azur, Azariah, and Ezri.
Esdras (French, Spanish); *Esra* (German); *Ezera* (Hawaiian)

—————————————— F ——————————————

Faber German form of Fabian, "bean grower."

Fabian Latin: "bean grower."
Fabyan (English); *Fabien, Fabert* (French); *Fabio, Fabiano* (Italian); *Fabius* (Latvian, Lithuanian); *Fabek* (Polish); *Fabi, Fabiyan* (Russian)

Fadey Ukrainian form of Thad or Tad, "stouthearted," "courageous."

Fadil (FAH-deel) Arabic: "generous."

Fairleigh Old English: "from the bull meadow" or "from the ram meadow."
Fairlay, Fairlee, Fairlie, Farlay, Farlee, Farley, Farly, Lee, Leigh

Fath Arabic: "victory."

Faxon Teutonic: "long hair."

Fedor (fay-DOHR) Russian form of Theodore, "gift of God" or Francis, "free man."

Feliks Russian form of Felix, "fortunate" or "lucky."

Felipe (feh-LEE-peh) Spanish form of Philip, "lover of horses." See Philip.

Felix Latin: "fortunate" or "lucky."
Feliks (Bulgarian, Polish, Russian); *Fela* (Czech); *Bodog* (Hungarian); *Felo, Pitin, Pito* (Spanish)

Fidel Latin: "faithful and sincere."

Filip (FEE-leep) Popular form of Philip ("lover of horses") used today in Bulgaria, Czechoslovakia, Lithuania,

Poland, Rumania, Russia, Norway, and Sweden. For other forms see Philip.

Finley Irish Gaelic: "small, fair-haired, brave one" or "sunbeam."
Fin, Findlay, Findley, Finley, Finn

Finn Old German: "from Finland"; or "fair-haired, fair-skinned one." Also a short form of Finley.

Fisk Middle English: "fish." The fishes symbolize Pisces.
Fiske

Fitz Old English: "son." Also a short form of names starting with "*Fitz-*."

Fitzgerald Old English: "son of the spear-mighty" or "son of the ruler with a spear."
Fitz, Gerald, Gerrie, Gerry, Jerry

Fletcher Middle English: "arrow featherer." Refers to an archer's skill in putting feathers on his arrows. Appropriate for a child born under Sagittarius, the archer.

Flint Old English: "a stream." The name has come to mean "hard as flint stone."

Flynn Irish Gaelic: "son of the red-haired one."
Flin, Flinn, Flyn

Forbes Irish Gaelic: "prosperous one" or "owner of fields."

Fordel (FOHR-del) English Gypsy: "forgiving."

Forrest Middle English: "forest protector."
Forest, Forester, Forster, Foster

Francis Latin: "free man" or "Frenchman." Popular worldwide.
Fran, Frank, Frankie, Franky (English); *Franc* (Bulgarian); *Frants* (Danish); *Frans* (Finnish); *Francois, Franchot* (French); *Franz, Franzl* (German); *Palani* (Hawaiian); *Francesco* (Italian); *Franio, Franus* (Polish); *Chico, Chicho, Chilo, Chito, Currito, Curro, Farruco, Francisco, Frasco, Frascuelo, Paco, Pacorro,*

Pancho, Panchito, Paquito, Quico (Spanish); *Frans, Franzen* (Swedish, Norwegian)

Frank Old French: "free man." Also a short form of Francis.
Franki, Frankie (English); *Franc* (Bulgarian, French); *Frans* (Finnish); *Franz, Franzl* (German); *Franek, Franus, Franio* (Polish); *Cisco, Franco, Paco* (Spanish)

Frazer Old English: "curly-haired"; or Old French: "a strawberry."
Fraser, Frasier, Fraze, Frazier

Fred A short form of names containing *fred*, such as Alfred, Frederick, etc.

Frederick Old German: "peaceful ruler." With its many forms, this has been one of the most popular boys' names in the world for some two hundred years.
Fred, Freddie, Freddy, Frederic, Fredric, Fredrick, Fritz, Ric, Rick, Rickie, Ricky (English); *Bedrich, Fridrich* (Czech); *Friedel, Friedrich, Fredi, Fritz, Fritzchen* (German); *Federico, Federigo* (Italian); *Fredek* (Polish); *Fridrich* (Russian); *Federico, Federoquito, Fico, Lico* (Spanish); *Frederik, Fritz* (Swedish)

Fritz Short form of Frederick, "peaceful ruler." See Frederick.

Fynn Ghanaian: "the River Offin." Many Ghanaian names come from rivers, rocks, mountains, trees, animals, and other elements in nature.

G

Gabi Hebrew: "God is my strength." This is a modern Israeli form of Gabriel.

Gabriel Hebrew: "God's hero" or "God is my strength." Popular in the United States, Germany, Czechoslovakia, France, Spain, and many other countries.
Gab, Gabe, Gabie, Gabby (English); *Gavril* (Bulgarian,

Russian); *Gabko, Gabo, Gabris, Gabys* (Czech); *Gabi,*
Gabor (Hungarian); *Gabriele, Gabrielli, Gabriello*
(Italian); *Riel* (Spanish)

Gadi (GAH-dee) Arabic: "my fortune." Common today in
Israel.
Gadiel

Gale Old English: "gay and lively"; or Irish Gaelic:
"stranger."
Gael, Gail, Gayle

Galen Irish Gaelic: "little bright one."
Gale, Gayle (English); *Galeno* (Spanish)

Galt Old Norse: "high ground." Popular in Norway.

Galvin Irish Gaelic: "a sparrow" or "brightly white."
Gal, Galvan, Galven

Gan Vietnamese: "to be near."

Gannon Irish Gaelic: "fair-skinned."

Garai (GAH-rah-ee) Mashona, Rhodesia: "to be settled."

Garridan (GAH-ree-duhn) English Gypsy: "you hid."

Garth Old Norse: "enclosure" or "protection" or "from
the garden." Popular in Scandinavia and the United
States.

Gary Old English *gari*: "a spearman."
Gari, Garey, Garri, Garry

Gaspar (gahs-PAHR) Persian: "master of the treasure." A
Spanish form of Casper.

Gavin Old Welsh: "white hawk" or "from the hawk field."
Gav, Gavan, Gaven, Gawain, Gawen

Gavril (gahv-REEL) Russian form of Gabriel, "God's hero"
or "God is my strength."

George Latin: "farmer" or "land worker."
Georgi, Georgie, Georgy, Jorge (English); *Georg, Georgi*
(Bulgarian); *Durko, Jur, Juraz, Jiri, Jurko, Juro, Jurik*

(Czech); *Georges* (French); *Jeorg, Juergen, Jurgen* (German); *Georgios, Giorgis, Giorgos, Gogos* (Greek); *Jurgis* (Lithuanian); *Jurek* (Polish); *Egor, Georgiy, Jurgi, Yegor, Yura, Yurchik, Yurik, Yusha, Yurko, Zhorka* (Russian); *Jorge, Jorrin, Yoyi* (Spanish); *Georg, Goran, Joergen, Jorgen* (Swedish, Norwegian)

Gerald Old German: "spear brave" or "spear strong."
Gerhard, Gerrard, Gerry, Jerry (English); *Geralde, Geraud, Giraud, Girauld* (French); *Gellart, Gellert* (Hungarian); *Geraldo, Giraldo* (Italian); *Gerek* (Polish); *Garald, Garold, Garolds, Kharald* (Russian); *Geraldo* (Spanish)

Gerhard Scandinavian form of Gerald, "spear brave" or "spear strong."

Gerik (GAI-rik) Polish form of Edgar, "wealthy spearman."

Germain Middle English: "a sprout" or "a bud." Also for girls.
Germaine, Jermain, Jermaine, Jermayne

Giamo (JAH-mo) Italian form of James.

Gibor (gee-BOHR) Hebrew: "strong." Modern Israeli name.

Gideon Hebrew: "a destroyer" or "feller of trees." In the Bible Gideon was a judge who delivered the Israelites from captivity and ruled Israel for forty years.
Gedeon (Bulgarian, French); *Gideone* (Italian); *Hedeon* (Russian)

Gil Spanish form of Giles, "young goat," or "youthful, downy-bearded one."

Gilad Arabic: "a camel hump." Especially popular in Israel.
Giladi, Gilead

Giles Greek: "young goat" or Old French: "youthful, downy-bearded one." Saint Giles was the patron saint of beggars.
Gilles (French); *Egidius* (German, Dutch); *Gil* (Spanish)

Gillie English Gypsy: "a song."

Ginton (geen-TOHN or anglicized to GIN-tuhn) Hebrew: "a garden." Modern Israeli form of the original Hebrew name Ginson.

Giovanni Favorite Italian form of John, "gracious gift of God."

Givon (gee-VOHN) Hebrew: "hill or heights." Most common today in Israel.

Goel (go-AYL or anglicized to rhyme with *Joel*) Hebrew: "the redeemer."

Goran Scandinavian form of George, "farmer" or "land worker." Popular today in Sweden.

Gorman Irish Gaelic: "little, blue-eyed one" or "man of clay."

Gosheven (go-SHAY-ven) North American Indian: "the great leaper."

Gowon (GO-wohn) Tiv, Nigeria: "rainmaker." In Africa, where this name originated, the name is given to a child born during a storm.

Gozal (go-SAHL) Hebrew: "a bird."

Graham Old English: "dweller in the gray land or gray home."
Graeham, Gram

Grant Middle English: "great."

Gray Popular short form of Grayson, "the bailiff's son."

Grayson Middle English: "the bailiff's son."
Gray, Grey, Greyson

Greg Short form of Gregory now used as a full given name.

Gregory Latin: "watchful one."
Greg, Gregg, Greggory (English); *Grigor, Grigoi* (Bulgarian); *Gregoire* (French); *Gregorios, Grigorios* (Greek); *Gregorio* (Italian, Portuguese, Spanish); *Gregors* (Latvian); *Gries* (Swedish)

Guido Spanish form of Guy, "life."

Gunnar Icelandic and Norwegian form of Gunther.

Gunther Old Norse: "warrior" or "battle army."
Gun, Guntar, Gunter, Gunthar (English); *Gunter* (French);
Gunter, Guenter, Guenther (German); *Guntero* (Italian);
Gunnar (Norwegian, Icelandic)

Gur (goor) Hebrew: "lion cub." Many Israeli names come
from this root, including Guri ("my lion cub"); Guriel
("God is my lion" or "God is my strength and
protection"), and Gurion ("a lion"), connoting strength.
In astrology the lion is the symbol of the sign Leo.

Gus Greek form of Constantine, "firm and constant."

Gustaf (goo-STAHF) Swedish: "staff of the Goths" or
"God's staff." Especially popular in Sweden.
Gus, Gussie, Gussy, Gustave, Gustus (English); *Gustav,
Gusti, Gustik, Gusty* (Czech); *Gustaff* (Dutch); *Kosti*
(Finnish); *Gustav* (French, German, Rumanian); *Gustavo*
(Italian); *Gustavs* (Latvian); *Gustavo, Tabo, Tavo* (Spanish)

Guy Latin: "life"; or Old German: "a warrior."
Guyon (English); *Gui, Guy, Vitus* (French); *Guido*
(Spanish, Italian)

Guyapi (goo-YAH-pee) North American Indian: "candid."

Gyasi (JAH-see) Akan, Ghana: "wonderful child."

---------------------------- **H** ----------------------------

Habib (hah-BEEB) Arabic: "beloved." A favorite in Tunisia
and Syria and popular in all Moslem countries.

Hadad (hah-DAHD) Arabic: "the Syrian god of virility."
Adad

Hadden Old English: "child of the heather-filled valley"
or "child from the heather hill."
Haddan, Haddon

Hadley Old English: "child from the heather meadow."
Hadlee, Hadleigh, Lee, Leigh

Hadrian Popular Swedish form of Adrian, "dark one."
See Adrian for other forms.

Hahnee (HAH-nee) North American Indian: "a beggar."
Originally bestowed by the Indians to fool evil spirits
into thinking the child was unloved and hence not
worth bothering with.

Haidar (HIGH-dahr) Arabic: "lion." Used in India and
Moslem countries.

Hakan (hah-KAHN) North American Indian: "fiery."

Hakeem (HA-keem or hah-KEEM) Arabic: "wise." One
of the ninety-nine qualities of God listed in the Koran.
Hakim

Hakem (HA-kem) Arabic: "ruler." In Algeria, Afghanistan,
Iran, Iraq, Jordan, Saudi Arabia, Yemen, and many
other countries, Hakem is also a title name meaning
"governor."

Hakim Ethiopian: "doctor."

ARABIC OCCUPATION AND
TITLE NAMES

Arabs often use names denoting a father's occupation.
Among these occupation names are:

Wakil ("lawyer"), Dabir ("secretary"), Khatib ("religious
   minister"), Haddad ("smith"), Ferran ("baker"), Kateb
   ("writer"), Khoury ("priest"), and Samman ("grocer").
Title names are also common. Among them: Rais ("cap-
   tain"), Wazir ("minister"), Arif ("corporal"), Amid ("general"), Fariq ("lieutenant general") and Zaim ("briga-
   dier general").

Hakon Old Norse: "of the high or exalted race." Many Norwegian kings have had this name.
Haakon, Hako (Norse)

Hale Old English: "from the hall" or "a healthy hero." Also a Hawaiian form of Harold, "army ruler." See Harold.

Halian (hah-lee-AHN) Zuni Indian: "belonging to Julius." Julian is the English equivalent.

Halil (huh-LIL) Turkish: "intimate friend."

Halim (hah-LEEM or HAH-leem) Arabic: "mild," "gentle," or "patient." Popular in Saudi Arabia, Iran, Jordan, Egypt, Turkey, and other Moslem countries.

Hamal (HA-mal or hah-MAHL) Arabic: "lamb." Hamal is also a bright star in the constellation Aries, the ram, and so appropriate for an Aries child.

Hamid Favorite form of Muhammad in Iran and other Moslem countries.

Hamilton Old English: "from the proud or home-lover's estate."
Hamel, Hamil, Hamill, Tony

Hamlin Old English: "lover of home."

Hanan (hah-NAHN) Hebrew: "God is gracious" or "gracious gift of God." Modern Hebrew form of John.

Hanif (HAH-neef or hah-NEEF) Arabic: "true believer (in the Moslem religion)."

Hank A familiar form of Henry; see Henry.

Hans Scandinavian and German form of John, "gracious gift of God." See John.

Hanuman (hah-noo-MAHN) Hindi: "the monkey chief." A Hindu monkey chief and one of the favorite characters in Hindu literature, Hanuman could fly, and many stories are told about his fantastically long tail. Once Hanuman was sent by the god Rama to fetch some healing herbs from a mountain before the moon rose. When the monkey god could not find the herbs, he carried the whole mountain back to his master. Uprooting the mountain took him so long, he could not finish the job before the moon came up, so Hanuman ate the moon and coughed it up again when he replaced the mountain.

Harb Arabic: "war."

Harel (hah-RAYL) Hebrew: "God's mountain." Currently popular in Israel.

Hari (HAH-ree) Hindi: "tawny." Hari is another name for the Hindu god Vishnu, the protector in the Hindu triad. A common variant is Haridas, the -*das* suffix indicating humility and complete subjection to Hari.

Harith (HA-rith or hah-REETH) Arabic: "ploughman."
Harithah (Arabic)

Harley Teutonic: "archer" or "deer hunter"; or Old English: "from the rabbit pasture." Appropriate for a Sagittarius child.

Harold Old Norse: "army ruler." Used in the United States, France, Bulgaria, Germany, Hungary, and Norway. Spelled *Harald*, this name is very popular in Denmark and Sweden.
Hal, Harry (English); *Jindra* (Czech); *Arry* (French); *Henrik* (Hungarian); *Aralt* (Irish); *Araldo, Aroldo, Arrigo* (Italian); *Haralds* (Latvian); *Haroldas* (Lithuanian); *Heronim, Hieronim* (Polish); *Haroldo* (Portuguese); *Enric* (Rumanian); *Garald, Garold, Gerahd* (Russian); *Harailt* (Scottish); *Haraldo* (Spanish)

Haroun (hah-ROON) Arabic form of Aaron, "lofty" or "exalted." See Aaron.

Harrison Old English: "Harry's son." Made well known by actor Harrison Ford.
Harris, Harrisen

Hasad (huh-SUHD) Turkish: "harvest" or "reaping."

Hashim (HA-shim or hah-SHEEM) Arabic: "broker" or "destroyer (of evil)." Hashim was a descendant of the Prophet Muhammad. Popular in Moslem countries.

Hasin (hah-seen) Hindi: "laughing."

Haskel Hebrew: "wisdom" or "understanding." Also a short form of Ezekiel, "strength."
Haskell

Hassan (HA-san) Arabic: "handsome." Among traditional Moslems, children of the same family often receive similar names. Hence, one family might have a Hassan, Muhassan, Husain, Khalid, Khallad, and Makhlad, all of which come from the word *salima*, "to be safe." The Hausa of Nigeria give this name to a first-born male twin; the second twin, if a boy, is named Husseini.

Hassel Teutonic: "a man from Hassall (the witches' corner)" or "one who lives near a hazel tree."
Hassal, Hassall, Hassell

Hastin (hah-steen) Hindi: "elephant." The name refers to a legendary hero in Hindu mythology who was born in an elephant lake.

Hayden Old English: "son of the rose-hedged valley."

Hedeon (heh-DAY-ohn) Russian form of Gideon, "destroyer" or "tree cutter." See Gideon.

Helaku (heh-LAH-koo) North American Indian: "sunny day."

Helki (HEHL-kee) Miwok Indian *hele*: "to touch." The connotation is "jacksnipe digging into the ground with its bill."

Heman (HAY-man) Hebrew: "faithful."

Henry Old German *heri-mann*: "ruler of a home or estate" or "heir"; or Latin *herminius*: "a person of high rank."
Hagan, Hal, Hank, Harry, Hendrik, Henri (English); *Henri, Henrim* (Bulgarian); *Hinrich, Jindra, Jindrich*

(Czech); *Henri* (French); *Heiner, Heinrich, Heinz, Hinrich* (German); *Bambis, Enrikos, Haralpos, Khambis, Kharlambos, Lambos* (Greek); *Hanraoi* (Irish); *Henrik* (Hungarian, Finnish); *Arrigo, Enrico, Enzio* (Italian); *Heniek, Henier, Honok* (Polish); *Henrique* (Portuguese); *Enric* (Rumanian); *Enrique, Kiki, Quico, Quinto, Quiqui* (Spanish); *Hersz* (Yiddish)

Hersh Yiddish: "a deer." Used today in Israel as well as the United States.
Hersch, Herschel, Herzl, Hirsch, Hirschel

Hilary Latin: "cheerful." Also used today for girls.
Hilery, Hillary, Hillery

Hilel (hi-LEL) Arabic: "the new moon." Arabic nature name. In astrology the moon governs the sign of Cancer, the moon card in the tarot pack corresponds to the sign of Pisces.

Hilmar Old Norse: "famous noble." Scandinavian name.

Hilton Old English: "from the town or estate on the hill."

Hinun (hee-NOON) North American Indian: "god of clouds and rain."

Hiroshi (hee-RO-shee) Japanese: "generous."

Hisoka (hee-SO-kah) Japanese: "secretive" or "reserved."

Ho Chinese: "the good."

Hod Hebrew: "vigorous" or "splendid." Used in Israel.

Hogan Irish Gaelic: "youthful one."

Holic (HO-lik) Czech: "barber." Czech occupation name.

Holleb "like a dove" or "one who lives at the sign of the dove," a symbol of peace. Used in Poland and Germany.
Hollub, Holub

Hollis Icelandic: "of the great hall" or "island man"; or Old English: "from the grove of holly trees."

Holt Old English: "son of the unspoiled forests."

Honon Miwok Indian: "bear."

Honovi (ho-NO-vee) North American Indian: "strong."

Hototo (ho-TO-to) North American Indian: "the whistler."

MIWOK INDIAN BEAR NAMES

The Miwok Indians of California have a special fondness for naming babies after the bear, the most powerful animal of the forest. Among these many colorful Miwok Indian bear names are:

ANAWUYE–"stretching a bear's hide to let it dry."

ESEGE–"bear showing its teeth when cross."

HATAWA–"bear breaking the bones of people or animals."

HOHO–"bear growing."

HULWEMA–"dead grizzly which has been shot and killed."

HUSLU–"bear with lots of hair."

LIWANU–"bear growling" (from *liwani*, "to talk").

NOTAKU–"growling of a bear as someone passes by."

SEWATI–"curving of the bear's claws."

TUKETU–"bear making dust as it runs."

UTATCI–"bear scratching itself."

YELUTCI–"bear traveling through brush and over rocks without making a sound."

For other Miwok Bear names, see Elki and Honon in the boys' name list and Sapata and the accompanying box in the girls' list.

Howe Middle English: "hill"; or Old German: "high or eminent one."

Howi Miwok Indian: "turtledove."

Howin Chinese: "a loyal swallow." Oriental nature name.

Hubert Old German: "brilliant mind" or "brilliant spirit."
Bert, Bertie, Berty, Hobart, Hubbard, Hube, Huber, Hubie, Huey, Hugh, Hugo (English); *Hubert, Hubertek, Berty* (Czech); *Berdy* (Russian); *Berto, Hubi, Huberto, Uberto* (Spanish)

Hugh Old English: "intelligent one." Also a short form of Hubert.
Huey, Hughie (English); *Hugo* (Danish, Dutch, German, Spanish, Swedish); *Hugon* (Spanish)

Hugo Popular international form of Hugh, "intelligent one."

Hunt Old English: "the hunt." Also short for all boys' names beginning with *Hunt-*.

Hunter Old English: "hunter."
Hunt

Huntington Old English: "the hunters' estate."
Hunt

Hurley Irish Gaelic: "child of the sea and tides." Appropriate for a boy born under one of the water signs: Pisces, Cancer, or Scorpio.
Hurlee, Hurleigh

Husain (hoo-SAYN) Arabic: "little beauty." Hussein was a descendant of the Prophet Muhammad.
Hussein

Hute (HOO-te) North American Indian: "star." Indian name for a star in the handle of the constellation Ursa Major, also known as the Big Dipper.

Huxley Old English: "from Hugh's meadow."
Hux, Lee, Leigh

———————————— I ————————————

Ian Scotch form of John, "gracious gift of God."

Ibrahim Arabic form of the Hebrew Abraham, "father of a mighty nation." One of the most popular Moslem names in Turkey, Iran, India, Arabia, Egypt, and Jordan. The patriarch appears in both the Old Testament and the Koran.

Igasho (ee-GAH-sho) North American Indian: "a wanderer."

Ilias (ee-LEE-ahs) Modern Greek form of Elijah, "Jehovah is my God."

Ilom (ee-LOHM) Ibo, Nigeria: "my enemies are many." Ilom is an abbreviated form of the longer name Ilomerika.

Inger Old Norse: "son's army." Popular today in Scandinavia.
Ingar

Ingmar Old Norse: "famous son." Popular in Scandinavia, especially Sweden. Namesake: filmmaker Ingmar Bergman.
Ingamar, Ingemar

Iniko (ee-NEE-ko) Efek, Ibo, Southern Nigeria: "time of trouble." In Africa this name is given to a child born during a time of civil war, invasion, or other disaster.

Inteus (een-TAY-oos) North American Indian: "he shows his face." In other words, he is not ashamed.

Ioakim (ee-o-AH-keem) Russian form of the Hebrew name Joachim, "God will establish."
Akim, Iov, Jov, Yov (Russian)

Ira Hebrew: "watchful one" or "descendants."

Isaac Hebrew: "he will laugh." Isaac was the most popular
   Jewish name during the twelfth century. Its popularity
   gradually dwindled until it was seldom used. But today
   the name is appearing more frequently, particularly in
   the United States.
   Ike, Ikey, Ikie (English); *Isak* (Bulgarian, Swedish,
   Norwegian, Russian); *Izak* (Czech); *Isaak* (German,
   Greek); *Aizik, Icek, Isaak, Izik, Yitzhak* (Yiddish)

Isak Form of Isaac, "he will laugh," used in Bulgaria,
   Sweden, Norway, Russia, and other countries in the
   world. Also said to be a magical name meaning "identical point," used in incantations to invoke the powers
   of God.

Isas (i-SAHS) Japanese: "meritorious one."

Istu (EES-too) Miwok Indian: "sugar-pine sugar."

Ivan Popular in Russia as a form of John, "gracious gift of
   God." See John.

Ivar (EE-vahr) Old Norse: "yew-bow army." Popular in
   Sweden.
   Iver, Ivor (English); *Yvor* (Russian)

Ives Old English: "son of the yew bow" or "little archer."
   Appropriate for a boy born under Sagittarius, the archer.
   Yves (French)

Ivon (ee-vohn) Teutonic: "archer."
   Yvon

Iye (EE-yeh) North American Indian: "smoke."

--------------------------- **J** ---------------------------

Jacinto (hah-SEEN-to or anglicized to jah-SIN-to) Spanish:
   "hyacinth." The feminine form is Jacinta.

Jackson Old English: "Jack's son."
   Jack, Jackie, Jacky, Jakson

Jacob Hebrew *Ya'aqob:* "the supplanter."
Cob, Cobb, Jake, Jakie, Jakob (English); *Ikov* (Bulgarian); *Jakub, Jokubas, Kuba, Kubes, Kubik, Kubo* (Czech); *Jacques, Jacquet* (French); *Jacob, Jakob, Jockel* (German); *Iakov, Iakobos, Iakovos* (Greek); *Jakab, Kobi* (Hungarian); *Giacobbe, Giacomo, Giacopo* (Italian); *Jeks, Jeska* (Latvian); *Jecis, Jekebs, Jokubas* (Lithuanian); *Jakub, Jakubek, Jalu, Kuba, Kubus* (Polish); *Jaco, Jaime* (Portuguese); *Jakov, Jasha, Jakiv, Yakov, Yanka, Yashko* (Russian); *Jacobo* (Spanish)

Jacques French form of Jacob, "the supplanter."

Jacy North American: "the moon." In Tupi-Guarani legend, Jacy, the moon, is the creator of all plant life. The name can also refer to the planet Venus.

Jael (yah-AYL) Hebrew: "mountain goat." Used in Israel as well as the United States. Also a girls' name.

Jafar (jah-fahr) "a little stream." Contemporary Moslem name popular in India.

Jagger North English: "to carry things in a cart" or "carter." Gaining popularity in the United States, possibly because of singer Mick Jagger.

Jahi (JAH-hee) Swahili: "dignity."

Jaime One of the most popular names in Portuguese- and Spanish-speaking countries. A form of James, "the supplanter." See also Jacob.

Jake Popular contemporary form of Jacob, "the supplanter."

Jakob A favorite form of Jacob in Denmark. Also used in other Scandinavian countries, the United States, and Germany.

Jal English Gypsy: "he goes." Referring to a wanderer.

Jamal Arabic: "handsome." See Jamil.

James Hebrew: "the supplanter." Originally an English form of Jacob. One of the most popular names in the world. For other forms, see Jacob.

Jamie, Jaymie, Jim, Jimmie, Jimmy (English); *Seamus* (Irish); *Giamo* (Italian); *Diogo, Jaco, Jaime, Jayme, Tiago* (Portuguese); *Chago, Chango, Chanti, Diego, Dieguito, Jaime, Jaimito, Jayme, Santiago, Tiago* (Spanish)

Jamie Once a nickname for James, now popular as an independent name in the United States.

Jamil (jah-MEEL) Arabic: "handsome."
Jamal, Jameel

Jan Popular Slavic and Dutch form of John, "gracious gift of God." One of the most common Christian names in Slavic countries. See John.

Jared Hebrew: "the descendant" or "one who gains an inheritance." Popular contemporary U.S. name.

Jarek (YAH-rek or anglicized to JAIR-ik) Polish form of Janus, "born in January."

Jaron (YAH-rohn or anglicized to JAIR-uhn, to rhyme with *Aaron*) "to cry out" or "to sing."

Jaroslav (YAH-ro-slahf or anglicized to JAIR-o-slav) Slavic: "glory of spring." One of the most popular names in Czechoslovakia.

Jarvis Old German: "keen with a spear" or "a leader in war."
Jervis

Jason Greek: "a healer." Jason was the author of the book Ecclesiasticus and a kinsman of Saint Paul, who was persecuted. Some name experts believe Jason was an English translator's form of a Greek name, which in turn was a form of the Hebrew Joshua or Jesus.

Jasper Old French: "the jasper stone" or a form of Casper, "master of the treasure."

Javas (JAH-vahs) Sanskrit: "swift" or "quick." Used in India and the United States.

Javier (hah-vee-AIR) Spanish (Basque): "owner of the new house"; or Arabic: "bright."

Javin (jah-VEEN or JA-vin to rhyme with *Gavin*) English form of the Hebrew name Yarin, "to understand" or "understanding one."

Jawhar (jah-oo-HAR) Arabic: "jewel" or "essence."

Jay Old French: "blue jay."

Jayme Contemporary Spanish form of James, "the supplanter."

Jean French development of John, "gracious gift of God." By far the most popular boys' name in France.

Jed Arabic: "the hand." Also a modern short form of the older name Jedediah, "beloved by the Lord."

Jedrek (YED-rik or anglicized to JED-rik) Polish form of Andrew, "strong and manly." See Andrew.

Jeff Modern short form of Jeffrey, "divinely powerful one."

Jeffrey Old French: "divinely powerful one."
Geoffrey, Jeff, Jefferey, Jeffry, Jeffy (English); *Geoffroi, Geoffroy, Jeoffroi* (French); *Gottfried* (German); *Gottfrid* (Hungarian); *Geoffredo, Giotto* (Italian); *Gotfrids* (Latvian); *Fotfryd, Fred* (Polish); *Geofri, Godoired* (Rumanian); *Gotfrid* (Russian); *Bogomir* (Serbian); *Fredo, Godofredo, Gofredo* (Spanish)

Jeks Modern Latvian form of Jacob, "the supplanter." See Jacob.

Jens Popular Swedish, Norwegian, and Danish form of John, "gracious gift of God." See John.

Jeremy Hebrew: "appointed by God." A contemporary form of Jeremiah.
Jem, Jemmie, Jemmy, Jerr, Jerrie, Jerry (English); *Jeremias* (Dutch, Finnish, German, Portuguese, Spanish); *Jereme, Jeremie* (French); *Ember, Jeremiah, Katone,*

Nemet (Hungarian); *Geremia* (Italian); *Jeremija, Yeremey* (Russian); *Jeremia* (Swedish)

Jerome Latin: "holy name."
Gerome, Gerrie, Gerry, Jerrome, Jerrie, Jerry

Jerry Popular contemporary short form of Gerald, Jeremy, and Jerome.
Jere, Jerrie

Jesse Hebrew: "wealthy one."
Jess, Jessie, Jessy

Jibben English Gypsy: "life." Similiar is the English Gypsy name Jivvel, "he lives."

Jim A short form of James, "the supplanter."
Jimmie, Jimmy

Jin Chinese: "gold." The name is occasionally used by Chinese astrologers if a child's horoscope is found to have too many wood influences. It is thought such names can overcome the evil in the stars because metal conquers wood.

Jiro (ji-RO) Japanese: "the second male."

Jivin (jee-veen or anglicized to JI-vin) East Indian: "to give life."

Jo Japanese form of the Biblical Joseph, "God will increase."

Joab Hebrew: "praise the Lord."

Jock A familiar form of Jacob ("the supplanter") and John ("gracious gift of God").
Jocko

Jody Popular modern short form of Joseph, "God will increase."
Jodi, Jodie

Joe Short form of Joseph, "God will increase."
Joey

Joel Hebrew: "God is willing" or "Jehovah is the Lord." In the Bible Joel was a Hebrew prophet.

Johan (YO-hahn) One of the most popular names in Scandinavia, a Scandinavian form of John.

John Hebrew *Yohanan:* "gracious gift of God" or "God is gracious." The most common first name in the Western world, John owes its popularity to the fact that two people associated with Christ—John the Baptist and John the Apostle—had this name.
Jack, Jacki, Jackie, Jock, Johan, Johnie, Johnnie, Johnny, Jon, Jonni, Jonnie, Jonny, Zane (English); *Hovhannes* (Armenian); *Iban* (Basque); *Johan* (Bavarian); *Jan, Jehan* (Belgian); *Ioan, Ivan* (Bulgarian); *Hanus, Honza, Ianos, Jan, Janco, Janek, Jano, Jenda* (Czech); *Hans, Jan* (Danish); *Johan* (Estonian); *Hannes, Hannu, Janne, Juhana, Juho, Jukka, Jussi* (Finnish); *Jean, Jeannot, Jehan* (French); *Haensel, Hans, Hansel, Hansl, Johann, Johannes* (German); *Giannes, Giannis, Giannos, Ioannes, Ioannis,* (Greek); *Jancsi, Jani, Janika, Janko, Janos* (Hungarian); *Sean, Seann, Shane* (Irish); *Gian, Gianetto, Giannini, Giovanni, Vanni* (Italian); *Joba, Jofan* (Lapp); *Jonas, Jonelis, Jonukas, Jonutis* (Lithuanian); *Jens, Johan* (Norwegian); *Jehan* (Persian); *Ignac, Iwan, Jan, Janek, Jankiel, Jas, Jasio* (Polish); *Joao* (Portuguese); *Iancu, Ioan, Ionel* (Rumanian); *Ioann, Ivan, Ivanchik, Ivano, Ivas, Vanek, Vanka, Vanko, Vanya, Yanka* (Russian); *Ian* (Scottish); *Juan, Juanch, Juancho, Juanito* (Spanish); *Hans, Hansel, Hasse, Hazze, Jan, Jens, Johan, Jonam* (Swedish); *Ohannes* (Turkish); *Evan, Jone* (Welsh); *Yochanan* (Yiddish)

Joji (JO-ji) Japanese form of George, "farmer."

Jolon (JO-lohn) North American Indian: "valley of the dead oaks."

Jon Contemporary short form of John or Jonathan.

Jonah Hebrew: "dove." In the Bible Jonah was swallowed by a whale.
Jonas (English, French, Spanish, Swedish, Icelandic); *Giona, Guiseppe* (Italian); *Iona, Yona* (Russian)

Jonathan Popular in the United States, from Hebrew, "gracious gift of God." See John.
Johnathan, Johnathon, Jon, Jonathon

Jone Welsh form of John, "gracious gift of God."

Jordan Hebrew: "descender," or "flowing downward."
Jordon, Jori, Jory (English); *Jourdain* (French); *Jared* (Hebrew); *Giordana* (Italian)

Jorge Spanish form of George, "farmer" or "land worker." See George.

Jori (JO-ree or YO-ree) Contemporary U.S. and Hebrew form of Jordan, "descender."

Joseph Hebrew: "God will increase," in the sense that "He shall add to His powers."
Jodi, Jodie, Jody, Joe, Joey, Jojo (English); *Iosif, Yosif* (Bulgarian); *Josef, Joza, Jozef, Jozka, Pepa, Pepik* (Czech); *Joosef, Jooseppi* (Finnish); *Josephe* (French); *Beppi, Josef, Jupp, Peppi, Sepp* (German); *Iosif* (Greek); *Joska, Joszef, Jozsef, Jozsi* (Hungarian); *Guiseppe, Pino* (Italian); *Jo* (Japanese); *Jazeps* (Latvian); *Josef, Jozio, Juzef, Juziu* (Polish); *Jose, Josef, Zeusef* (Portuguese); *Iosif, Osip, Osya, Yeska, Yesya, Yusif, Yusup, Yuzef* (Russian); *Josep, Josip, Joze, Jozef, Jozhe, Jozhef* (Serbian); *Che, Cheche, Chepe, Chepito, Jobo, Jose, Josecito, Joseito, Joselito, Pepe, Pepillo, Pepin, Pepito, Pipo* (Spanish); *Yusuf* (Swahili); *Josef* (Swedish, Norwegian); *Osip* (Ukrainian); *Josef, Yousef* (Yiddish)

Josha (JO-shuh) East Indian: "satisfaction."

Joshua Hebrew *Yoyoshua:* "God of salvation."
Josh (English); *Josue* (French); *Josua* (German); *Jozsua* (Hungarian); *Giosia* (Italian); *Joaquim* (Portuguese); *Iosua* (Rumanian); *Joaquin, Josue* (Spanish); *Josua* (Swedish); *Yehosha* (Yiddish)

Jotham Hebrew: "God is perfect."

Jov Short form of the Russian name Ioakim, "God will establish."

Juan (hwahn or wan) A favorite in Spanish-speaking countries, this is a Spanish form of John, "gracious gift of God."

Judd Hebrew: "praised." A modern development of Judah.

Jude Hebrew: "praised." Contemporary Israeli form of the older name Judah.
Juda, Judas, Judd

Jules Modern short form of Julius, used in the United States and France. Made famous by writer Jules Verne.

Julian Latin: "one belonging to Julius." Popular in Spanish-speaking countries.
Julio (Spanish); *Halian* (Zuni Indian)

Julius Latin: "youthful" or "downy-bearded."
Jule, Jules (English); *Julio* (Spanish)

Jumah (JOO-mah) Swahili: "born on Friday," the holy day in the Moslem religion.
Jimoh, Juma

Jun (joon) Chinese: "truth"; or Japanese: "obedient." Also a girls' name.

Juri (YOO-ree) Estonian form of George, "farmer" or "land worker." See George.

Justin Old French: "upright and just." Popular in the United States, Germany, Czechoslovakia, and France.
Justen, Justis (English); *Iustin* (Bulgarian); *Jusa, Justyn* (Czech); *Just, Justus* (German); *Guistino* (Italian); *Justins, Justs* (Latvian); *Justas, Justinas, Justukas* (Lithuanian); *Inek, Justek, Justyn* (Polish); *Iustin, Ustin, Yusts, Yustyn* (Russian); *Justino, Justo, Tuto* (Spanish); *Justinus* (Swedish, Norwegian)

K

Kabil Turkish: "possessed." The English form of this name is Cain.

Kadar (KAH-dahr) Arabic: "powerful."
Kedar

Kadin (kah-DEEN) Arabic: "friend," "companion," or "confidant."
Kadeen

Kadir (KAH-deer) Arabic: "green" or "green crop (of grain)," connoting freshness and innocence.
Kadeer

Kaga (KAH-gah) North American Indian: "writer" or "chronicler."

Kai (kigh) Hawaiian: "sea" or "seawater." Also for girls.

Kakar (KUH-kuhr) Todas, India: "grass."

Kala (KAH-lah) Hindi: "black" or "time." One of the many names for the Hindu god Siva.

Kalb Arabic form of Caleb, "dog." The name is rarely used in the Arabic world today unless a family has lost many children and is trying to make the evil spirits believe the child is worthless to them.
Kilab (Arabic)

Kale (KAH-le or anglicized to KALE) Hawaiian form of Charles, "strong and manly."

Kaleb Variant spelling of Caleb, "bold and impetuous" or "a dog." See Caleb.

Kalil (kah-LEEL) Arabic: "good friend." In Israel the same name means "crown" or "wealth."
Kahlil, Khaleel, Khalil

Kaliq (KAH-liq) Arabic: "creative." The name refers to a quality of God.

Kalkin (kahl-KEEN or anglicized to KAHL-kin) Hindi: "The god Kalkin." In Hindu literature Kalkin is the tenth incarnation of the god Vishnu and will come during the Age of Darkness. Some Hindu scholars say Kalkin is yet to come, others say he is already here. It is believed that Vishnu as Kalkin, or Kalki, will appear riding a white horse.

Kalle (KAH-le) A favorite in Scandinavia, particularly in Sweden and Finland, Kalle is a form of Charles, "strong and manly." See Charles.

Kalman (KAWL-mahn) Hungarian form of Charles.

Kaloosh (kah-LOOSH) Armenian: "blessed coming" or "blessed advent."

Kamali (kah-MAH-lee) Shona, Southern Rhodesia: "the kamali spirit." Among the Mashona people Kamali is a spirit believed to help a newborn baby live when other children in the village are dying.

Kami (KAH-mee) Hindi: "loving." Another name for Kama, the handsome black Hindu god of love who is said to ride a parrot and carry a bow of sugarcane strung with bees and flower-tipped arrows.

Kamil (kah-MEEL) Arabic: "perfect." One of the ninety-nine qualities of God listed in the Koran. Popular especially among Moslems.
Kameel

Kane Japanese: "golden"; or Hawaiian: "man" or "the eastern sky."

Kaniel (kah-nee-AYL or anglicized to rhyme with *Daniel*) Hebrew: "stalk" or "reed."
Kan, Kani, Kanny

Kantu Hindi: "happy." Another name for Kama or Kami, the Hindu god of love.

Kara (KAH-rah) Banti Eskimo: "broken-fingered one." Nickname for an Eskimo boy who has broken a finger.

Kardal (KAHR-dal) Arabic: "mustard seed."

Kareem (ka-REEM) Arabic: "generous, friendly, precious, and distinguished," often interpreted as simply "generous." Generosity is one of the ninety-nine qualities

of God listed in the Koran. The name is a favorite among Moslems and gaining popularity in the United States, possibly because of basketball player Kareem Abdul-Jabbar.
Karim

Karl Popular German form of Charles, "strong and manly." Also used in Bulgaria, Hungary, and Scandinavia.

Karmel (kahr-MEHL) Hebrew: "vineyard," "garden," or "farm." Used in Israel for boys and girls.

Kaseko (kah-SEH-ko) Shona, Southern Rhodesia: "to mock" or "to ridicule." A Mashona woman who has been scorned because she has no children may proudly name her first born son Kaseko.

Kasib (KA-sib or ka-SEEB) Arabic: "fertile."
Kaseeb

Kasim (kah-SEEM) Arabic: "divided."
Kaseem

Kasimir (KAH-se-mer) Old Slavic: "commands peace."

Kasper Greek: "precious stone"; or Persian: "master of the treasure." Especially popular in Germany. See Casper.

Kass German: "like a blackbird." Popular in Germany.
Kaese, Kasch, Kase

Kayin (kah-YEEN) Yoruba, Nigeria: "celebrated." Name used by the Yoruba for a long-hoped-for child.

Keahi (ke-AH-hee) Hawaiian: "fire." Also a girls' name.

Keb Egyptian: "the Egyptian god Keb." A mystical name from the Egyptian *Book of the Dead*. Keb was an ancient earth god upon whose back grew the world's trees and plants. He is sometimes pictured with a goose on his head and is often called the great cackler because he supposedly laid the egg from which the world sprang. In pyramid texts, he is the god of the dead, representing the earth in which the dead are buried.

Kedar (KEH-dahr) Hindi: "mountain lord." One of the 1,008 names for the Hindu god Siva. See Siva. Also a variation of the Arabic Kadar, "powerful."

Keddy Scottish variation of Adam, "man of the red earth." See Adam.
Keady, Keddie

Kedem (KE-dem) Hebrew: "ancient," "old," or "from the east."

Keegan Irish Gaelic: "little fiery one." Astrological name for a boy born under one of the fire signs: Aries, Leo, or Sagittarius.

Keir Celtic: "dark-skinned."

Keith Irish Gaelic: "one from the battle place"; or Old Welsh: "from the forest."

Kekoa (ke-KO-uh) Hawaiian: "the fire-leafed koa tree on the beautiful green ridges of the Koolau (mountains)." This name is a short form of the long Hawaiian name Kekoalauliionapalihauliuliokekoolau.

Kelby Old German: "from the farm by the spring."
Keelby, Kelbee, Kelbie, Kellby

Kele Hopi Indian: "sparrow hawk." Used by Hopis in the rattlesnake cult.
Kelle

Kelemen (KEL-e-men) Hungarian form of Clement, "gentle" or "kind."

Kelii (ke-LEE) Hawaiian: "the chief."

Kell Old Norse: "from the spring." Might be given to a boy born under one of the water signs: Pisces, Cancer, or Scorpio.

Kelly Irish Gaelic: "a warrior." Also a girls' name.
Kele, Kellen, Kelley

THE LONGEST NAME IN
THE UNITED STATES

Long Hawaiian names often seem peculiar to Americans, but we also have long names in our country. In his book *Treasury of Name Lore*, onologist Elsdon Smith reports the longest name in the United States belonged to a Philadelphian named Hubert Blaine Wolfeschlegelsteinhausenbergerdorff. If pressed, Hubert would explain that his full name was Adolph Blaine Charles David Earl Frederick Gerald Hubert Irvin John Kenneth Lloyd Marin Nero Oliver Paul Quincy Randolph Sherman Thomas Uncas Victor William Xerxes Yancy Zeus Wolfeschlegelsteinhausenbergerdorffvoralternwarengewissenhaftschaferwessenshafswarenwohlgefutternundsorgfalugkeitbeschutzenvorangriefendurchihrraubgierigfeinds, Senior. Imagine trying to squeeze that on a birth certificate.

Kem English Gypsy: "the sun." In astrology the sun rules the sign of Leo.

Ken Short form of Kenneth.

Kenn Old Welsh: "clear, sweet water."

Kenneth Old English: "a royal oath"; or Irish Gaelic: "handsome."
Ken, Kenney, Kenny (English); *Kenya, Kesha* (Russian) *Chencho, Incencio, Inocente* (Spanish)

Kent Old Welsh: "brightly white."

Kerel Afrikaans: "young man."

Kerem (ke-REM) Turkish: "noble and kind."

Kerey (KEH-ree) English Gypsy: "homeward bound."
Keir, Ker, Keri

Kern Irish Gaelic *ceirin:* "little black one."
Kearn, Kerne, Kieran

Kerr Irish Gaelic: "dark one" or "a spear."

Kerry Irish Gaelic: "son of the black one" or simply "black one."
Keary

Kers Todas, India: "the wight plant." The name refers to a plant known to botanists as *eugenia arnottiana*.

Kersen Indonesian: "cherry."

Kerwin Irish Gaelic: "little jet-black one." Used in Ireland and the United States.
Kerwen, Kerwinn, Kirwin

Kesar (keh-SAHR) Russian form of Caesar, "hairy" or "long-haired." Also used in the Ukraine.

Kesin (keh-SEEN) Hindi: "long-haired beggar." A title name occasionally used for a child.

Kesse (KEH-se) Fanti or Ashanti, Africa: "fat at birth."

Kevin Irish Gaelic: "lovable and gentle one."
Kev, Kevan, Keven, Kevvy

Kibbe (KEEB-beh) American Indian, Nayas: "the night bird."

Kijika (kee-YEE-kah or anglicized to ki-JEE-kah) North American Indian: "walks quietly."

Killian Irish Gaelic: "small and warlike."
Kilian, Killie, Killy

Kim Vietnamese: "gold" or "metal"; or Old English: "ruler." In the Orient this name is sometimes given to restore the balance of metal and wood influences in a child's horoscope.

Kin Japanese: "golden."

Kingsley Old English: "one from the king's meadow."
King, Kingsly, Kinsley

Kingston Old English: "from the king's estate."
King, Kinston

Kipp Old English: "one from the pointed hill."
Kip, Kipper, Kippie, Kippy

Kiral (ki-RUHL) Turkish: "king."

Kirby Old Norse: "one from the church village."
Kerby

Kiril (KI-ril) Bulgarian form of Cyril, "lordly."

Kiritan (keer-ee-TAHN) Hindi: "wearing a crown." Another name for the Hindu gods Vishnu and Indra.

Kirk Old Norse: "from the church."

Kistna (KIST-nah) Hindi: "the sacred Kistna River." Also a short form of Krishna, "delightful."

Kistur (KEE-stoor) English Gypsy: "a rider."

Kit Popular short form of Christopher, "Christ-bearer."
Kitt

Kito (KEE-to)—Swahili: "jewel." Implies the child is precious.

Kivi (KEE-vee) Hebrew: "supplant," "protected," or "held by the heel." Used today in Israel as well as the United States.
Akiba, Akiva, Kiva

Kiyoshi (kee-YO-shee) Japanese: "quiet," an admirable Oriental virtue.
Yoshi

Kizza (keez-SAH) Uganda, Africa: "born after twins."

Kliment Russian form of Clement or Clemens, "gentle" or "kind." See Clement.

Knox Old English: "one from the hills."

Knud Danish: "kind." A favorite in Denmark.

Knut Old Norse: "knot." Popular today in Norway and Sweden.
Canute (English); *Knute* (Danish)

Kokudza (ko-KOOD-zah) African: "the child shall not live long." Like many African names, this one reveals a preoccupation with death and may be given to trick the demons into believing no one cares if the child dies.

Kolya Popular pet form of Nicholas ("victorious army" or "victorious people") used in Russia.

Konane (ko-NAH-ne) Hawaiian: "bright as moonlight."

Konni (KO-nee or anglicized to KAHN-nee) German form of Conrad, "bold counselor." See Conrad for other forms.

Kono (KO-no) Miwok Indian: "a tree squirrel biting through the middle of a pine nut."

Kontar (KOHN-tar) Akan, Ghana: "only child."

Korb German: "basket."

Korudon (ko-ROO-dohn) Greek: "helmeted one" or "crested one."
Corydon, Coryell (English)

Kostas (KO-stahs) Modern Greek form of Constantine, "firm and constant." See Dinos.

AMERICAN INDIAN NATURE NAMES

The American Indians have created some of the most detailed, elaborate of all nature names. The very meanings of these names reveal how closely the Indians have observed the natural world. Among these colorful names are: Kalmanu ("lightning striking a tree"), Nikiti ("round and smooth like an abalone shell"), Siwili ("long tail of the fox which drags along the ground"), Tiktcu ("jacksnipe bird digging wild potatoes"), Wenutu ("sky clearing after being cloudy"), and Yotimo ("the yellow jacket carrying pieces of meat from a house to its nest").

Kosti (KO-stee) Finnish form of Gustaf, "staff of the Goths."
See Gustaf.

Kovar (KO-vahr) Czech: "smith."

Krishna Hindi: "delightful."
Kistna, Kistnah, Krisha, Krishnah

Krispin Czech, German, Hungarian, and Slavic form of
Crispus, "curly-haired." See Crispus.

Kriss Contemporary U.S. and Latvian form of Christopher,
"Christ-bearer."

Krister (KREE-ster) Swedish form of Christian, "believer
in Christ, the anointed one." See Christian.

Kristian Form of Christian popular in Russia, Sweden, and
the United States. See Christian.

Kristo Modern Greek form of Christopher, "Christ-bearer."

Kruin (KROO-in) Afrikaans: "top of a tree" or "mountain peak."

Kuper Yiddish: "copper." For a boy with reddish or gold-
en hair.

Kurt German and U.S. form of Conrad, "bold counselor."

Kuzih (KOO-zhi) Carrier Indian: "great talker."

Kwaku (KWAH-koo) Akan, Ghana: "born on Wednesday."

Kwam Zuni Indian form of Juan, which is a Spanish form
of John, "gracious gift of God."

Kwame (KWAH-me) Akan, Ghana: "born on Saturday."
The feminine form is Ama.

Kwamin (KWA-men) Ga, Africa: "born on Saturday."

Kwesi (KWEH-see) Ochi, Africa: "born on Sunday."

Kyle Yiddish: "crowned with laurel," a victory symbol; or
Irish Gaelic: "one from the strait."
Kiel, Kile, Kiley, Ky, Kylie

───────────────── **L** ─────────────────

Laban Hebrew: "white."

Ladd Middle English: "an attendant."
Lad, Laddie, Laddy

Lado (LAH-do) Bari, Southern Sudan: "second-born boy.'
Common among the Bari of Southern Sudan, Ladi is
often used for a second-born twin, along with Ular
("first-born twin").

Lais (lays) East Indian: "lion." Common especially among
Moslems in India.

Lal Hindi: "beloved." Another name for Krishna.

Lamar Latin: "close to (or related to) the sea"; or Old
German: "land famous."

Lance Old German: "land." Made famous by Sir Lancelot
of Arthurian legend.
Lancelot, Launce, Launcelot

Landon Old English: "from the open, grassy meadow."
Landan, Landen

Lane Middle English: "one from the narrow road."

Lang Old Norse: "tall man." Popular in Scandinavia.

Langdon Old English: "from the long hill."
Lang, Langston

Langley Old English: "from the long meadow or forest."
Lang, Langly

Langston Old English: "from the tall man's town or estate."
Lang, Langsdon

Langundo (lahn-GOON-do) North American Indian: "peaceful."

Lani Hawaiian: "sky." This is also a common element in
many longer Hawaiian names. See Lani, listed in
the girls' section.

Lanu (LAH-noo) Miwok Indian: "people passing one another at the *pota* ceremony when running around the pole." Miwok names frequently refer to tribal customs.

Lars One of the most popular Norwegian names, Lars is a Scandinavian form of Lawrence, "crowned with laurel." See Lawrence.

Lashi (LAH-shee) English Gypsy form of Louis, "famous warrior."
Lash, Lasho

Lathrop Old English: "from the barn farmstead."
Lathe, Lathrope, Lay

Lavi (LAH-vee) Hebrew: "lion." In astrology the lion is the symbol of Leo.
Leib, Leibel (Yiddish)

Lawrence Latin: "crowned with laurel." First popularized by Saint Laurence, a third-century martyr.
Larrance, Larrence, Larry, Lauren, Laurence, Lawrance, Lary, Lon, Lonnie, Lonny, Lorn, Lorne, Lorrie, Lorry, Loren, Lorence, Lorin (English); *Lauritz, Lorenz* (Danish); *Laurens* (Dutch); *Lauri* (Finnish); *Laurent* (French); *Lorenz* (German); *Lenci, Lorant, Lorinc* (Hungarian); *Labhras* (Irish); *Lorenzo, Loretto, Renzo* (Italian); *Brencis, Labrencis* (Latvian); *Raulas, Raulo* (Lithuanian); *Inek, Lorenz* (Polish); *Lourenco* (Portuguese); *Labrentsis, Larka, Larya, Lavr, Lavrik, Lavro* (Russian); *Labhruinn* (Scottish); *Chencho, Laurencio, Lencho, Lorenzo* (Spanish); *Lars, Larse, Laurans, Lorens* (Swedish, Norwegian)

Lawton Old English: "from the town or estate on the hill."
Laughton, Law

Leander Greek: "like a lion."

Leben (LAY-ben) Yiddish: "life."

Lee Irish Gaelic: "a poet"; or Old English: "from the meadow." Also a short form of names containing *lee*.
Leigh

Leif Old Norse: "beloved." Extremely popular in Norway.
Lief

Leighton Old English: "one from the meadow farm."
Lay, Layton, Leigh

Lel (layl) English Gypsy: "he takes."

Len Hopi Indian: "flute." From the Hopi flute cult. Also short for all names containing *len*. The Hopis often combine this name with other words to create new names, such as Lenmana ("flute maiden") and Lenhononoma ("standing flute"), referring to the flute ceremony.

Lenci (LEN-tsee) Hungarian development of Lawrence, "crowned with laurel." See Lawrence.

Lenn A familiar form of Leonard, "lionlike." See Leonard.

Lenno (LEHN-no) North American Indian: "man."

Lennor (LEH-nohr) English Gypsy: "spring" or "summer."

Lensar (LEHN-sahr) English Gypsy: "with his parents."
Variation: Lendar ("from his parents").

Leo Latin: "lion." Astrological name for a boy born under the sign of Leo.

Leon French: "like a lion." Used in France, Germany, Poland, Rumania, Spanish-speaking countries, and the United States. Also a form of Leonard.
Leo, Leosko, Lev (Czech); *Leonidas* (Greek); *Leone* (Italian); *Leonas, Liutas* (Lithuanian); *Leonek, Leos* (Polish); *Leao, Leonardo* (Portuguese); *Lev, Leva, Levka, Levko* (Russian)

Leonard Old Frankish: "brave as a lion." Used in many countries.
Lee, Len, Lenard, Lenn, Lennard, Lennie, Lenny, Leo, Leon, Lon, Lonnie, Lonny (English); *Lienard* (French); *Leonhard* (German); *Leonardo* (Italian, Portuguese, Spanish); *Leonhards, Leons* (Latvian); *Leonards* (Lithuanian); *Leonek, Linek, Nardek* (Polish); *Leonid, Lonya* (Russian); *Leontes* (Swedish, Norwegian)

Leor (leh-OHR) Hebrew: "I have light." Popular today in Israel. Also a girls' name.

Leron (leh-ROHN) Hebrew: "song is mine." Modern Israeli name.
Lerone, Liron, Lirone

Les Modern form of Lester ("from the chosen camp") or Leslie ("from the gray fortress").

Lev Czech and Russian form of Leo or Leon, "like a lion."

Levi (LAY-vee or anglicized to LEE-vigh or LEH-vee) Hebrew: "joined to" in the sense of being joined with God. Popular Israeli name.
Lev, Levey, Levy, Lewi (Israeli)

Lewis See Louis.

Liam (LEE-uhm) One of the most popular names in Ireland, Liam is a shortened form of William, "unwavering protector."

Liang (lee-AHNG) Chinese: "good" or "excellent."

Liko (lee-koo) Chinese: "Buddhist nun." This unusual Chinese name is given to boys to suggest to the demon world that the child is of little value and at the same time is protected by Buddha.

Lincoln Old English: "from the poolside colony." The name is often bestowed to honor the sixteenth U.S. President, Abraham Lincoln.
Linc, Link

Linfred Old German: "gentle peace." Modern German name.

Lio (LEE-oh) Hawaiian development of Leo, "lion."

Lise (LEE-se) Miwok Indian: "salmon's head just coming out of the water." According to one legend, the salmon were once locked away from the Indians by two old demons. The coyote, who was talkative and polite in those days, tricked the demons into giving him the key to the salmon and freed the river for the Indians.

Liu (LEE-oo) African: "voice." Used by the Ngoni-speaking people of Malawi.

Liwanu (lee-WAH-noo) Miwok Indian: "bear growling."

Loe (LO-e) Hawaiian form of Roy, "king."

Lokni (LOHK-nee) Miwok Indian: "rain coming through a small hole in the roof." Possibly given to a boy born during a rainstorm.

Loman (LO-mahn) Serbo-Croatian: "delicate."

Lon Irish Gaelic: "fierce and strong." Also a short form of Lawrence, "crowned with laurel."
Lonnie, Lonny

Lonato (lo-NAH-to) North American Indian: "flint."

Lono (LO-no) Hawaiian: "god of peace and agriculture."

Lorant (LO-rawnt) Hungarian form of Lawrence, "crowned with laurel." See Lawrence.

Lorens Form of Lawrence popular in Norway, Sweden, and Denmark.

Lorne A modern form of Lawrence, "crowned with laurel."
Lorn

Lothar German form of Louis, "famous warrior."

Loudon Teutonic: "from the low valley."
Lowden

Louis Old German: "a famous warrior."
Lew, Lewes, Lewis, Lon, Lou, Louie (English); *Lude, Ludek, Ludko, Ludvik* (Czech); *Ludirk* (Finnish); *Clovis, Louis* (French); *Lothar, Ludwig* (German); *Ludovici, Luigi* (Italian); *Ludis* (Latvian); *Ludwik, Lutek* (Polish); *Luis* (Portuguese, Spanish); *Ludis* (Russian); *Ludvig* (Swedish, Norwegian)

Luis A Spanish and Portuguese form of Louis, "famous warrior."

Luister Afrikaans: "a listener."

Luke Latin: "light," "bringer of light," or "bringer of knowledge." Biblical name made popular because of Saint Luke. Popular in Germany and the United States. *Lucas, Lucian, Lucien, Lucius, Luck, Lucky* (English); *Lukas* (Czech); *Luce, Lucien, Lucius* (French); *Lucius, Lukas* (German); *Loukas* (Greek); *Lukacs* (Hungarian); *Lukass* (Latvian); *Lukasz* (Polish); *Lucas* (Portuguese, Spanish); *Luchok, Luka, Lukash, Lukasha, Lukyan,* (Russian); *Lukas* (Swedish); *Lusio* (Zuni Indian)

Lunt Old Norse: "from the grove." Scandinavian name.

Lutherum (LOO-theh-ruhm) English Gypsy: "slumber." English Gypsy name for a child who sleeps a lot.

Luyu (LOO-yoo) Miwok Indian *luyani*: "to shake the head," the connotation being "dove shaking its head sideways."

Luz (loos) Spanish: "light." Also a girls' name.

Lyle Old French: "from the island."
Ly, Lyell

Lyndon Old English: "from the linden-tree or lime tree hill."
Lin, Lindon, Lindy, Lynn

Lyron (lee-ROHN) Hebrew: "lyric" or "lyrical." Israeli name.
Liron

M

Mac Scottish Gaelic: "son of." Also a shortened form of all boy's names starting with *Mac-*.

Macdougal Scottish Gaelic: "the dark stranger's son."
Mac, Mack, Dougal

Macmurray Irish Gaelic: "the mariner's son."
Mac, Mack, Murray, Murry

Madison Old English: "the mighty warrior's son."
Maddie, Maddy

Mahir (mah-HEER) Hebrew: "industrious" or "expert."

Maimun (MIGH-moon) Arabic: "lucky."

Makis (MAH-kees) Modern Greek form of Michael, "who is like God?" See Michael.

Maksim (mahk-SEEM) Russian form of Maximilian, "greatest in excellence." See Maximilian.

Malik (MAH-lik) Arabic: "master." According to some Moslems, the name God dislikes most is Malik Al-Amlak, which means "king of kings."

Mallory Old German: "an army counselor"; or old French: "unfortunate and strong."
Mal, Malory, Lory

Mamo (MAH-mo) Hawaiian: "saffron flower" or "yellow bird." Also a girls' name.

Manchu Chinese: "pure."

Manco (MAHN-ko) Inca, Peru: "king."

Mandek (MAHN-dek) Polish form of Armand, "army man."

Mander (MAHN-der) English Gypsy: "from me."

Mando (MAHN-do) Spanish form of Armand, "army man."

Manipi (mah-NEE-pee) North American Indian: "a walking wonder."

Mansa (MAHN-sah) African: "king." In ancient Egypt the mansa rulers basked in elegance. One mansa was always accompanied by at least three hundred servants and musicians, the latter carrying gold and silver guitars. Another, from Mali, was so extravagant that when he passed through Cairo on a pilgrimage to Mecca, he and his followers threw such a quantity of gold on the market that they undermined the price of the Egyptian dinar.

Mansur (mahn-SOOR) Arabic: "divinely aided." Popular Arabic name.

Manu (mah-NOO) Akan, Ghana: "second-born son." Used by the Ghanaian people for the second boy in a row.

Manuel Hebrew: "God be with us." The older form of this name is Emanuel. Used in Spain, Russia, and the United States.
Eman, Emanuel (Czech); *Maco, Mano* (Hungarian); *Emek* (Latvian); *Mango, Manny, Manolon, Manue, Mel, Minel* (Spanish); *Emmanuil, Manuil, Manuyil* (Russian); *Immanuel* (Yiddish)

Marar (mah-RAHR) Wataware, Southern Rhodesia: "dirt." *Marara*

Marc A French form of Mark, "warlike one."

Marcus Popular modern U.S. form of Mark. See Mark.

Marid (MAH-rid) Arabic: "rebellious."

Mark Latin: "warlike one." Popular worldwide due to the Biblical Saint Mark. See also Martin.
Marc, Marcus, Markus (English); *Marcus, Marek, Marko* (Czech); *Markus* (Danish, Dutch, German, Swedish); *Marc* (French); *Marinos, Markos* (Greek); *Marci, Marcilka, Markus* (Hungarian); *Marco* (Italian); *Markus, Marts* (Latvian); *Marcos* (Portuguese, Spanish); *Mark, Marka, Markusha* (Russian); *Marko, Mari* (Slovenian)

Marnin (mahr-NEEN) Hebrew: "one who creates joy" or "one who sings." Currently used in Israel.

Mart Turkish: "born during the month of March." Also a short form of Martin, "warlike."

Martin Latin *martinus*: "warlike." An international name used in the United States, Czechoslovakia, Estonia, Rumania, Russia, Sweden, Norway, Spanish-speaking countries, and elsewhere.

Mart, Martan, Marten, Martey, Marti, Martie, Marton, Marty (English); *Martinka, Tynek, Tynko* (Czech); *Mertin* (French); *Martel* (German); *Martinos* (Greek); *Marci, Marcilki, Martino, Marton* (Hungarian); *Martino* (Italian); *Martins* (Latvian); *Martinas* (Lithuanian); *Marcin* (Polish); *Martinho* (Portuguese); *Martyn* (Russian); *Martiniano, Marto* (Spanish); *Marten* (Swedish); *Marti* (Swiss and Slovenian)

Marty Popular contemporary U.S. form of Martin.

Mary Old English: "friend of the sea."

Maska (MAHS-kah) North American Indian: "powerful."

Maslin Old French: "little twin." An astrologer may use this name for a boy born under the sign of Gemini, the twins.

Mason Old French: "stoneworker."

Masud (mah-SOOD) Arabic: "fortunate." Commonly used by Swahili-speaking people in Africa.

Mato (MAH-to) North American Indian: "brave."

Matope (mah-TO-peh) Mashona, Southern Rhodesia: "this shall be the last child." -

Matt Popular contemporary form of Matthew, "gift of Jehovah."

Matthew Hebrew: "gift from Jehovah." One of the most popular names in the world, made famous by Saint Matthew, one of Christ's twelve apostles.
Mat, Mathew, Mathia, Mathias, Matt, Mattias, Mattie, Matthia, Mattmias, Matty (English); *Matei* (Bulgarian); *Matek, Matus* (Czech); *Matt* (Estonian); *Mathieu, Matthieu* (French); *Mathe, Matthaus, Matthias* (German); *Matthaios* (Greek); *Mate* (Hungarian); *Matteo* (Italian); *Matteus* (Norwegian); *Matyas* (Polish); *Mateus* (Portuguese); *Matheiu* (Rumanian); *Matfei, Matvey, Mayfey, Motka, Motya* (Russian); *Mata* (Scottish); *Mateo, Matias* (Spanish); *Mathias* (Swedish)

Mauli (MOW-lee) Hawaiian: "dark-skinned."

Maximilian Latin: "greatest in excellence."
Mac, Mack, Max, Maxie, Maximillian, Maxy (English); *Maxi, Maxim* (Czech); *Maxime* (French); *Maximalian* (German); *Maks, Makszi, Miksa, Maxi* (Hungarian); *Massimiliano, Massimo* (Italian); *Makimus, Maksymilian* (Polish); *Maximiliano* (Portuguese); *Maksim, Maksym, Maksimka, Sima* (Russian); *Max, Maxi, Maximo, Maximino, Maximiliano* (Spanish)

Mayer Germanic: "overseer or farmer." One of the commonest names in Austria.

Mead Old English: "from the meadow."
Meade

Mehmet (ME-met) A form of Muhammad particularly popular in Turkey. See Muhammad.

Mehtar (meh-tahr) East Indian: "prince." Used to indicate noble ancestry, but also popular among India's poorer castes.

Melvern North American Indian: "great chief."

Menachem Yiddish: "comforter." Made famous worldwide by Israeli Prime Minister Menachem Begin.
Mendeley (Yiddish)

Mendel East Semitic *min'da*: "wisdom" or "knowledge."

Mendeley (men-de-LAY) Russian name either from the Yiddish for "comforter" or the Latin for "of the mind." Also a Yiddish form of Menachem.

Mered (me-REHD) Hebrew: "revolt."

Merrill Old French: "small and famous."
Meril, Merill, Merle, Merrel, Merrell, Meryl

Merripen (MEH-ree-pen) English Gypsy: Paradoxically, this name can mean either "life" or "death."

Mestipen (MESS-ti-pen) English Gypsy: "fortune" or "luck."

Meyer German: "farmer." Popular in Belgium.

Michael Hebrew: "Who is like God?" In its many variations, this is one of the most popular names in the world. The spelling Michael is popular in Germany as well as English-speaking countries.
Mickel, Mickie, Micky, Mike, Mitch, Mitchel, Mitchell (English); *Mihail* (Bulgarian); *Michal, Min, Minka, Misa, Miso, Misko* (Czech); *Mihkel, Mikk* (Estonian); *Mikko* (Finnish); *Dumichel, Michau, Michel, Michon* (French); *Makis, Michail, Mihail, Mikhail, Mikhalis, Mikhos* (Greek); *Mihal, Mihaly, Misi, Miska* (Hungarian); *Michele* (Italian); *Mikelis, Miks, Mikus, Milkins* (Latvian); *Mikkel* (Norwegian); *Machas, Michak, Michal, Michalek, Mietek* (Polish); *Miguel* (Portuguese); *Mihail, Mihas* (Rumanian); *Michail, Mika, Mikhail, Mikhalka, Misha, Mischa* (Russian); *Micheil* (Scottish); *Micho, Mickey, Miguel, Migui, Miki, Mique* (Spanish); *Mickel, Mihalje, Mikael* (Swedish); *Mihailo* (Ukrainian); *Michael* (Yiddish)

Miles Latin: "soldier" or "warrior"; or Old German: "merciful one."
Myles

Mimis Popular in Greece as a pet form of Dimitri, "belonging to Demeter."

Mingan (MEEN-gahn) North American Indian: "the gray wolf."

Mischa Russian pet form of Michael, "Who is like God?"

Misu (MEE-soo) Miwok Indian: "rippling water."

Mitch Contemporary form of Mitchell, which in turn is a form of Michael, "Who is like God?"

Mitchell A form of Michael which has been used since the twelfth century. See Michael.
Mitch

Mohan (MO-hahn) Hindi: "delightful." Another name for Krishna, the most celebrated Hindu god.

Mojag (MOH-yahg) North American Indian: "never quiet." Indian name for a baby who cries a lot.

MIWOK WATER NAMES

Water names are common among the Miwok Indians of
California. Examples include: Iskemu ("water running gently
when the creek dries"), Miltaiye ("water in waves"), Uhubitu
("foul, stinking, stagnant water"), and Yottoko ("black mud
at the edge of the water"). Such names often refer to the
way a nearby stream looked when the baby was born.

Montague French: "from the pointed hill."
Montagu, Monte, Monty

Monty A short form of names containing *mont*, especially
Montague.

Morris Latin: "dark-skinned one." A modern English form
of Maurice.
Maurey, Maurie, Maury, Morey, Morie, Morrie, Morry

Morven Scottish Gaelic: "child of the sea" or "a mariner"; or Irish Gaelic: "great, fair-skinned one." Astrological name for a boy born under one of the water
signs: Pisces, Cancer, or Scorpio.

Moses Hebrew: "saved (from the water)."
Moe, Mose, Moshe, Moss (English); *Moisei* (Bulgarian);
Moise (French); *Moisis* (Greek); *Mozes* (Hungarian);
Moise, Mose (Italian); *Moze* (Lithuanian); *Moshe, Mosze,
Moszek* (Polish); *Moïses* (Portuguese); *Moisey, Mosya*
(Russian); *Moises, Moshe, Mozes* (Yiddish)

Moshe (mo-SHAY) Hebrew and modern U.S. form of Moses,
"saved (from the water)."

Mosi (MO-see) Swahili: "first-born."

Moswen African: "light in color." From Botswana.

Motega (mo-TEH-gah) North American Indian: "new arrow."

Muhammad Arabic *hamida*: "the praised one." The Prophet Muhammad universalized this name. With its many

variations, Muhammad is the most popular boys' name among Moslems and the most common boys' name in the world. A Moslem saying goes, "If you have a hundred sons, name them all Muhammad." Among the more than five hundred variations:
Ahmad, Ahmed, Amad, Amed, Hamid, Hamdrem, Hamdun, Hammad, Hammed, Humayd, Mahmud, Mahmoud, Mehemet, Mehmet, Mohamet, Mohammad, Mohammed, Muhammed

Mundan (MOON-dahn) Southern Rhodesian: "garden." *Munda*

Muraco (MOO-rah-cho) North American Indian: "white moon."

Musenda (moo-SEHN-dah) Baduma, Africa: "nightmare." Among the Baduma people of Africa, this name is given to a child when the mother has a vivid dream right before the baby's birth.

---------------- **N** ----------------

Nabil (nah-BEEL) Arabic: "noble."

Nagid (nah-GEET or anglicized to nah-GEED) Hebrew: "ruler" or "prince."

Nahele (nah-HEH-le) Hawaiian: "forest" or "grove of trees."

Nahma (NAH-mah) North American Indian: "the sturgeon."

Nalren (NAHL-rehn) Dene Indian: "he is thawed out."

Namid (NAH-meed) North American Indian: "star dancer." This Indian name probably refers to the vain coyote, who wanted to dance with the stars. One night he asked a star to sail by a mountain and take him by the paw, which she did. The next night, impatient for the star's return, the coyote jumped off the mountain himself, thinking that if the star could fly, so could he. The legend says that he was "ten whole snowfalls in falling, and when he landed, he was squashed as flat as a willow mat.''

Namir (nah-MEER) Hebrew: ''leopard,'' connoting swiftness. Modern Israeli name.

Nandin (NAHN-deen) Hindi: ''destroyer.'' One of the 1,008 names for the Hindu god Siva, the destroyer.

Narain (nah-RIGHN) Hindi: ''the god Vishnu,'' another name for Vishnu, the Hindu god believed to be the protector and sustainer of the world.

Nard Persian: ''the game of chess.''

Nasser (NAS-ser) Arabic: ''victorious.'' A favorite among Moslems, this name refers to one of the ninety-nine qualities of God listed in the Koran.
Nassor (Swahili)

Natal (nah-TAHL) Spanish form of Noel, ''born on Christmas.''

Nathan Hebrew: ''a gift.'' In a recent survey of the one hundred most popular boys' names in the United States, Nathan ranked forty-first, just below Zachary and above Patrick. The longer Nathaniel ranked ninety-second. This name is also popular in France, Italy, Sweden, and Norway.
Nat, Nate, Nathen, Nathon, Natt, Natty (English); *Natan* (Hungarian, Polish, Russian, Spanish)

Nathaniel Hebrew: ''given by God.'' See Nathan.
Nat, Nate, Nathan, Nathon, Natt, Natty (English); *Nathanael* (French); *Nataniele* (Italian)

Nav (nahv) Hungarian *nev*: ''name.'' Coined by the English Gypsies.

Nawat (NAH-waht) North American Indian: ''left hand.''

Nayati (nah-YAH-tee) North American Indian: ''the wrestler.''

Ned A familiar form of names beginning with *Ed-*, such as Edgar, Edmund, and Edward. Also used today as an independent name.

Nehru East Indian *nahar*: "canal." The late Indian Prime Minister Nehru was so named because a canal passed by his family's ancestral estates.

Neil Irish Gaelic: "a champion."
Neal, Neale, Neill, Neils, Nels, Nial, Niels, Niles (English); *Nilo* (Finnish); *Nil, Nilya* (Russian); *Nels, Niels, Nils* (Scandinavian); *Niall* (Scottish)

Nelek (NEL-ek) Polish pet form of Kornelek, "horn-colored" or "like a horn." The English equivalent is Cornel.

Nels A Scandinavian and modern U.S. form of Neil, "champion."

Nen Egyptian: "the spirit of Nen." Occult name from the Egyptian *Book of the Dead*. Nen personified the inert, motionless primeval waters and was sometimes pictured with a human body and a frog's head.

Neper (NEH-pair) Spanish name meaning "of the new city."
Napier

Nero Latin: "strong" or "stern."
Neron (Bulgarian, French, Spanish); *Nerone* (Italian)

Neto (NEH-to) Spanish form of Ernest, "earnest one."
Ernst (German, Norwegian, Swedish); *Ernesto, Ernestino* (Spanish)

Nevin Irish Gaelic: "the saint's worshiper"; or Old German: "nephew."
Nev, Nevins, Niven

Newlin Old Welsh: "son of the new pool." Given to a child whose home is beside a pool.
Newlyn

Nibaw (NEE-baw) North American Indian: "I stand up."

Nicabar (nee-kah-BAHR) Spanish Gypsy: "to take away" or "to steal."

Nicanor (nee-kah-NOR) Spanish form of Nicholas, "victorious army" or "victorious people."

Nicholas Greek: "victorious army" or "victorious people." A favorite in the United States.
Claus, Cole, Nic, Nichol, Nick, Nicky, Nicol, Nik, Nikki, Nikky (English); *Nikita, Nikolas* (Bulgarian); *Nikula, Nikulas* (Czech); *Nicolaas* (Dutch); *Nikolai* (Estonian); *Colar, Colin, Nicolas, Nicole* (French); *Claus, Klaus, Nikolaus* (German); *Nikolaos, Nikolos, Nikos* (Greek); *Micu, Miki, Niki, Niklos* (Hungarian); *Cola, Niccolo, Nicola* (Italian); *Kola, Niklavs, Nikolais* (Latvian); *Nicolai* (Norwegian); *Mikolai, Milek* (Polish); *Nicolau* (Portuguese); *Kolya, Nikolai* (Russian); *Nicolas* (Spanish); *Niklas, Nils* (Swedish)

Nigan (NEE-gahn) North American Indian: "ahead."

Nigel Latin: "black" or "dark."

Niki Polish form of Dominick, "born on Sunday" or "belonging to God." In Greece Niki is a girls' name meaning "victorious army."

Nils A Scandinavian form of Neil ("a champion") and a Swedish form of Nicholas ("victorious army" or "victorious people").

Nissan Hebrew: "flight."

Nissim (nees-SEEM) Hebrew: "sign" or "miracle."

Nitis (NEE-tes) North American Indian: "friend" or "good friend."
Netis

Nnamdi (nahm-DEE) Nigerian: "my father is still alive." Given in Nigeria to a child thought to be the reincarnation of his father.

Noah Hebrew: "quiet peace" or "rest." In the Bible Noah was chosen by God to build the Ark so his family would survive the flood. The most popular spelling of this name in the world is *Noe,* used in Czechoslovakia, France, Greece, Hungary, Italy, Rumania, Spain, and many other countries.
Noi (Bulgarian); *Noach* (Dutch); *Noi, Noy* (Russian); *Noel* (Spanish); *Noak* (Swedish, Norwegian)

Nodin (NO-din) North American Indian: "the wind."
  Knoton, Noton

Noel French: "born on Christmas." Also a Spanish form of
  Noah, "quiet peace" or "rest."
  Nowell (English); *Natale* (Italian); *Natal* (Spanish)

Nolan Irish Gaelic: "noble and famous."

Norris Old French: "one from the north."
  Norrie, Norry

NICKNAMES:
INSULTING OR FLATTERING?

Some nicknames are almost impossible to avoid. If your
last name were Rhodes, for example, it would be almost
impossible for your son to avoid the nickname Dusty. And
if your surname was Waters, some wag would inevitably
call your child Muddy Waters at school. Though some
psychologists insist an extremely insulting nickname like
"Fatso" or "Stinky" can leave lasting psychological scars
on a child, more recent research suggests this may not be
so. In fact, a team of Oxford University researchers head-
ed by Rom Harre found that in all cultures, having a
nickname—even an insulting one—is better than having
no nickname at all. The Oxford researchers concluded that
being nicknamed at least entitles a child to *some* social
attention, whereas a child with no nickname is viewed as
something of a nonperson.

How to help your child avoid an unfortunate nickname if
you want to? You might choose a "good" nickname for
your child from the start. If you name your son Benjamin
James and then call him "B.J." yourself, chances are his
school chums won't name him Benji (after the famous
dog). Likewise, when your baby is small, avoid "cutesy-
pie" names he or she may later become saddled with.
(Studies have shown kids especially abhor nicknames
like Sweetie-pie, Goo-Goo, and Honeybunch.)

Nowles (nolz) Middle English: "from the grassy slope in the forest." Earth name for a boy born under one of the earth signs: Capricorn, Taurus, or Virgo.
Knolls, Knowles

Noy Hebrew: "beauty." Used in Israel.

Numair (noo-MIGHR) Arabic: "panther."

Nuri (NOO-ree) Hebrew: "fire." Used today in Israel.
Nur, Nuria, Nuriel

Nuru (NOO-roo) Swahili: "light." Given to a child born during daylight.

Nusair (noo-SIGHR) Arabic diminutive of *Nasr*, "vulture."

───────────────── O ─────────────────

Odell Middle English: "from the wooded hill"; or Scandinavian: "little and wealthy."
Dell, Ode, Odey, Odie, Ody

Odin Scandinavian: "the god Odin." Odin is the chief god in Norse mythology, source of all wisdom, patron of culture, and champion of heroes.

Odinan (o-dee-NAHN) Ochi and Ga, Africa: "fifteenth-born child."

Odion (O-dee-ohn) Benin, Nigeria: "first of twins."

Odissan (o-DEES-sahn) Ochi and Ga, Africa: "thirteenth-born son."

Odon (O-dohn) Contemporary Hungarian form of Edmund, "wealthy protector," or French form of Otto, "prosperous one."
Odi

Ogden Old English: "dweller in the oak valley."
Ogdan, Ogdon

Ogun (o-GOON) Yoruba, Nigeria: "god of war." In Yoruba legend, Ogun is the god of war and the son of the river and lake goddess.

Ohanko (o-HAHN-ko) North American Indian: "reckless."

Ohin (oh-HEEN) Akan, Ghana: "chief."

Oko (o-KOH) Yoruba, Nigeria: "the god Ogun."

Okon (o-KOHN) Efik, Africa: "born at night."

Olaf Old Norse *anleifr*: "ancestral relic." A favorite in Norway, this was the name of five Norwegian kings. *Olin* (English); *Olafur* (Icelandic); *Olav* (Norwegian)

Olery Old German: "ruler of all." Used especially in France.

Oles (O-les) Polish form of Alexander, "helper and defender of mankind." See Alexander.

Olin An English form of Olaf, "ancestral relic."

NIGERIAN HOLY NAMES

Like all people around the globe, the Yoruba-speaking people of Nigeria frequently name their babies after gods or religious figures. Whereas Christians the world over are fond of the Apostle names Matthew, Mark, Luke, and John, and Moslems favor variations of the name Muhammad, Nigerian parents often name their babies after Ogun, their god of war. Examples include: Ogunkeye ("Ogun has earned honor"), Ogunsanwo ("Ogun gives help"), and Ogunsheye ("Ogun has performed honorably"). Other Nigerian baby names referring to God are: Olufemi ("God loves me"), Olujimi ("God gave me this"), Olukayode ("my Lord brings happiness"), Olushegun ("God is the victor"), and Olushola ("God has blessed me").

Olorun (o-lo-ROON) Yoruba, Nigeria: "belonging to the god Olorun." The supreme god of the Yoruba pantheon, Olorun was born from Olokun, the mighty ocean of the sky. This ancient deity is no longer worshiped.

Omar (O-mahr) Arabic: "first son," "most high," or "the Prophet's follower."
Omer

Onan (o-NUHN) Turkish: "prosperous." Also a Turkish surname.

Onani (o-NAH-nee) Ngoni, Malawi: "look!"

Orban Hungarian name from Latin: "city boy" or "born in the city." See Urban.

Ordando (or-DAHN-do) Spanish form of Roland, "from the famous land."
Orlando (Spanish, Italian)

Oren Hebrew: "ash tree."

Orji (OR-jee) Ibo, Nigeria: "mighty tree."

Orson Latin: "little bear"; or Old English: "the spear man's son."
Sonnie, Sonny, Urson

Orunjan (o-ROON-jahn) Yoruba, Nigeria; "god of the midday sun."

Osgood Old English: "divinely good."
Ozzi, Ozzie, Ozzy

Osmond Old English: "a divine protector."
Osman, Ozzi, Ozzie, Ozzy (English); *Osmen, Osmanek* (Polish); *Osmundo* (Spanish)

Otadan (o-TAH-dahn) North American Indian: "plenty."
Tadan

Ottah (o-TAH) Urhobo, Nigeria: "thin one." Used by the Urhobo-speaking people of Nigeria for a child who is thin at birth.

Otto Old German: "prosperous one." Modern German form

of an older name—Odo—which was introduced into England by the Normans and was used occasionally in England in the nineteenth century. Otto is now used in many countries, including Czechoslovakia, Hungary, Rumania, Russia, Sweden, and the United States.
Otik, Oto (Czech); *Odon, Othon* (French); *Otho, Otfried, Ottocar, Ottomar* (German); *Othon* (Greek); *Otello, Ottone* (Italian); *Audr, Odo* (Norwegian); *Onek, Otek, Oton, Otton, Tonek* (Polish); *Otilio, Otman, Oto, Oton, Tilo* (Spanish)

Ouray (o-RAY) North American Indian: "the arrow." In astrology the archer is the symbol of Sagittarius.

Owen Form of Evan, "young warrior" or "young bowman." See Evan.

Oxford Old English: "from the place where the oxen cross the river."
Ford

————————————— **P** —————————————

Pablo (PAH-blo) Spanish form of Paul, "little." See Paul.

Paco North American Indian: "bald eagle." Also Spanish form of Francis or Frank.

Paddy Contemporary American creation from Patrick, "noble one." Also an Irish form of Patrick.

Page French: "young attendant."
Padget, Padgett, Paget, Paige

Paki (PAH-kee) South African: "witness."

Pal (pahl) English Gypsy: "brother." Also a form of Paul, "little."

Palani (pah-LAH-nee) Hawaiian form of Francis, "free one" or "Frenchman."

Pallaton (PAHL-ah-tohn) North American Indian: "fighter."
Palladin, Pallaten (English)

Palmer Old English: "a crusader" or "a pilgrim bearing palms."

Pancho Popular Spanish form of Francisco, which is a form of Francis, "free one" or "Frenchman." See Francis.

Parker Middle English: "protector (or keeper) of the park."
Park, Parke

Parlan Popular Scottish form of Barth, "a farmer" or "son of the earth." See Barth.

Parnell Old French: "little Peter." In the twelfth century this was a feminine form of Peter in England until it came to mean a promiscuous woman and fell into disfavor. Today Parnell is enjoying a revival as a boys' name.
Parnel, Parrnell, Pernel, Pernell

Pascal Italian: "pass over" or "born at Easter or Passover." Hebrew name for a child born during the Passover season.
Pascual, Pace, Pasqual

Pat North American Indian: "fish." Also a short form of names containing *Pat*, especially a nickname for Patrick. In astrology the fishes are the symbol of Pisces.

Patamon (PAH-tah-mahn or anglicized to PAT-a-muhn) North American Indian: "raging."

Patrick Latin: "noble one." The name honors Saint Patrick, the patron saint of Ireland, and is one of the most popular names in Ireland and the United States.
Pat, Paddy (English); *Patrice* (French); *Patricius, Patrizius* (German); *Padraic, Padraig* (Irish); *Patrizio* (Italian); *Patek* (Polish); *Patricio* (Portuguese); *Padruig* (Scottish); *Patricio, Ticho* (Spanish)

Patrin English Gypsy: "leaf trail." This English Gypsy name refers to a trail Gypsies make from handfuls of leaves or grass which are thrown along the way to guide those behind.

Pattin English Gypsy: "a leaf," connoting freshness. Also a form of the name Patton, "from the warrior's estate."

Patton Old English: "from the warrior's estate."
Pat, Paten, Patin, Paton, Patten, Pattin

Patwin (PAT-win) North American Indian: "man." According to Liwaito Indian legend, a great flood covered the Sacramento Valley and destroyed all but one man. After an earthquake opened the Golden Gate and drained off the water, this man mated with a crow and repopulated the earth with Patwin, modern man.

Paul Latin: "little." Often bestowed in honor of Saint Paul. *Pol, Paulis* (English); *Pavel* (Bulgarian, Czech); *Poul* (Danish); *Pal, Pali, Palika* (Hungarian); *Pall* (Icelandic); *Paolo, Paulo* (Italian); *Pauls, Pavils* (Latvian); *Poul* (Norwegian); *Inek, Paulin, Pawel* (Polish); *Pasha, Pashka, Pavel, Pavlik, Pavlo, Pawl* (Russian); *Oalo, Pablo, Paulino, Paulo* (Spanish); *Pal* (Swedish)

Pavel Czech, Bulgarian, and Russian form of Paul, "little."

Paxton Old English: "from the peaceful town."
Pax, Paxon

Payat (PAY-yaht) North American Indian: "he is coming."
Pay, Payatt

Paz (pahz) Spanish: "peace." Also a girls' name.

Pepin Old German: "perseverant one" or "one who petitions."
Pepi, Peppi, Peppie, Peppy

Perry Old French: "little Peter"; or Middle English: "a pear tree."

Peter Latin: "rock" or "stone." Introduced into England by the Normans, Peter was associated with the papacy in Rome and was a great favorite until Henry VIII broke with the Pope in 1534. For nearly three centuries the name was an outcast, considered rustic and old-fashioned. Peter came into vogue again in the early

1900s, with the sudden enormous popularity of James
M. Barrie's 1904 play *Peter Pan*.
Pete, Petey, Petie (English); *Petr, Piotr* (Bulgarian);
Pieter (Dutch); *Peet, Peeter* (Estonian); *Pierre, Pierrot*
(French); *Panos, Petros, Takis* (Greek); *Pedro, Pero,
Piero, Pietro* (Italian); *Petras, Petrelis, Petrukas*
(Lithuanian); *Peder, Petter* (Norwegian); *Pictrus, Pietrek,
Piotr, Piotrek* (Polish); *Petar, Petru* (Rumanian); *Perka,
Petinka, Petr, Petro, Petruno, Petrusha, Pyatr* (Russian);
Peadair (Scottish); *Pedrin, Pedro, Perequin, Perico,
Pequin, Petronio, Peyo, Piti* (Spanish); *Peder, Per*
(Swedish)

Peyton Old English: "from the fighter's estate."
Pate, Payton

Phil Short form of Phillip, "lover of horses."

Phillip Greek *philippos*: "lover of horses."
Phil, Philip, Phill, Phillipp (English); *Filip* (Bulgarian,
Czech, Lithuanian, Norwegian, Rumanian, Serbian,
Swedish); *Philippe, Philippel* (French); *Philipp* (Ger-
man); *Phillipos* (Greek); *Fulop* (Hungarian); *Filib, Pilib*
(Irish); *Filippo* (Italian); *Filips* (Latvian); *Fil, Filip,
Filipek* (Polish); *Feeleep, Filip, Filipp, Filya* (Russian);
Felipe, Felipino, Filipp (Spanish); *Fischel* (Yiddish)

Pias (PEE-ahs) English Gypsy: "fun."

Pierce Old Anglo-French: "rock or stone." An early form
of Peter used before the fifteenth century, Pierce has
made a comeback as a modern U.S. name. Popularized
by actor Pierce Brosnan.
Pearce, Piers, Pierse

Pierre A French form of Peter, "rock" or "stone."

Pilar (pee-LAHR) Spanish: "pillar" or "fountain base."
Refers to Mary the mother of Jesus, pillar of the
Christian religion. Also a girls' name.

Pili (PEE-lee) Swahili: "second-born son."

Pillan (pee-LAHN) Araucanian Indian: "supreme essence." A major deity among the Araucanian Indians, Pillan is the god of thunder, lightning, and other natural phenomena.
Pilan

Pirro (PEER-ro) Greek: "with flaming hair." Popular Spanish name.

Platon Spanish: "broad-shouldered."

Pol Greek: "crown." A shortened form of Pollux, the name of an orange star, the brighter of two first-magnitude stars in the constellation Gemini, the Twins. Also a short modern form of Paul, "little."

Porter Latin: "a porter" or "gatekeeper."

Pov (pohv) English Gypsy: "earth."

Powa (PO-wah) North American Indian: "rich."

Prentice Middle English: "an apprentice."
Prent, Prentiss

Prescott Old English: "from the priest's home."
Prescot, Scot, Scott, Scottie, Scotty

Preston Old English: "from the priest's estate."

Price Old Welsh: "the ardent one's son."
Pryce

Pryor Latin: "head of the monastery."
Prior, Pry

Putnam Old English: "one who lives by the pond."

———————————— Q ————————————

Quico (KEE-ko or anglicized to KWEE-ko) Short form of many Spanish names, including Enrique (a form of Henry) and Francisco (a form of Francis).

Quillan (KWIL-luhn) Irish Gaelic: "cub." Astrological name for a child born under the sign of Leo, the lion.

Quimby Old Norse: "one living at the woman's estate."
Quenby, Quim, Quin, Quinby

Quinlin Irish Gaelic: "strong one."
Quinn, Quinley

Quinn Irish Gaelic: "intelligent" or "wise." Also a form of Quinlin, Quintin, and other names starting with *Quin-*.

Quintin Spanish: "fifth-born child."
Quito

Quirin "The quirin stone." Exact origin unknown. The quirin is a magic stone supposedly found in the lapwing's nest and also known as the traitor's stone. According to legend, when placed on a sleeping person's head, the stone causes him to reveal his innermost thoughts.

R

Rabi (ra-BEE) Arabic: "breeze," connoting the fragrance, for example, of new-mown hay or the earth after a spring rain.

Rad Short modern U.S. name originally a nickname for any name containing *rad*.
Radd

Radburn Old English: "one from the red stream."
Burnie, Burny, Rad, Radd, Radborn, Radborne, Radbourne, Radburne

Radcliff Old English: "from the red cliff."
Cliff, Rad, Radd, Radcliffe

Radman (RAHD-muhn) Slavic: "joy."

Radomil (RAD-o-mil) Slavic: "lover of peace." Popular in Czechoslovakia.

Rafael A favorite in Spanish-speaking countries, Rafael is a form of Raphael, "God has healed." Also used in Rumania.

Rafe Short form of Raphael ("God has healed") or Rafferty ("rich and prosperous").

Rafferty Irish Gaelic: "rich and prosperous."
Rafe, Rafer, Raff, Raffer

Rafi (rah-FEE or anglicized to RAH-fee) Arabic: "exalting." The Prophet Muhammad objected to this name because he thought it too proud. Also a familiar form of Raphael ("God has healed").

Ragnar (RAG-nar) Old Norse: "mighty army." Popular in Norway and Sweden.
Ragnor, Rainer, Rainier, Rayner, Raynor (English)

Rahman (rah-MAHN) Arabic: "compassionate" or "merciful." Popular Moslem name referring to qualities of God listed in the Koran. A favorite combination is Abdul Rahman or Abd-al-Rahman ("servant of the Merciful One"), which Moslems consider one of the two names God loves best. The other name is Abdul Allah or Abd-Allah ("servant of God").
Rahmet (Turkish)

Raiden (RIGH-den) Japanese: "thunder god." Raiden, the Japanese thunder god of legend, is usually depicted as a red demon carrying a drum and having two claws on each foot.

Raini North American Indian: "the Creator." In Tupi-Guarani Indian legend, the god Raini created the world by placing it in the shape of a flat rock on another god's head.

Raleigh Old English: "from the deer meadow."
Lee, Leigh, Rawley, Rawleigh

Ramadan (rah-mah-DAHN) Swahili: "born in the month of Ramadan." Ramadan is the ninth month of the Moslem year, during which pious Moslems fast from sunrise to sunset.

Ramon (rah-MOHN) Spanish form of Raymond, "wise protector."

Ramsden Old English: "ram's valley." In astrology the ram symbolizes Aries.

Ramsey Old English: "ram's island" or "the raven island." *Ramsay, Ramsy*

Rance African: "borrowed all"; also a short form of Ransom. *Rancel, Rancell, Ransel, Ransell*

Rand A short form of Randall or Randolph. Means simply "shield."

Randall Contemporary U.S. form of Randolph, "shield-wolf." This name, which has come into vogue only recently, was quite popular in the Middle Ages. *Rand, Randal, Randel, Randell, Randi, Randie, Randy*

Randolph Old English *rand-wulf*: "shield-wolf." This name came into vogue in the eighteenth century as a then "modern" form of Randal. *Rand, Randal, Randall, Randel, Randell, Randi, Rancie, Randy*

Randy A short form of Randall or Randolph now used as an independent name. *Randi, Randie*

Ranier English form of Ragnar, "mighty army." See Ragnar.

Ranon (rah-NOHN) Hebrew: "to sing" or "to be joyous." Modern Israeli name. *Ranen*

Ransom Old English: "son of the shield." *Rance, Ransome, Ranson*

Rapier Middle French: "strong as a sword." James T. Rapier (1839–1884) was a black congressman from Alabama who called for strong enforcement of the civil rights legislation passed during Reconstruction. Rapier urged blacks to unite and form labor unions and organized the first conclave of black working men.

Rashid (rah-SHEED) Swahili *rashidi*: "one of good council." Popular modern U.S. name.

Ravi Hindi: "conferring." One of the titles of the Hindu sun god Surya, who is considered one of the twelve guardians of the months of the year. In India the Ravi River is a tributary of the sacred Indus.

Raviv (rah-VEEV) Hebrew: "rain" or dew."

Raymond Old German: "wise protector." Used also in Russia and France.
Ray, Raymund (English); *Rajmund* (Czech); *Raimund* (German); *Raimondo* (Italian); *Raimundo* (Portuguese); *Reimond* (Rumanian); *Raimundo, Ramon, Mundo* (Spanish)

Razi (RAH-zee) Aramaic: "my secret." Popular in Israel.
Raz, Raziel

Reece Old Welsh: "ardent" or "rash."
Rees, Reese (English); *Rhett* (Welsh)

Reed Old English: "red-haired" or "ruddy-skinned."
Read, Reade, Reid

Reeve Middle English: "a bailiff."
Reave, Reeves

Regan Irish Gaelic: "little king."
Reagan, Reagen, Regen

Remington Old English: "from the estate of the raven family."
Rem, Remy

Rendor (REN-dohr) Hungarian: "policeman."

René (re-NAY) French: "reborn."

Rey Spanish form of Roy, "king." See Roy.

Reyhan (REH-hahn) Arabic: "favored by God."

Rez Hungarian: "copper." For a boy with coppery or reddish hair.

THE MOST "AU COURANT" BABY NAMES

Popular names for babies go in and out of fashion. In the nineteenth century, names of famous statesmen and politicians were "in" and many babies were called Washington, Hamilton, Jefferson, Lincoln, Madison, and Monroe. This trend continued into the twentieth century and when Franklin Delano Roosevelt was president, thousands of babies were called Franklin. More recently Jacqueline Kennedy Onassis, who was a popular first lady, spawned a rage of baby Jacquelines.

Novelists and poets were once influential baby-name trendsetters. Sixteenth-century poet Sir Philip Sidney invented the popular name Pamela ("all-honey") and Stella ("a star"). Occasionally a character in a novel will capture the public imagination; the lead character in Eric Segal's *Love Story*, for example, spawned an enormous number of Jennifers in the early 70s. But the characters that most inspire baby name fads today are those on television. For example, several years ago Erin became fashionable, when both B.J. on *M.A.S.H.* and the family on *The Waltons* had little girls with that name. More recently, soaps such as *Dallas* and *Dynasty* inspired parents both in this country and in Europe to name their babies Alexis, Krystal and Sue Ellen.

Though we can understand why TV shows might inspire names, other fads are harder to fathom. Though no one knows why, there's recently been an explosion of both boys' and girls' names starting with the letter J. Among them: Jaime, Jared, Jason, Jennifer, Jeremy, Jill, Joshua, Jeffrey, Joel, Julia, Jonathan, Jonas, Jessica, Jed, and Justin.

Which names are currently the very most popular? That depends on which region of the country you survey. Kizzie is presently enjoying popularity in Florida, while Ona is fairly common in Detroit. In New York City, which contains a wide cross-section of parents from all backgrounds and social classes, here (in order of popularity) are the most popular names for babies—then and now.*

1898: Mary, Catherine, Margaret, Annie, Rose, Marie, Ester, Sarah, Francis, Ida
John, William, Charles, George, Joseph, Edward, James, Louis, Francis, Samuel

1928: Mary, Marie, Annie, Margaret, Catherine, Gloria, Helen, Teresa, Jean, Barbara
John, William, Joseph, James, Richard, Edward, Robert, Thomas, George, Louis

1948: Linda, Mary, Barbara, Patricia, Susan, Kathleen, Carol, Nancy, Margaret, Diane
Robert, John, James, Michael, William, Richard, Joseph, Thomas, Stephen, David

1964: Lisa, Deborah, Mary, Susan, Maria, Elizabeth, Donna, Barbara, Patricia, Ann(e) and Theresa (Ann and Theresa tied for tenth place)
Michael, John, Robert, David, Steven, Anthony, William, Joseph, Thomas, Christopher, Richard

1972: Jennifer, Michelle, Lisa, Elizabeth, Christine, Maria, Nicole, Kimberly, Denise, Amy
Michael, David, Christopher, John, James, Joseph, Robert, Anthony, Richard, Brian

1975: Jennifer, Michele, Christine, Lisa, Maria, Melisa, Nicole, Elizabeth, Jessica, Erica
Michael, John, Robert, David, Christopher, Anthony, Joseph, Jason, Jose

1985: Jennifer, Jessica, Christina, Stephanie, Melisa, Nicole, Elizabeth, Amanda, Danielle, Lauren
Michael, Christopher, Daniel, David, Anthony, Joseph, Jonathan, Jason, John, Robert

*Information provided by the New York City Health Department

Rhett Possibly a Welsh form of Reece, "ardent" or "rash." Made popular by Rhett Butler, the rakish hero of Margaret Mitchell's novel *Gone with the Wind*.

Richard Old German: "powerful ruler"; or Old English: "brave and powerful." Commonly used in many countries, including the United States, Bulgaria, France, Czechoslovakia, Germany, and England.
Dick, Dickie, Dicky, Ric, Ricard, Rich, Richerd, Rick, Rickert, Rickie, Ricky, Ritch, Ritchie, Ritchy (English); *Risa* (Czech); *Arri, Juku, Riki, Riks, Rolli* (Estonian); *Reku, Rikard* (Finnish); *Richart* (German); *Rihardos* (Greek); *Riczi, Rikard* (Hungarian); *Riccardo, Ricciardo* (Italian); *Richards, Rihards* (Latvian); *Risardas* (Lithuanian); *Rikard* (Norwegian); *Rye, Rysio, Ryszard* (Polish); *Dic* (Rumanian); *Rostik, Rostislav, Rostya, Slava, Slavik, Slavka* (Russian); *Ricardo, Richi, Ricky, Rico, Riqui* (Spanish); *Rickard* (Swedish)

Rico Spanish form of Richard, "powerful ruler" or "brave and powerful." See Richard.

Rida (REH-dah) Arabic: "favor," implying the child is in God's favor.

Riki Estonian form of Fredrick ("peaceful ruler") and Henry ("ruler of a home or estate").

Rimon (ri-MOHN) Hebrew: "pomegranate." A favorite in Israel.

Ringo Japanese: "apple." The apple is an Oriental symbol of peace and this name has the connotation "peace be with you."

Rip Dutch: "ripe" or "full-grown." Also a modern short form of Ripley, "from the shouter's meadow."

Ripley Old English: "from the shouter's meadow."
Lee, Rip, Ripp

Roald Old German: "famous ruler." One of the most popular names in Norway, made famous by Norwegian polar explorer Roald Amundsen and children's book writer Roald Dahl.

Rob Modern short form of Robert, "shining with fame."
Robb, Robbie, Robby

Robert Old English: "shining with fame." Extremely popular worldwide, Robert is used not only in the United States and other English-speaking countries, but also in Bulgaria, Czechoslovakia, France, Germany, Hungary, Poland, Sweden, and Norway. The name was made world famous in the fourteenth century by Robert the Bruce, King of Scotland, and has been a favorite ever since.
Bert, Bob, Bobbi, Bobbie, Bobby, Rab, Rob, Robb, Robbi, Robbie, Robby, Robertson, Robin, Robinson, Rupert (English); *Berty, Bobek, Rubert* (Czech); *Robers, Robin, Robinet* (French); *Rudbert, Ruprecht* (German); *Robi* (Hungarian); *Riobard* (Irish); *Roberto, Ruberto, Ruperto* (Italian); *Roberts* (Latvian); *Rosertas* (Lithuanian); *Robin* (Rumanian); *Berto, Bobby, Rober, Roberto, Ruperto, Tito* (Spanish)

Robi Hungarian nickname for Robert, "shining with fame." See Robert.

Robin Popular modern form of Robert, "shining with fame."

Rock Old English: "from the rock."
Rockie, Rocky

Rod A contemporary short form of many names, including Roderick, Rodger, and Rodman. Now popular as an independent name.
Rodd

Rodas (ROH-dahs) Spanish name from the Greek meaning "place of roses."

Roderick Old German: "famous ruler."
Broderick, Rick, Ricky, Rod, Roddie, Roddy, Roderic, Rodrich, Rodrick, Rory (English); *Rodrique* (French); *Roderich* (German); *Rodrigo* (Hungarian, Italian); *Rurich, Rurik* (Russian); *Rodrigo, Ruy* (Spanish)

Rodger A variant spelling of Roger, "famous spear."

Rodman Old English: "famous" or "heroic."
Rod, Rodd, Roddie, Roddy

Roger Old German: "famous spear." A favorite in England in the Middle Ages, Roger fell out of favor in the sixteenth century, when it was associated with any vagabond or rogue. Once again popular today. Well-known namesakes: baseball star Roger Maris, anchorman Roger Mudd.
Rodge, Rodger, Rog, Rutger, Ruttger (English); *Rudiger* (German); *Rogerios* (Hungarian); *Ruggero* (Italian); *Gerek* (Polish); *Rogelio, Rogerio* (Spanish)

Rohan (RO-hahn) Hindi: "sandalwood," connoting the fragrance of sweet incense.

Rohin (ro-HEEN) East Indian: "on the upward path."

Roi Form of Roy ("king") used today in India.

Roland Old German: "from the famous land."
Orland, Rolland, Rollin, Rollins, Rollo, Rolly, Rowe, Rowland (English); *Orlando, Rudland, Ruland* (German); *Lorand, Lorant* (Hungarian); *Orlando, Rolando* (Italian, Spanish); *Rolek* (Polish); *Lando, Olo, Orlo, Roldan, Rolon, Rollon* (Spanish)

Rolf (rohlf) Old German: "swift wolf" or "wolf counsel." Currently popular in Sweden and Norway.

Rolon (ro-LOHN or anglicized to RO-lun) Spanish name originally from Old German and meaning "famous wolf."

Romney Old Welsh: "curving river." Appropriate for a boy born under one of the water signs: Pisces, Cancer, or Scorpio.

Roni (RO-nee or anglicized to RAH-nee) Hebrew: "my joy." Modern Israeli variations: Ron ("joy" or "song"), Ronel ("joy or song of God"), and Ronli ("joy or song is mine").

Rory Irish Gaelic: "red king." Also a modern U.S. and Irish form of Roderick, "famous ruler."

Ross Scottish Gaelic: "one from the peninsula." Especially popular in the United States.
Rosse, Rossie, Rossy

Roth Old German: "red-haired or ruddy-skinned." Popular in Germany.

Roy French: "king."
Roi (French); *Loe* (Hawaiian); *Rey* (Spanish)

Royce Old English: "the king's son."

Royd Old Norse: "from the forest clearing."

Ruben Hebrew: "behold a son." Used in France, Russia, and Spanish-speaking countries, as well as all English-speaking regions of the world. The variation *Rubin* is used not only in the United States, but also Russia, Norway, Sweden, Rumania, and Israel.
Reuben, Reuven, Rube, Rubin, Ruby (English); *Reuben* (French, German); *Rouvin* (Greek); *Ruvim* (Russian)

Rudo (ROO-doh) Shona, Zimbabwe: "love."

Rudolf Slavic and Scandinavian form of Rudolph, "famous wolf."

Rudolph Old German: "famous wolf."
Dolf, Rolf, Rolfe, Rollo, Rolph, Rudie, Rudolf, Rudy (English); *Ruda, Rudek, Rudolf* (Czech); *Rodolphe* (French); *Ralph, Rudolf, Rutz* (German); *Rezso, Rudi* (Hungarian); *Rudolfo, Rodolfo* (Italian); *Rudolfs* (Latvian); *Dodek, Rudek* (Polish); *Dolfe, Dolfi, Rude, Rudi* (Slavic); *Rodolfo, Rolo, Rudolfo, Rudi, Rudy, Rufo* (Spanish)

Rurik Slavic form of Rory, "red king," or Roderick, "famous ruler."

Russ Short form of Russell, "red-haired."

Russell Old French: "red-haired."
Rus, Russ, Rustie, Rusty (English); *Rosario* (Italian)

Ryan Irish Gaelic: "little king." Currently popular in the United States.
Ryon

S

Saburo (sah-boo-ro) Japanese: "third-born male."

Sahale (sah-HAH-leh) North American Indian: "above."

Sahen (shah-hehn or anglicized to SAH-hen) Used in India, this name means "falcon."

Sakima (sah-KEE-mah) North American Indian: "king."

Salih (SAH-lee) Arabic: "good" or "right."

Salim (sah-LEEM) Arabic: "peace." Swahili name. Also popular in Arabic countries, where the name is pronounced SA-lim and means "safe."
Saleem

Salmalin (sahl-mah-leen) Hindi: "taloned." Another name for Garuda, the half-giant, half-eagle vehicle of the Hindu god Vishnu. Garuda is pictured with the body, arms, and legs of a man, the talons, beak, and head of an eagle, and a white face, red beak, and golden body. According to legend, he was hatched from a monstrous egg five hundred years after his mother laid it.

Salomon (sah-lo-MOHN) Spanish form of Solomon, "peaceful."

Salvador (sahl-vah-DOHR or anglicized to SAL-vah-dor) Spanish name meaning "the Savior." See Xavier.

Samein (sa-MIGH-an) Arabic form of Simon, "to hear" or "to be heard."

Sammon Arabic: "grocer."

Samson Hebrew: "like the sun." Used not only in the United States and England, but also Bulgaria, France, Rumania, and Russia.
Sam, Sammie, Sammy, Sampson, Sanson, Sansum (English); *Sansone* (Italian); *Sansao* (Portuguese); *Sanson* (Spanish); *Simson* (Swedish)

Samuel Hebrew: "His name is God" or "God has heard." This ever-popular name from the Bible is used in the United States, England, Czechoslovakia, France, Germany, Hungary, Poland, Spanish-speaking countries, Sweden, Norway, and Russia. A true whole-world name.
Sam, Sammie, Sammel, Sammy, Sem, Shem (English); *Samuil* (Bulgarian); *Samko, Samo* (Czech); *Zamiel* (German); *Samouel* (Greek); *Samie, Samu* (Hungarian); *Somhairle* (Irish); *Salvatore, Samuele* (Italian); *Samaru* (Japanese); *Samuelis* (Lithuanian); *Samuil, Samvel* (Russian); *Shem, Shemuel, Schmuel* (Yiddish)

Santo Spanish, Italian: "sacred" and "saintly."

Sarad (SAH-rahd) Hindi: "born in autumn."

Sarngin (SAHRN-geen) Hindi: "archer." Another name for the Hindu god Vishnu, the protector, who carries a bow called the *sarnga*.

Sarojin (sah-RO-jeen) Hindi: "lotuslike." The lotus is revered by Hindus because Brahma was born in the center of this sacred flower.

Scott Old English: "a Scotsman."
Scot, Scotti, Scottie, Scotty

Sean Irish form of John currently in vogue in the United States. See John.
Shaun, Shawn

Sef Egyptian: "yesterday." An Egyptian lion god in the *Book of the Dead.* In astrology the lion governs the sign of Leo.

Segel Hebrew: "treasure." Derived from the biblical phrase *Am Segulah*, "a treasured people," often used to refer to Israel.

Seif (SIGH-eef) Arabic: "sword of religion."

Senon (SEH-nohn) Spanish: "living" or "given by Zeus."

Senwe (SEHN-weh) Baduma, Africa: "a dry stalk of grain." Given to a frail child who resembles a thin stalk.

Sepp German form of Joseph, "God will increase." See Joseph.

Sergei Latin: "an attendant." The most popular boys' name in Russia today.
Serge (English); *Sergius* (German); *Sergio* (Italian, Spanish); *Serg, Sergiusz, Sewek* (Polish); *Serge, Sergey, Sergeyka, Sergi, Sergie, Sergo, Sergunya, Serzh, Serhiy, Serhiyko, Syarhey* (Russian)

Seth Hebrew: "appointed one." Seth was Adam's third son.

Sevilen (se-vi-LEN or anglicized to SEV-i-len) Turkish: "beloved."

Shalom (sha-LOHM) Hebrew: "peace."
Sholom

Shamir (shuh-MEER) Hebrew: "the shamir stone." Refers to a hard precious stone believed to have been used in building Solomon's temple.

Shamus An Irish form of James, "the supplanter." See James.

Shanahan Irish Gaelic: "wise one."
Shan, Shana, Shane

Shandy Old English: "little and rambunctious."
Andy, Shan, Shandie

Shane Modern Irish form of John, "gracious gift of God."
Shaine, Shayn, Shayne

Shannon Irish Gaelic: "little, old, and wise." Popular modern U.S. name.
Shannan

Shanon Hebrew: "peaceful" or "secure." Popular today in Israel.
Shanan

Sharif (shah-REEF) Arabic: "honest." A popular name in Arabic countries, made well-known in the United States probably by actor Omar Sharif.

Shawn Popular modern U.S. variation of John, "God is gracious." See John and Sean.

Sheehan Irish Gaelic: "little peaceful one."

Shem Yiddish: "name." A short form of the Yiddish Shemuel, "His name is God." See Samuel.

Shen Egyptian: "sacred amulet." This magical name comes from the Egyptian *Book of the Dead*. The name refers to an Egyptian amulet that symbolized eternal life and was often placed by the feet of the dead.

Sherborn Old English: "from the clear, pure brook." An astrological and ecological water name.
Sherborne, Sherburn, Sherburne

Shing (sheeng) Chinese: "victory."

Shiro (shee-ro) Japanese: "fourth-born son."

Sidney Old French: "from the city of St. Denis, France."
Cid, Cyd, Si, Sid, Sidon, Syd, Sydney, Sydny (English); *Sidonio* (Spanish)

Sigfrid Old German: "peaceful" or "victorious." Popular especially in Germany.
Siegfried, Sig, Sigfried, Singefrid (English); *Siffre, Sigfroi* (French); *Siegfried, Seifert, Seifried* (German); *Szigfrid, Zigfrid* (Hungarian); *Sigefriedo* (Italian); *Zigfrids* (Latvian); *Sigvard, Siurt* (Norwegian); *Zygfryd, Zygi* (Polish); *Fredo, Siguefredo* (Portuguese); *Zigfrids* (Russian); *Sigfrido, Sigifredo* (Spanish)

Sigurd Old Norse: "victorious guardian." Sigurd was a major hero in Norse myth, and the name is still extremely popular in Scandinavian countries.

Silvain Latin: "from the forest." Used in France.
Silvanus, Sylvester (English)

Simen English Gypsy: "alike," "equal," or "it is we." The name implies a resemblance between the newborn baby and his parents.

Simon Hebrew: "to hear" or "to be heard."
Si, Simeon, Symon (English); *Samein* (Arabic); *Simion, Simeon* (French); *Simeon, Sim, Simmy* (German); *Semon* (Greek); *Simone* (Italian); *Simao* (Portuguese); *Simion* (Rumanian); *Simeon* (Russian); *Shimon* (Yiddish)

Siva (SHEE-vah or anglicized to SIV-uh) Hindi: "the god Siva." This popular Hindu name refers to the god Siva, the destroyer.

Sivan (SEE-vahn) Hebrew: "born in the ninth month." This name comes from the ninth month of the Jewish calendar, corresponding in astrology to Gemini, the Twins.

Skelly Irish Gaelic: "a storyteller."
Skelley, Skellie

Skip Old Norse: "ship master."
Skipp, Skipper, Skippie, Skippy

Slade Old English: "child from the valley."

Slane Czech: "salty."

Slavik (SLAH-vik) Russian pet form of Stanislav, "glorious position." See Stanislav.

Slevin Irish Gaelic: "mountaineer."
Slaven, Slavin, Slevin

Sloan Irish Gaelic: "a warrior or fighter."
Sloane

Sofian (SO-fee-an) Arabic: "devoted."

Sol Latin: "the sun" or "child of the sun." Astrological name for a boy born under Leo, the lion, which is ruled by the sun. Also short for Solomon, "peaceful."

Solomon Hebrew: "peaceful."
Salom, Selim, Sol, Solaman, Soloman, Sollie, Solly

(English); *Salamun* (Czech); *Lasimonne, Salaun, Salomon*
(French); *Salomo* (German, Swedish); *Salamon* (Hungarian); *Salomone* (Italian); *Solomonas* (Lithuanian);
Salomon (Norwegian, Spanish); *Salamen* (Polish);
Shelomoh, Shlomo (Yiddish)

Songan (SOHN-gahn or anglicized to SAHN-gun or SAHN-jun) North American Indian: "strong."

Stan A short form of many boys' names containing the syllable *stan-*. Now an independent name in the United States.

Stancio (STAN-see-o) Spanish form of Constantine, "firm and constant."

Stane Serbian diminutive of Stanislav, "glorious position."

Stanislav Slavic: "glorious position." One of the most popular names in Russia, also common in Serbia, Czechoslovakia, and the Ukraine.
Stan, Stanislas, Stanislus (English); *Stana, Stando, Stano* (Czech); *Stanislas* (French); *Stanislau* (German);
Stanislao (Italian); *Stanislaw, Stasiek, Stasio* (Polish);
Slava, Slavik, Slavka, Stas, Staska, Stashko (Russian);
Stane (Serbian); *Estanislao, Lao, Tano, Tanix, Tilo* (Spanish)

Starr Middle English: "a star."

Steele Sanskrit: "he resists"; or Middle English: "hard as steel."
Steel

Stephen, Steven Greek *stephanos*: "crowned." Popularized worldwide by Saint Stephen, the first Christian martyr, and by Saint Stephen, a Hungarian king during the tenth century.
Stef, Steffen, Steph, Steve, Stevie, Stevy (English);
Stefan (Bulgarian, Czech, Polish, Swedish); *Tapani, Teppo* (Finnish); *Etienne, Tiennot* (French); *Stefan, Steffel* (German); *Stamos, Stefanos, Stefos, Stephanos, Stavros* (Greek); *Isti, Istvan* (Hungarian); *Stefano* (Italian); *Stefens* (Latvian); *Steffen* (Norwegian); *Estevao* (Portuguese);

Stefan, Stenya, Stepan, Stepanya, Stepka (Russian); *Esteban, Stevan, Teb* (Spanish)

Stiggtur (STEEG-gur) English Gypsy: "gate."

Stoffel German form of Christopher, "Christ-bearer." See Christopher.

Sudi (SOO-dee) Swahili: "luck." A favorite in East Africa.

Sultan Swahili: "ruler."

Sven Scandinavian: "youth." One of the most popular names in Norway, in part because of the Scandinavian trend toward choosing more Norse-sounding names. *Svend* (Danish)

T

Tab Old German *tabbert:* "brilliant one among the people"; or Middle English: "drummer."

Tabib (tuh-BIB) Turkish: "doctor" or "physician."

Tabor (TAH-bor) "from the camp" or "from the fortified encampment." Used in Hungary and Turkey.

Tad Old Welsh: "father." Also a form of Thad, "praiser" or "courageous and stouthearted." See Thad. *Tadd*

Tadeo (TAH-deh-o) Spanish form of Thad, "praiser" or "courageous and stouthearted." See Thad.

Tadi (TAH-dee) Omaha Indian: "wind." The feminine form of this name is Tadewi.

Tadzi (TAHD-zee) Carrier Indian, Canada: "the loon."

Tahir (TAH-hir) Arabic: "pure." A popular Moslem name in Egypt, Turkey, Saudi Arabia, Jordan, and India.

Tait Scandinavian: "cheerful." *Taite, Tate*

Takis (TAH-kis) Modern Greek form of Peter, "rock" or "stone."

Tal Hebrew: "dew" or "rain." Used in Israel for both boys and girls. Also short for names starting with *Tal-*.

Talbot Middle English: "woodcutter"; or Old German-French: "valley bright."
Tal, Talbert, Tallie, Tally

Talib (TAH-lib) Arabic: "seeker." A child who seeks after truth.

Talli (TAHL-lee) Lenape Indian: meaning uncertain. In Lenape Indian lore Talli led the tribe after the great flood to the Snake Land, where they rebuilt civilization.

Talman (TAHL-mahn) Aramaic: "to injure" or "to oppress."
Tal, Tallie, Tally, Talmon

Talor Hebrew: "dew of the morning." Popular in Israel.
Tal

Taman Serbo-Croatian: "dark" or "black."

Tamas Hungarian form of Thomas, "twin." See Thomas.

Tanek Polish name originally from Greek: "immortal." The English form of this name, which is no longer used, is Athanasius.
Arius (German); *Atanazy, Atek* (Polish); *Afon, Afonya, Fonya, Opanas, Panas, Tanas* (Russian)

Tani (TAH-nee) Japanese: "valley." Also a girls' name.

Tanner Old English: "a tanner or leather worker."
Tan, Tann, Tanney, Tannie, Tanny

Tano (TAH-no) Ghanaian: "the River Tano." Many names in Ghana are taken from nature.
Tanno (African)

Taro (TAH-ro) Japanese: "first-born male." Loosely translated, Taro means "big boy."

Tas English Gypsy: "a bird's nest."

Tate North American Indian: "windy" or "a great talker"; or Middle English: "cheerful one."
Tait, Taite

Tauno Contemporary Finnish form of Donald, "world mighty" or "world ruler."

Tavish Scotch Gaelic: "twin." A Scottish form of Thomas.
Tavis, Tevis, Tevish

Tawno English Gypsy: "small" or "tiny." The feminine equivalent is Tawnie.

Tayib Arabic: "good" or "delicate." Common in India.

Taylor Middle English: "a tailor."
Tayler, Taylour

Ted A short form of Theodore ("God's gift") and names begging with *Ted-* or *Ed-*.
Tedd, Teddie, Teddy

Telek (TE-lek) Polish: "iron cutter."

Telem (TEH-lem) Hebrew: "ford near a cliff" or "a furrow." The English equivalent is Clifford.

Tem English Gypsy: "country"; or Egyptian: "the Creator god Tem." In the Egyptian *Book of the Dead*, Tem is the oldest of the gods and the Creator who lived when "not was sky, not was earth, not were men, not were born the gods, not was death." He dwelled in the celestial waters and thought of the creation of the world. When Tem's ideas were spoken aloud, the world came into being.

Teman (TAY-muhn) Hebrew: "right side," referring to the south. Modern Israeli name.

Terril Old English: "the thunder ruler." English variation of the Old Norse name Thor.
Terrell, Terrie, Terrill, Terry, Tirrell, Tyrrell

Teva (TAY-vah) Hebrew: "nature."

Thad Latin: "praiser"; or Greek: "courageous and stout-hearted." Contemporary short form of the older name

Thaddeus, one of Christ's twelve apostles. Many scholars believe that Thaddeus was also known as Saint Jude.

Tad, Tadd, Taddy, Thadd, Thaddy (English); *Tadeas, Tades* (Czech); *Thadee* (French); *Thaddaus* (German); *Tade* (Hungarian); *Taddeo, Thaddeo* (Italian); *Tadek, Tadzio* (Polish); *Faddei, Fadey, Tadey* (Russian); *Tadeo* (Spanish)

Thane Old English: "attendant warrior" or "follower."
Thain, Thaine, Thayne

Thanos (THAN-nohs) Contemporary Greek form of Arthur, "noble" or "bear man." See Arthur.

Theodore Greek: "God's gift." Several saints have borne this name.
Ted, Tedd, Teddie, Teddy, Theo, Theodor, Tudor (English); *Feodor* (Bulgarian); *Bohdan, Fedor, Tedik, Teodor, Teodus* (Czech); *Tewdor, Theodor* (German); *Tivadar, Todor* (Hungarian); *Teodoro* (Italian); *Fedor, Teodor, Teos, Teodorek, Tolek* (Polish); *Feodor, Feodore, Fedinka, Fedir, Fedar, Fedya, Teodor, Todor, Todos* (Russian); *Teodoro, Teodomiro* (Spanish)

Theodoric Old German *theuda-ricja*: "ruler of the people." In the thirteenth century the most common form of this name was Terry, which is again popular today.
Derek, Derk, Derrick, Ric, Rick, Ricky, Ted, Teddie, Teddy, Terrie, Terry

Theron (THAIR-uhn) Greek: "a hunter." Possible astrological name for a boy born under Sagittarius, the archer.

Thomas Greek: "a twin." With the spelling *Tomas*, this name is used today in the United States, Ireland, England, Canada, Czechoslovakia, Lithuania, Portugal, Russia, Sweden, Norway, and Spanish-speaking countries. Owes its worldwide popularity to Saint Thomas, one of Christ's twelve apostles.
Massey, Tam, Tameas, Tammany, Tammen, Tammy, Thom, Tom, Tomm, Tommie, Tommy (English); *Toomas* (Esto-

nian); *Tuomas, Tuomo* (Finnish); *Thumas* (French); *Thoma*
(German); *Tamas, Tomi* (Hungarian); *Tomasso, Masaccio*
(Italian); *Tomelis* (Lithuanian); *Tomcio, Tomek, Tomislaw,
Slawek* (Polish); *Tomaz, Tome* (Portuguese); *Foma, Fomka*
(Russian); *Tavis, Tavish, Tevis, Tevish* (Scottish); *Chumo*
(Spanish)

Thor Old Norse: "thunder." From the Old Norse thunder
god Thor, this is one of the most popular names in
Denmark.
Tor (English, Norwegian)

Thornton Old English: "dweller at the thorny estate."
Made famous by author Thornton Wilder.
Thorn, Thorne

Thorpe Old English: "dweller in the village."

Tilden Old English: "from the valley of the good, liberal
one."

SCANDINAVIAN MYTHOLOGY NAMES

Old Norse mythology is the basis for many modern
Scandinavian names. Such names as Sigurd, Sigmund,
and Siegfried (or Sigvard) are drawn from medieval folk
tales. Thor, the Old Norse god of thunder, is also the
source of many modern Scandinavian names. Among
them: Thorbjorn ("Thor's bear" or "thunder bear"), Thorleif
("Thor's beloved"), and Thorvald ("thunder ruler"). Many
English names secretly commemorate Thor as well, including: Thorburn ("Thor's bear" or "thunder bear"), Thorley
("Thor's meadow"), Thormond ("Thor's protection"), Thurlow
("from Thor's hill"), Thorald ("Thor-ruler" or "thunder ruler"), Thorbert ("Thor's brilliance"), and Thurston ("Thor's
stone or jewel"). As man's benevolent friend and protector,
Thor is represented as a god of fabulous strength who
rode in a goat-drawn chariot the rolling wheels of which
sounded of thunder and who slew giant demons with a
thunderbolt. The English Thursday was originally "Thor's
day."

Tilford Old English: "from the ford belonging to the good, liberal one."

Tilton Old English: "from the good, liberal one's estate." *Tiltan, Tilten, Tiltin*

Timin (tee-MEEN) Arabic *tinnin:* "sea serpent." Timin is a huge, famous fish in Hindu mythology. Even bigger is Timin-gila, "swallower of Timin," and bigger still is Timin-gila-gila, who swallows Timin-gila. The Sea Monster is the Hindu symbol for the lunar month corresponding to our astrological sign Capricorn.

Timothy Greek *timotheos*: "honoring God." The apostle Saint Timothy made this name popular in many forms around the world.
Tim, Timkin, Timmie, Timmy, Timon (English); *Timotei* (Bulgarian); *Timo* (Finnish); *Timothee* (French); *Timotheus* (German); *Timotheos* (Greek); *Timot* (Hungarian); *Tiomoid* (Irish); *Timoteus* (Norwegian, Swedish); *Tymek, Tymon* (Polish); *Timoteo* (Portuguese, Italian, Spanish); *Tima, Timka, Timofei, Timofey, Timok, Tisha, Tishka* (Russian)

Timur (tee-MOOR) Hebrew: "tall" or "stately."

Tino (TEE-no) Modern Spanish short form of Augustino, "the exalted one's son."

Tito Spanish and Italian form of Titus, "of the giants."

Titus Greek: "of the giants." In Greek myth the giant Titus was slain by Apollo. Used in Bulgaria, Germany, and English-speaking countries.
Tite (French); *Titos* (Greek); *Tito* (Italian, Spanish); *Titek, Tytus* (Polish)

Tivon (tee-VOHN) Hebrew: "naturalist" or "lover of nature."

Tobal (to-BAHL) Spanish pet form of Cristobal, which is a Spanish form of Christopher, "Christ-bearer." See Christopher.

Tobbar (TOH-bahr) English Gypsy: "road." *Boro-tobbar-killipen* is the Gypsy term for high toby, or highway robbery.

Toby Diminutive of the Hebrew Tobias, "God is my good."
Popular today, particularly in Ireland.
Tobey, Tobie

Todd North English: "a fox." Popular modern U.S. name.
Tod

Todor (TOH-dohr) Used in Hungary, Russia, and the Ukraine,
Todor is a form of Theodore, "God's gift."

Tohon (to-HOHN) North American Indian: "cougar."

Tolek (TOH-lek) A favorite nickname in Poland, used as a
short form of Anton (the Polish form of Anthony) and
Todor (the English equivalent is Theodore).

Tomas The most popular form of Thomas in the world,
used in Czechoslovakia, Lithuania, Portugal, Russia,
Sweden, Norway, Spanish-speaking countries, and other regions. See Thomas.

Tomi (TOH-mee) Kalabari, Nigeria: "the people"; Japanese:
"rich"; also a modern Hungarian form of Thomas.
This is an example of how the same name can be
created and used by widely separated cultures.

Tomlin Old English: "little twin." A diminutive form of
Thomas. Astrological name for a child born under
Gemini, the twins. See also Thomas.
Tomkin

Toni Slavic and Hungarian form of Anthony, "inestimable" or "priceless." See Anthony.

Topwe (TOHP-way or anglicized to TOP-wee) Southern
Rhodesian: "the topwe vegetable." This is an example
of a Southern Rhodesian "second name," given when a
child reaches maturity, usually at age twelve or four-
teen. This particular name suggests a personal quirk,
Topwe referring to a vegetable the child loved to eat.

Tor Tiv, Nigeria: "king." In Scandinavia the same name is
a popular variation of Thor. See Thor.

Torin Irish Gaelic: "chief."

Toshio (to-SHEE-o) Japanese: "year boy." Popular in Japan.
Toshi

Tovi (TOH-vee) Hebrew: "my good."
Tov

Tracy Latin: "bold and courageous"; or Irish Gaelic: "a fighter."
Trace, Tracey, Tracie

Travis Old French: "from the crossroads."
Traver, Travers, Travus

Tremain Celtic: "from the house by the rock."
Tremaine, Tremayne

Trent Latin: "the rapid stream."

Trevor Irish Gaelic: "wise, discreet one."
Trev, Trevar, Trever

Trey Middle English: "third-born."

Troy Irish Gaelic: "a foot soldier"; or Old French: "from the curly-haired people's region."

Tukuli (too-KOO-lee) Miwok Indian: "caterpillar traveling headfirst down a tree during the summertime." The name is derived from *tukini*, "to throw oneself endwise."

Tully Irish Gaelic: "quiet and peaceful," "devoted to God's will," or "living with God's peace."
Tull, Tulley, Tullie

Tunu (TOO-noo) Miwok Indian: "deer thinking about going to eat wild onions."

Tupi (TOO-pee) Miwok Indian *tupi:* "to pull out" or "to pull up." The elaborate connotation is "throwing a salmon onto the riverbank."

Turi (TOO-ree) Nickname for the Spanish Arturo, which is a Spanish form of Arthur, "noble" or "bear man."

Tyee (TIGH-ee) North American Indian: "chief." Another form is Tyonek, "little chief."

Tyler Middle English: "tile-maker" or "roofer."
Ty

MIWOK INDIAN INSECT NAMES

Insect names are common among the Miwoks and often reveal these Indians' subtle observations of the natural world. Examples include: Hesutu ("lifting a yellow jacket's nest out of the ground"), Momuso ("yellow jackets piled up in their nest during the winter"), Muata ("little yellow jackets in the nest"), Nokonyu ("katydid's nose being close to its mouth"), Patakasu ("small ant biting a person hard"), and Tiimu ("black-and-white caterpillar coming out of the ground").

Tymon Polish form of Timothy, "honoring God." See Timothy.

Tyrone Greek: "sovereign one"; or Irish Gaelic: "from Owen's land."
Ty, Tye

―――――――――――――――― U ――――――――――――――――

Ulan Bari, Southern Sudan: "first-born twin." See also Lado.

Ulric Old German: "ruler of all" or "wolf-ruler."
Alaric, Ric, Rich, Richie, Richy, Rick, Rickie, Ricky, Ulrich, Ulrick

Upton Old English: "from the upper town or estate."

Urban Latin: "one from the city."
Orban, Urbane (English); *Urbain, Urbaine* (French); *Orban* (Hungarian); *Urbano* (Italian, Portuguese, Spanish); *Urvan* (Russian)

Urie Hebrew: "God is my light," or "Jehovah's flame."
Uri, Uriah, Uriel

Uzoma Ibo, Nigeria: "born during a journey."

V

Vadin (VAH-deen) Hindi: "speaker," implying scholarly or learned discourse.

Valin (VAH-leen) Hindi: "the monkey king." See Balin.

Van Dutch: "son of." Originally a nickname, this has now become a given name. Many old Dutch names have this prefix. Van is also a feathered monster or dragon in Armenian myth.
Vann

Vance Middle English: "a thresher."
Van

Varden Old French: "from the green hills."
Vardon, Verden, Verdon

Vartan Armenian: "rose."

Vasilis (vah-SEE-lees) Greek form of Basil, "kingly" or "magnificent." See Basil.

Vasin East Indian: "ruler" or "lord."

Vassily (vah-SEE-lee) Russian form of Basil ("kingly," "magnificent") or William ("unwavering protector.") See Basil or William.

Vaughn Old Welsh: "small."

Vencel (VEN-tsel) Hungarian: "wreath" or "garland."

Vered Hebrew: "a rose."

Vern Latin: "youthful" or "like spring." A short form of Vernon.

Vernon Latin: "youthful" or "like spring."
Vern, Verne

Vic Modern short form of Victor, now used in the United States as an independent name. See Victor.

Victor Latin: "a conqueror."
Vic, Vick (English); *Viktor* (Bulgarian, Hungarian,

Russian, Swedish); *Victoir* (French); *Vittore, Vittorio* (Italian); *Wiktor, Witek* (Polish); *Vitor* (Portuguese); *Vika, Vitenka, Vitka, Vitya* (Russian); *Victorio, Victorino, Vito, Vitin* (Spanish)

Vidor (VEE-dohr) Hungarian name from Latin, "cheerful." The English equivalent is Hilary or Hillery.

Viljo (VEEL-yo) Very popular name in Finland, this is a Finnish form of William, "unwavering protector."

Vincent Latin: "conquering."
Bink, Vin, Vince, Vinn, Vint (English); *Vincenc, Vinco* (Czech); *Vincenz* (French, German); *Binkentios* (Greek); *Vinci* (Hungarian); *Enzo, Vicenzo, Vincenzo* (Italian); *Wicek, Wicent, Wicus* (Polish); *Kesha, Vika, Vikent, Vikenti, Vikesha* (Russian); *Chenche, Vincente* (Spanish)

Vinson Old English: "Vincent's son."

Vito (VEE-to) Latin: "relating to life." Popular in Spanish-speaking countries. Also a Spanish form of Victor, "a conqueror."

Vladimir Old Slavic: "powerful warrior" or "army ruler." Form of Walter popular in Russia. For variations around the world, see Walter.

Vladlen (VLAHD-len) Russian creation from Vladimir plus Lenin. Became popular in Russia after Lenin came into power.

--------------------------------**W**--------------------------------

Waban (wah-BAHN) North American Indian: "the east wind."

Wade Old English: "from the river crossing."

Wakiza (wah-KEE-zah) North American Indian: "desperate fighter."

Walden Old English: "child of the forest valley." Closely associated with Thoreau's Walden Pond.
Wald, Waldon

Wallace Old English: "a Welshman."
Wallie, Wallis, Wally, Walsh, Welch, Welsh

Walt Short form of Walter, "powerful warrior" or "ruler of an army," used today as an independent name. Well-known namesakes: poet Walt Whitman and Walt Disney.

Walter Old German: "powerful warrior" or "ruler of an army."
Wallie, Wally, Walt (English); *Valtr, Vladko, Waltr* (Czech); *Gauther, Gautier* (French); *Walli, Walther, Waltli* (German); *Gualtiero* (Italian); *Valter, Valters* (Latvian); *Vacys, Vanda, Vandele, Waldemar* (Lithuanian); *Ladislaus* (Polish); *Dima, Dimka, Vladimir, Volya, Vova, Vovka* (Russian); *Gualberto, Bualterio, Gualtero, Gualterio, Gutierre, Waterio* (Spanish)

Wapi (WAH-pee) North American Indian: "lucky."

Ward Old English: "a guardian" or "watchman."

Warner Old German: "the defending army" or "defending warrior."

Wayne Old English: "a wagon maker." Originally a short form of Wainwright, but long used as an independent name.
Vaino (Finnish)

Webb Old English: "a weaver."
Web

Welby Old English: "from the farm by the spring."

Wemilat (weh-MEE-laht) North American Indian: "all given to him." Indian name for a child born to wealthy parents.

Wemilo (weh-MEE-lo) North American Indian: "all speak to him," implying all respect him.

Wen English Gypsy: "born in winter."

Wesh English Gypsy: "from the forest" or "woods."

Westbrook Old English: "dweller near the west-brook."
Brook, Brooke, Wes, West, Westbrooke

Wicent Polish form of Vincent, "conqueror." See Vincent.

Wichado (wee-CHAH-do) North American Indian: "willing."

Wilanu (wee-LAH-noo) Miwok Indian: "pouring water on acorn flour in a leaching place."

Wildon Old English: "from the wild valley."
Will

Will Old English: "unwavering and determined." A short form of William used today as an independent name. Also a short form of other names starting with *Wil-*.

William Old German: "unwavering protector."
Bill, Billie, Billy, Will, Willi, Willie, Willis, Willy, Wilson, Williamson (English); *Vilhelm* (Bulgarian); *Vila, Vilek, Vilem, Viliam, Vilko, Vilous* (Czech); *Guillaume, Guillaums* (French); *Wilhelm, Willi, Willy* (German); *Vasilios, Vassos* (Greek); *Vili, Vilmos* (Hungarian); *Uilliam* (Irish); *Vas, Vasili, Vasiliy, Vasilak, Vaska, Vassili, Vasya, Vasyl* (Russian); *Vilhelm, Ville, Wilhelm, Willie* (Swedish); *Velvel, Welfel, Wolf* (Yiddish)

Wilny North American Indian: "eagle singing while flying."

Wilton Old English: "from the farm with a spring."
Will, Willie, Willy, Wilt

Wilu (WEE-loo) Miwok Indian: "chicken hawk calling *wi*."

Winfield Teutonic: "friend of the soil" or "friend of the earth."
Field, Win, Winn, Winny, Wyn

Wingi (WEEN-gee) North American Indian: "willing."

Winston Old English: "from a friend's town."
Win, Winn, Winsten, Wyn

Winward Old English: "my friend's (or brother's) forest" or "my brother's keeper."
Ward, Win, Winn, Wyn

Woodrow Old English: "from the hedge near the forest."
Wood, Woody

Woody Short form of names containing the syllable *wood*. Now used today as an independent name, possibly because of its fame due to director, actor, writer Woody Allen and singer Woody Guthrie.

Worth Old English: "from the farmstead."

Wuliton (WOO-li-tuhn) North American Indian: "to do well."

Wunand (WOO-nahnd) North American Indian: "God is good."

Wuyi (WOO-yee) Miwok Indian: "turkey vulture soaring."

Wyatt Old French: "little warrior."
   Wiatt, Wyat

Wynn Welsh: "fair one."
   Win, Winn, Wyn

Wynono (wi-NO-no) North American Indian: "first-born son."

––––––––––––––––––––– X –––––––––––––––––––––

Xavier Arabic: "bright"; or Spanish: "owner of the new house." Xavier and Javier are also used in Spain.
   Javier (English); *Xaver* (German); *Saverio* (Italian)

Xenos Greek; "a guest" or "a stranger."

Xerxes Persian: "ruler." Name of a famous Persian king.

Xylon Greek: "dweller in the forest."

––––––––––––––––––––– Y –––––––––––––––––––––

Yadid (yah-DEED) Hebrew: "friend" or "beloved."

Yadin (yah-DEEN) Hebrew: "God will judge."
   Yadon

Yakecen (YAH-keh-shen) Dene Indian: "sky on song."

Yakez (YAH-kehz) Carrier Indian: "heaven." Shortened from the words *ya kezudzepe*, which mean "sky on his ears in," or "within heaven's ears."

Yale Old English: "from the slope" or "from the land corner."

Yancy North American Indian: "Englishman."

Yannis Modern Greek form of John, "gracious gift of God."

Yarb English Gypsy: "herb," implying a fragrant scent.

Yarin (yah-REEN) Hebrew: "to understand."
Javin (English)

Yasar (ya-SAHR) Arabic: "wealth." The Prophet Muhammad objected to this name because he considered it too proud.
Yaser, Yassar, Yasser

Yazid (YA-zid) Arabic name which dates to antiquity and is identical in meaning to the Hebrew Joseph, "He will increase," in the sense that his power and influence will grow. The only difference is the "he" in the Arabic name refers to the bearer of the name, whereas the Hebrew "He" refers to Jehovah.

Yemon (yeh-MOHN) Japanese: "guarding the gate."

Yerik Modern Russian form of Jeremy, "appointed by God." See Jeremy.

York Old Celtic: "from the yew estate"; or Old English: "from the estate of the boar."
Yorke

Yucel Turkish: "sublime."

Yukio (yoo-KEE-o) Japanese for "snow boy," implying "boy who goes his own way."
Yuki, Yukiko

Yule Old English: "born on Christmas." Popularized by actor Yul Brynner.
Yul

Yuma (YOO-mah) North American Indian: "the chief's son."

Yunus Turkish form of Jonah, "dove," the symbol of peace.

Yuri Popular in Russia as a Russian form of George, "farmer" or "land worker." See George.

Yusef (YOO-sef) Arabic form of Joseph, "he will increase." Also used today in Czechoslovakia, Germany, and Poland. See Joseph.
Yazid

Yutu (YOO-too) Miwok Indian: "coyote making a feint so he can seize a bird." From the Miwok Indian *yutme*, "to claw."

Yves French form of Ives, "little archer" or "son of the yew bow." In astrology the Archer is the symbol of Sagittarius. See Ives.

----------- Z -----------

Zach Short form of Zachary ("Jehovah has remembered") now used in the United States as an independent name.

Zachary Hebrew: "Jehovah has remembered."
Zach, Zacharia, Zack, Zak (English); *Sakari* (Finnish); *Zacharie* (French); *Sacharja, Zacharia* (German); *Zacharias, Zako* (Hungarian); *Zacarias* (Portuguese, Spanish); *Sachar, Zakhar* (Russian); *Sakarias, Sakarja, Zakris* (Swedish, Norwegian)

Zahid (za-HED) Arabic: "self-denying" or "ascetic."

Zahur (zah-HOOR) Swahili: "flower."

Zaid Shortened Arabic form of Yazid, a development of Joseph. See Yazid.

Zaki (ZA-kee) Arabic: "intelligent."

Zamir (zah-MEER) Hebrew: "a bird" or "a song." Currently popular in Israel.
Zemer

Zane An English form of John, "gracious gift of God." See John.

Zareb (za-REB) Sudanese: "protector against enemies."

Zared Hebrew: "ambush."

Zarek (ZAH-rek) Polish name derived from the Greek and meaning "may God protect the king."

Zeeman Dutch: "seaman." For a boy born under one of the water signs: Pisces, Cancer, or Scorpio.

Zeheb (ze-HEB) Turkish: "gold."

Zeke Modern short form of Zechariah, "the memory of the Lord." Also Aramaic: "spark" or "shooting star."

Zeki (ze-KI) Turkish: "intelligent" or "quick-witted."

Zelimir Slavic: "he wishes peace."

Zenon Greek: "living" or "given life by Zeus."
Zeno (French); *Zewek* (Polish); *Zinon* (Russian); *Cenon,*
Zenon (Spanish)

Zenos "Jupiter's gift." Astrological name for a boy born under Sagittarius or Pisces, both signs ruled by Jupiter.

Zesiro (zeh-SEE-ro) Luganda, Uganda: "elder twin." Common name in Uganda in Africa.

Ziven Slavic: "vigorous and alive." Used especially in Czechoslovakia, Poland, and Russia.
Ziv, Zivon

Zorya Ukrainian: "star."

GREAT PARENTING BOOKS

___SUPER WORKING MOM'S HANDBOOK
by Roseann Hirsch   (U38-037, $8.95, U.S.A.)
            (U38-074, $11.95, Canada)

This is an indispensible compendium of time-saving, useful suggestions for working mothers, ranging from psychological advice on alleviating stress to household tips and recipes. Organized for fast and easy reference in an appealing almanac format, this is the ultimate guide to juggling household management and childrearing with job demands.

Available in large-size quality paperback

___MOTHER CARE, OTHER CARE   (U32-936, $4.50, U.S.A.)
by Sandra Scarr   (U32-937, $5.95, Canada)

Today, the majority of mothers with preschool children must address the issue of child-care while they work outside the home. In more than six million American families, both parents work. For all the parents who have been raised believing that any disruption of the traditional mother-child relationship is potentially damaging to the child, either psychologically, emotionally, or intellectually, this book is a comforting source of information that shatters all the myths about child care.

___PARENTS AND KIDS TOGETHER   (U37-014, $8.95, U.S.A.)
by Lisa Lyons Durkin   (U37-017, $11.95, Canada)

This book offers many creative ways to make all the time busy parents have with their children really count. It shows how everyday activities can be transformed into fun and rewarding growth experiences that teach children basic skills, motivate them to learn, strengthen parent-child bonds, build a child's self-esteem, and inspire children's independence, curiosity and creativity.

Available in large-size quality paperback

WARNER BOOKS
P.O. Box 690
New York, N.Y. 10019

Please send me the books I have checked. I enclose a check or money order (not cash), plus 50¢ per order and 50¢ per copy to cover postage and handling.*
(Allow 4 weeks for delivery.)

_____ Please send me your free mail order catalog. (If ordering only the catalog, include a large self-addressed, stamped envelope.)

Name _____

Address _____

City _____

State _____ Zip _____

*N.Y. State and California residents add applicable sales tax.   164